AF265544

DR. JOHN CONDIT

HISTORY

OF

THE ORANGES

TO 1921

Reviewing the Rise, Development and Progress of an
Influential Community

DAVID LAWRENCE PIERSON
THE AUTHOR

VOLUME III

ILLUSTRATED

Lewis Historical Publishing Company, New York
1922

Copyright
Lewis Historical Publishing Company
1922

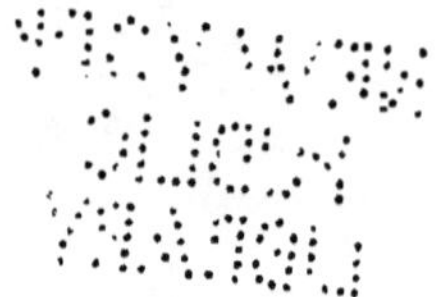

HISTORY OF THE ORANGES

CHAPTER LXXXII

ORANGE IN 1920

Orange in 1920 has a population of 33,268, all comfortably housed and enjoying blessings not dreamed of by the forebears of the pioneer period. So rapid have the various inventions and improvements come to us, lessening the tedium of the daily routine of home and business, that they have been appropriated as a matter of course. Sanitation has made wonderful changes in the general health of the city. Freedom from diseases formerly appearing with seasonal regularity, such as chills and fever (malaria), typhus fever, small pox, etc., is one of the greatest blessings of the era. Evenly heated homes and office buildings in the winter months, now the rule, was a few generations ago a very rare exception. Truly we have come into the enjoyment of multitudinous blessings. We have been accustomed to the rapidly moving trolley car, the speeding automobile, the railroad train gliding along under its superb equipment, the handy telephone and various other devices evolved for our convenience. It is a goodly heritage and we are not insensible of the toil of the years which has brought it to us.

The Commission form of government, adopted by the electorate in 1914, is in operation in 1920. William A. Lord, mayor, is Director of Public Affairs, and the other Commissioners are: Frank J. Murray, Director of Revenue and Finance; Isaac Shoenthal, Director of Public Safety; George Roach, Director of Streets and Public Improvements, and William F. Kearney, Director of Parks and Public Property. All the departments are in the City Hall, on Day street, with the exception of the Fire Department, which is occupying a central station at the corner of Lincoln and Central avenues. The assessed valuations of Orange in 1920 amount to $27,436,532 and the tax levy was $1,096,819.50, less $103,-069.54 expected from revenue. The item for local purposes was $832,-010.63, and for county and other demands, $264,808.87.

Orange has the largest amount of property exempted from taxation in the Oranges, and is also smallest in area. This unfair condition is partly caused by the erection of all the hospitals and several other public enterprises in the city, and also there are four cemeteries wholly or partly within its jurisdiction. Distribution of the burden among the other municipalities seems the logical way of assisting the city, which now needs increased funds for the departmental activities.

Main street, a source of worriment to the city officials for a score of years, because of its constant need of repair, has been relaid with wood block pavement and is giving very good service. The city, which inaugurated the system in New Jersey of paving as laid down by Telford and MacAdam, at the end of the decade of 1860, is now departing therefrom, it having been unsatisfactory since the advent of the automobile and its resultant heavy traffic. The old-style roads are also a nuisance in seasons of high winds, the dust being blown about, much to the discomfiture of the storekeeper and the householder. Under the direction of Commissioner Roach, who supervises much of the repairing, a plan of "carpet" treatment is followed by spreading a thick layer of asphalt over the old roadbed, which not only acts as a binder and makes a smooth surface, but proves most economical in its enduring qualities. The work continues, public approval being given the method adopted.

The Orange Free Library, while not an institution under city management, is enjoying a fixed place in the educational and constructive forces of the city. The building, at the corner of Essex avenue and Main street, is open to the public during the day and reading material placed at the disposal of every resident. Three branches have been established—the Valley Branch at 41 Tompkins street, the St. Cloud Branch in the Men's Club House, St. Cloud, and the Pleasantdale Branch, in the schoolhouse at Pleasantdale. Miss Elizabeth Howland Wesson has been the librarian for many years.

A problem again facing the city authorities is the inadequate water supply and the necessity of more liberal impounding in the season of rainfall. The upper reservoir, abutting on Northfield road, built forty years ago, stands well the wear of the years and is used for storage purposes. The lower reservoir, at Campbell's pond, continues to send its supply to the city, but there is need of another enclosure, the ravine just above the pond forming an ideal location. It is probable that within the next few years it will be selected for a new reservoir, which will be the means of conserving a vast amount of water now flowing away. The quality continues excellent and the people are practically immune from destructive fires because of the gravity pressure secured by the building of the tank on the mountainside.

Two amendments attached to the Federal Constitution during the World War vitally affected the community, as they did no doubt many others. The traffic in the sale of intoxicating liquor, starting locally from the very day of Puritan settlement, was abolished by the Eighteenth Amendment, which became effective on January 16, 1919. This was foreshadowed by the enforcement of the war measure which prohibited the sale of liquor after June 30, 1918. Not only was a large and valuable trade eliminated from the national life, but also a source of revenue to the Government in the excise tax imposed. Plants involving large sums of money and employing many operatives were brought to a state of idleness. The Orange Brewery, however, converted its large building on Hill street to the production of other commodities and thus suffered little or

ORANGE FREE LIBRARY, VALLEY BRANCH

no financial loss. A strong opinion was expressed by reasonable-minded men that the amendment was out of place in its attachment to the Constitution and that the same object could have been attained by legislation. The Prohibition Party had won in the long fight for its adoption.

The Nineteenth Amendment granted the right of suffrage to women, placing them upon the same footing with men in the exercise of the ballot. Advocates of general suffrage had persisted four score years or more that the normal way of choosing officials to conduct the public business was through a universal participation. Taxation without representation, they argued, was unfair and not in accord with the principles of the Consitution. It will be recalled that Lucy Stone defied Collector Mandeville to make her pay taxes in the days preceding the Civil War. The amendment was ratified August 26, 1920, and the first election at which the women cast their ballot was held on November 2, 1920, when they turned out en masse, wives accompanying their husbands, and in some instances several members of the family proceeding in a group to the ballot box. The vote in the Oranges was especially large, East Orange alone casting 19,699 ballots, or 94.2 per cent. of the entire registry, breaking all previous records. The Republican candidate for President received a total credit of 15,350 in the city.

Near the end of the United War campaign, the happy suggestion presented itself to the public-spirited men and women engaged therein to adopt a similar method for the collection of money to be used in the administration of the various charitable and philanthropic institutions of the Oranges. Each of them sent at least one appeal annually and not a few oftener to the people. By accurate tabulation the list of individuals who subscribed to these worthy objects numbered just 900. This was considered a very incomplete registry of public appreciation for the untiring work conducted by the various boards of direction. Now a change had come into the hearts of the people. They had familiarized themselves with the spirit of giving during the war, and the opportune time had arrived, it was adjudged by those more deeply interested in the charities and philanthropies of the community, to concentrate in one general movement for the annual collection of funds to sustain them. As an outcome the Welfare Federation of the Oranges was finally organized for this purpose. Following the close of the United War campaign, November 18, 1918, till June 25, 1919, the plan of organization was weighed from every angle. The constitution of the Federation adopted on this date provided for the selection of a board of directors, the membership of which was to be limited to one representative of the participating institutions, and for the commemoration of the activities of the Citizens War Committee of the Oranges, ten of its members were added to the Board.

The first officers chosen were: Chairman, Manton B. Metcalf; Vice-

Chairman, Charles F. Rand; Treasurer, Sidney M. Colgate, and Secretary, Clarence H. Potter. Nineteen organizations affiliated with the Federation during the first year, all willing to experiment with the novel idea of conducting one energetic campaign for the securing of necessary funds to carry on their work. They were the Orange Memorial Hospital, St. Mary's Hospital, New Jersey Orthopædic Hospital, Orange Orphan Society, Diet Kitchen of the Oranges, Young Men's Christian Association of the Oranges, Visiting Nurses' Association of the Oranges, Orange Valley Social Settlement, Day Nursery of the Oranges, Orange Fresh Air Fund, Orange Free Library, Comforts and Welfare Society of South Orange, Orange Public Bath Association, Young Women's Christian Association of the Oranges, East Orange Social Settlement, Orange Bureau of Associated Charities, Children's Aid and Protective Society of the Oranges, Anti-Tuberculosis League of the Oranges, West Orange Community League and the Young Men's Christian Association of the Oranges.

The object of the Federation was declared to be two-fold. First, to aid the members of the Federation in the most crucial part of their work —the money raising for operating expenses, repairs, replacing of equipment, improvements and interest on indebtedness. Each institution was obligated to submit on or before October 1, of each year, a budget for the twelve months beginning on January 1, which was carefully analyzed by the Board of Directors, and then included in the total amount to be solicited from the people. The Federation also promised to collect and distribute the needed money to the various members. The social service was a proposed feature which proved satisfactory, the public, through the solicitors and the publicity specially given, understanding as it had never before, the true worth of the social service field. After the finance committee had passed upon all the budgets offered, the total net sum to be raised the first year was set at $340,600. The campaign, however, did not begin till January 16, 1920. It continued till January 26, under the direction of the following chairmen: Orange, Judge Thomas A. Davis; East Orange, Clarence H. Kelsey; West Orange, Farnham Yardley; South Orange, Maplewood and Hilton, Arthur H. Muir; Industrial division, Mark M. Jones. The constitution provided that each subscriber could designate, if so inclined, the particular institution to which the donation may be applied.

At the close of the systematic house to house canvass, a total of 10,200 subscribers appeared on the list. The sum raised just went over the budget, amounting to $340,500. No more will the people be importuned to subscribe to entertainments and other means of raising money to sustain the needed work of relief and uplift. The Welfare Federation is now a reality and well proves its worthiness by relieving the institution of the financial cares.

No effort put forth by philanthropic men and women of the Oranges has produced more decided and helpful influence upon human kind than the fresh air work carried on each summer for twenty years, under the direction of the Orange Fresh Air Association. A home was purchased at Bradley Beach, and there the tired and weary women who have had an uneven existence are given a week's rest by the seashore, with warm and nourishing food and other comforts and an opportunity to secure a fresh grip upon life.

Advantages for securing an education at a minimum of expense and application were never so generously placed before the children of our homes as they are in this year of 1920. If the Federal Constitution, after setting the wheels of the governmental machinery in operation, had made possible only the institution of the public school, it would have well justified its adoption and ratification. Indeed, under the influence of this great instrument the progress of the human race, directly and indirectly, has been nothing short of marvelous. The training of the youth to accept its rightful place in the affairs of the daily routine is now generally acknowledged a necessity and not a luxury, so considered in the early days of our Republic. What a debt of gratitude we owe the old-time pedagogue, he who taught the district school of our great-grandfather's day! The name, for instance, of Colonel Chester Robinson, principal of the Orange Academy a century ago, who so sternly ruled the pupils committed to his care, but a most excellent instructor. His was the type of the noble educator who wrought strongly in the days of limited educational facilities. These pioneers were real constructionists in the sphere of education. They laid the foundation of the system of today so ably administered by worthy successors of their mantle long since laid aside.

Fifty-three years have passed since the New Jersey Legislature in 1868 passed the act establishing the Orange Board of Education. Each of the three wards of the town were represented on the board by three commissioners. In time there were five sub-divisions, increasing the membership to fifteen. Politics frequently crept into the deliberations of the commissioners, having an influence more or less harmful to the cause of education. Then the Legislature in 1908 passed an act, duly approved, providing for a Non-Partisan School Board of nine members, thus doing away with the old ward representation. The act was mandatory, and the vote at the November election was not upon its adoption but for a choice of commissioners to succeed the Board of Education of fifteen members. The new organization, according to law, was made on January 1, 1909. Arthur D. Chandler was chosen president and John J. Booth vice-president. The other commissioners were Herbert T. Abrams, L. Howard Brumbaugh, G. Wallace Hutchinson, Edward J. McCloskey, Henry Naulty, Laurence A. Norton and Frederick M. Struck. Superintendent James G. Riggs and Secretary William G. McCurdy were continued in their offices. The new management of the schools was accepted most cordially by the teaching force, and the spirit of coöperation strongly manifested. The law was later amended, reducing the representation from nine to five members. Mr. Booth, who has served faithfully as a commissioner ever since 1909, succeeded Sidney M. Colgate as president, in 1920. Mr. Colgate's constant aim was to sustain the school spirit, which he assisted so well in doing while holding the position of executive. At his own expense he provided a dental clinic for use by all the pupils of the schools, and when opened for the reception of patients it instantly proved its necessity. The other commissioners serving in 1920 are Mrs. L. Stowell Clark, Stephen L. Stetson, Harry D. Wethling and John Pitman.

The Orange schools hold the record for attendance of all the cities of the State, it being 94.67 per cent. for 1920, second of all municipalities in the county and third for the entire State.

Centrally located and convenient to the transportation lines passing through the city, the Orange High School, at the corner of Main and Cleveland streets, is also the administration building of the city. It is a handsome structure, built of brick, with wide sweeping lawn in front. The main entrance is reached from Main street, and at the right are the offices of Superintendent W. Burton Patrick, who has been in charge of the schools for the past six years. Stanley C. Dukeshire, one of the oldest principals in point of service, has his office on the opposite side of the entrance. There are eighteen class rooms in the High School building, the auditorium on the third floor having been converted to the use of the commercial department. There is an enrolment in all the classes of 417. The value of the plant is $152,000.

Urgent need for the accommodation of more classes in the grammar grades made obligatory the erection of a new building in the rear of the High School in 1914. Ground was broken on January 21 of that year, and on January 29, 1915, the completed structure was dedicated and formally named the Central School of Orange. Sidney M. Colgate, president of the Board of Education, presided, and praise was bestowed upon Commissioner Frederick M. Struck for his excellent supervision of construction as chairman of the building committee. State Commissioner of Education Calvin N. Kendall delivered an address and a handsome silk flag was presented to the school by David L. Pierson, president of Orange Chapter, New Jersey Society, Sons of the American Revolution, in behalf of that organization. It was accepted by Miss Nelle West, a student, for the faculty and pupils.

Eighteen class rooms are provided in the building and the auditorium will seat nearly 1,000. There is also a large gymnasium. Stanley C. Dukeshire, principal of the High School, was placed in charge of the Central School. A covered passageway connects the two buildings. The value of the plant is $279,000. The other schools are:

LAYING CORNERSTONE OF ORANGE HIGH SCHOOL, MAIN AND CLEVELAND STREETS, JUNE 22, 1906

Lincoln Avenue, corner of Jackson street, near the Orange Playground—Howard J. McNaughton, Principal; twenty-six class rooms; enrolment, 1,467. Value of plant, $527,000.

Park Avenue, nearly opposite North Center street—George B. Schulte, Principal; eighteen class rooms; enrolment, 765. Value of plant, $191,000.

Forest Street, corner of Valley road—Andrew Scarlet, Principal; twelve class rooms; enrolment, 742. Value of plant, $99,000.

Oakwood Avenue, about midway between Lackawanna Railroad and Central avenue—Howard L. Goas, Principal; eighteen class rooms. Subnormal school in North Center street, also under his supervision; total enrolment, 940. Value of Oakwood Avenue building and grounds, $135,000.

Cleveland Street—Frank L. Yost, Principal; eighteen class rooms; enrolment, 847. Value of plant, $184,000.

Tremont Avenue—Florence J. Lacey, Principal; ten class rooms; enrolment, 409. Value of plant, $85,000.

Recognizing the great underlying fundamentals of a healthy body and a clear mind of the pupil if the processes of imparting knowledge by the teacher are to have a beneficial effect, the Board of Education, through the continued watchfulness of Superintendent Patrick and his assistants, spare no expense in needed medical attention. In his annual report for 1920, Mr. Patrick dwells especially upon the value of the dental clinic, saying that "the Orange school system is fortunate indeed in having a citizen who is so vitally interested in the subject that he provides this service and equipment without any expense to the individual pupil or to the taxpayers, and years hence when the results of this work will be even more apparent to the pupil than they are now, I am sure that there will be additional appreciation to the donor of this essential attribute to the system." The clinic was set up in the Lincoln Avenue School building and the record for 1920 showed that 1,871 appointments were filled and completed work performed on 1,102 patients.

Dr. Ella A. Coughlan, the medical inspector, is assisted by three nurses who regularly visit the schools, looking after the health of the children. Examinations and inspections made on 5,162 pupils during the school year of 1919-1920 numbered 206,890, being eighty per cent. of the total enrolment. The fresh air class, opened in a building on Central avenue, near Essex avenue, on September 17, 1910, is very helpful to the under-nourished pupils. Artificial heat is not used in any way, and with the air in all seasons having full play through the room, teacher and pupils prosecute their work, well bundled in warm clothing when the temperature lowers. Food is supplied the children as exigencies require. The sub-normal classes studying in the North Center building, having an attendance of about sixty, are given special attention. So adept did the boys become in the making of brushes that a concern offered to purchase their entire product. A feature introduced in the Orange system in accordance with the new law, operative July 1, 1920, is the continuation school, for all boys between fourteen and sixteen years of age, and who have not obtained their required schooling. Thirty-six weeks of instruction, six hours each, three in academic and three in shop work, were given 128 applicants. Physical culture is taught by Carl Seibert most energetically, and under his direction the basket ball team became proficient and won the class B championship of the State for 1920. The gymnasium instruction has some excellent results. The Americanization work, night school and vocational training are specialized; the machine shop and printing office have a special lure for the boys; the girls of the dressmaking department have become expert in fashioning garments, and the cooking class disposes of its preparations to the faculty and pupils at the lunch hour at cost price. Garden cultivation in the summer of 1920 by the more ambitious boys was successful beyond the estimate made of those managing the enterprise. The total value of the vegetables raised by the boys amounted to $1,092.

There is a strong tendency in the High School toward studying in the commercial classes, four teachers being required to keep up with the work. The necessity of the average student to enter business after completing the course of study is responsible for the lessening number expressing a desire to study the classics and prepare for entrance into a college.

CHAPTER LXXXIII

SOUTH ORANGE

Originally the southerly boundary of Orange was at Camptown, now Irvington, but on April 14, 1835, the New Jersey Legislature created the township of Clinton, which included South Orange and Millburn. The latter was set off in 1857, and South Orange on January 26, 1861, the boundaries being described as follows:

Beginning at a point on the line between Orange and Newark, half a mile north of South Orange avenue; thence southerly along the middle of said avenue; thence to the bridge over the east branch of the Elizabeth River; in the road near the house of William Steckman, in Clinton; thence to the northwesterly corner of Daniel Hedden's house; thence to the bridge in the road near the house of Charles E. Lum; thence to the bridge near the residence of J. E. Courter; thence toward the late residence of Samuel Headley, deceased, to the boundary line of the township and Union county; thence westerly to the east branch of the Rahway River; thence to a bridge in the road near the house of Peter Failade; thence to "Rock Hole," in the Rahway River; thence along the river to Mark's Mill; thence to the northeasterly corner of James E. Smith's land on the top of the First Mountain, adjoining the Walker road; thence to a small bridge near Daniel Webb's; thence to the southwest corner of D. W. Smith's house on Scotland street; thence to a point in Center street to Abby Lindsley's land; thence to the place of beginning except the Orange Poor Farm.

Included in this territory were some of the choicest farms in New Jersey, several having been retained in family circles from the earliest years. The people were prosperous, the well cared for lands and buildings and the selected livestock indicating happiness and contentment. The center of the town was in the vicinity of South Orange avenue and Valley street, where the tavern conducted by Marcus Ball was retaining its popularity of more than a score of years under his management. Nearby were the Columbian school, the Presbyterian and Methodist churches, post office, a few stores and dwellings. Jefferson Village was the name applied to the southern part of the township on Independence Day, in 1798, by admirers of Thomas Jefferson and in his honor.

George E. Low, who has preserved local historical data, thus describes the manner in which the name of Jefferson Village was dropped in the early decade of 1860:

About 1860-1862, John W. Shedden bought thirty acres of land near the present Maple avenue, and laid it out in villa plots, the first improvements of this character made in the settlement. He built two cottages and persuaded a few of the residents to join with him in giving an acre of land to the Morris and Essex Railroad Company and building a station thereon, to be known as Maplewood. The name was suggested by Mrs. Elijah Gardner, then living on Ridgewood road, who thought it appropriate because of the large maple tree which stood near the station and because of the great maple swamp, a conspicuous feature of the place in former days. The village soon adopted the name applied to the station and the fine old name of Jefferson Village became a thing of the past.

"Records of the Revolutionary War history in Maplewood are not easy to find," says Mr. Low, "but we learn in the little Bear Lane Cemetery (removed in recent years) the remains of fifteen soldiers of the Revolution. Their names are not all preserved, but among them were Aline Little, J. Beldome, Joseph Lyon and Adjutant Durand, an uncle of Asher B. Durand, who served under General Washington. Upon the site of the Timothy Ball house, adjacent to the Selim Freeman homestead, on Ridgewood road, at the corner of Cedar lane, was located the cavalry scout stable, where accommodations were provided for forty mounts. Coon road, on the top of the mountain, was a watch tower. From Vauxhall was to come the alarm if the British were making a move for Morristown, and from Baldwin's station on Scotland road, if the Tories were coming from that direction."

Among the early settlers was Samuel Durand, of French descent, who in 1750 bought land and established a residence described as being six miles from Newark and two miles from Springfield. His son John erected a dwelling house on the site now known as the westerly corner of Durand road and Ridgewood road, where the Durand homestead has been standing for over one hundred and sixty years.

John Durand was a farmer possessed of unusual mechanical ability. He made tools and weapons, built his home and was so skilful in mending watches and clocks that he did a large business among his neighbors and in the adjacent villages. The incident is related that General Washington sent his spy-glass to Durand for some necessary repairs, which he did so skilfully as to win the cordial appreciation of the commander-in-chief. It is said that though having volunteered his services in the cause of Freedom, he was returned to his home for the purpose of making bayonets for the soldiers. There were eleven children in the family, the eighth, born August 21, 1796, being named Asher Brown Durand, who proved to be the most eminent man produced in Maplewood. Magnificent woodlands spread before his house, while at the rear unbroken forests stretched to the top of the mountain and far beyond over hill and valley for many miles. Game birds were plentiful, the streams abounding in trout and the forests in deer, raccoons and other wild animals. An occasional bear trespassed on the farm yard, many of them being tracked to their den and shot. The mountain trail down which the dead bears were dragged was known till recent years as Bear Lane, when, for some unaccountable reason the name was changed to Claremont avenue.

In this environment Asher Brown Durand spent his boyhood days. He early expressed an artistic temperament and during his career became an artist of world-wide renown. From 1845 to 1850 he was president of the National Academy of Design and was also an original member of the Century Club of New York. Known as the "father of American landscape painting," Mr. Durand was equally well accomplished in the art of engraving, in which, it was said, he was even more skilful than handling the brush. He was not set aside till after reaching his eightieth birthday.

In 1815 Jefferson Village numbered thirty families. A map of the village engraved at that time showed "Great Meadow Swamp" extending along the brook from the present Jefferson avenue in a northerly direction; "Little Maple Swamp," "Turtle Lake," "Factory Pond," "Crooked Brook," the east branch of the Rahway river winding its way to the south; a factory, sawmill, two mines (supposed to have been opened for copper), the Baptist Meeting House (called the Babel Chapel), and a fortification called "Bom Fort." Names of the village inhabitants noted on the map were "Captain Smith," "Captain Sam," "Aunt Rachel," and "Neighbor Joseph." Jefferson avenue was noted as Dominie Lane, where the preacher lived who held forth on Sundays in Babel Chapel and wove rag carpets at home on week days. Other quaint names were "Grub Street," "Heathern Street," and "Shag Poke Lane." "Necessity Corners" marked the site of the school house.

Important factors in the prosperity of Jefferson Village were the grist mills of the Piersons, well established institutions in 1740; the Dunnell paper mill, located on the east branch of the Rahway river, about in line with Oakland road of 1900; the blacksmith shop of Daniel Beach on Valley street, north of Parker avenue, and the general store of Henry Smith and later of Charles R. Crowell, on Valley street, south of Oakland road of later years. The present Pierson Mills were built in 1831, but the Pierson family had been owners of mills on the east branch of the Rahway river for a hundred years before that date.

A school house stood at "Necessity Corners" and was visited from time to time by an itinerant schoolmaster who instructed the youth of the neighborhood. Asher Brown Durand was a pupil, attending intermittently for about six years or until he was thirteen years old. The site of this structure was at the corner of Ridgewood road and Baker street. In 1833 the trustees parted with it for the sum of $70, $60 for the land, $10 for the building. A new school was then erected on the northwesterly side of Ridgewood road, opposite Highland place. This was abandoned in 1868, C. V. S. Roosevelt very generously paying $2,000 for the property. The first school teacher of record is Morris Baker, a native of South Jersey, who came to Jefferson Village about 1784 and taught in the district school. He was a farmer and purchased land on which his descendants have lived ever since. The length of his term of service is not disclosed, the records not being available before 1818. Amos Rich was engaged as the teacher in that year. The school was managed by an association which provided a building and invited a schoolmaster to undertake the tuition of such pupils as would each pay $1.75 per quarter. The schoolmaster was engaged to teach seven or eight hours a day, clean and heat his building, do his own collecting of tuition fees and assume all risk of financial loss. Under these circumstances it is not, perhaps, so very surprising that in the fifty years from 1818 to 1868 there were no less than fifty-one different teachers in charge of the school.

The present town building was the next school house erected, work being started August 25, 1869, and the dedicatory exercises held on January 31, 1870. The entire cost of building, furniture and ground was $7,500. The trustees were Daniel Morrison, Edward Crowell, Thomas A. Reeve and Daniel H. Carpenter. To the latter is due in very great measure the credit for providing the school accommodations, which for the time were adequate and comfortable and far superior to anything previously possessed by the school district. Mr. Carpenter was secretary and treasurer of the board of trustees for a number of years and the community profited greatly by his generous services and wise counsel.

The teacher who left upon Maplewood the imprint of his personality more strongly than any other man was James Ricalton, who taught the pupils from 1872 to 1891, with the exception of the years 1888-1889. He was and is a remarkable man, as many of those whom he instructed and who are active and prosperous citizens of today will gladly testify. He is an expert photographer, explorer and collector of curios, and is favorably known to the governments of several nations as well as our own, as an intrepid war correspondent and photographer of battle scenes.

In 1903 the present brick school house was built under the direction of William H. Kemp, chairman of the building committee of the Board of Education, and in 1911 it was enlarged by the addition of a wing.

A Baptist society was formed in 1810 at Jefferson Village, of which Elder Joseph Gildersleeve was pastor, his flock numbering eighteen communicants. He was described as a Godly man who served his neighbors well and faithfully for nearly fifty years. Caleb Durand donated the plot on December 7, 1811, at the northerly corner of Springfield road (now Ridgewood road) and Bear lane. Here was erected the first church edifice of Maplewood. It was occupied in 1812. Joseph Gildersleeve, the only pastor, died in 1845, and his remains were buried in the cemetery adjoining the church. The property was transferred to the Methodist Episcopal church of Jefferson Village on July 10, 1858. The name was changed to the First Methodist Episcopal Church of Maplewood in 1870

and it was again changed to the Morrow Memorial Methodist Episcopal
Church on December 12, 1897.

Modern Maplewood could not have been prophesied in 1868, when
there were only three commuters to New York, and the total population
did not exceed one hundred and fifty. Twenty years later the number of
residents making the daily trip to the metropolis did not exceed fifteen.
But the progressive decade of 1880 was witnessing many changes in the
Oranges and the township of South Orange was feeling the impetus after
a period of thirteen years, when only one house was built in the section
now known as Maplewood. Gradually new families were coming to the
open spaces in and about the settlement and its healthfulness made it
most adaptable for home making. During the first ten years of the Twentieth Century when the tide of settlers was in full strength, an average
of nearly fifty houses were erected annually. The frame building used
as the Maplewood station of the Lackawanna railroad was abandoned on
January 6, 1902, and the present one of brick with its wide plaza was
substituted. These improvements were part of the Lackawanna Railroad
Company's plan of abolishment of grade crossings by overhead construction. Maplewood's post office was opened in 1893, which proved a very
great convenience. Hitherto the people living in the southern part of the
township were compelled to make the long trip to the postal station on
South Orange avenue to secure their mail.

The assessed valuation of the town in 1900 was less than $1,000,000
and the population was 1,630. Communication with the outside world by
trolley had been in vogue about five years. Maplewood was being sought
more and more each year by families living in congested centers, who
found there the freedom and joyousness of living in an open country
round about them.

Twenty years have made wonderful impressions upon the township
of South Orange. The two settlements, Maplewood and Hilton, while enjoying the designation of a distinctive community life, are both under
the government of the township committee. Some day the confusion
arising out of the situation may lead to the recognition of each as a separate municipality and leaving to the Village of South Orange the name so
long associated with the territory.

The Township Committee in 1920 is composed of Ernest E. Mathi-
son, chairman; John S. DeHart, Jr., Charles D. Henley, Edward Horn-
beck and Harry C. Thompson. The assessed valuation of the township
had increased from $1,000,000 in 1900 to $11,850,900 in 1920, a phenomenal gain. The tax rate for this year is 2.76. The local budget amounts
to $159,645.73. Added to this are the county tax, $114,693.01, and the
school tax, $101,666.88. The population is 5,309.

The township is supplied with water by the Commonwealth Water
Company of Summit, and in 1920 the sum of $6,077.76 was paid for the

rental of hydrants placed at the service of the Fire Department. Sewer facilities are also enjoyed, arrangements having been made with the Village of South Orange and Irvington for rental (the former being paid $3,567.88 and the latter $100 in 1920) in the Trunk Line Outlet Sewer which extends across country to tidewater at Elizabethport.

Roosevelt Park, consisting of sixty-seven acres, was one of the largest single tract developments of Maplewood. The property was owned by Cornelius V. S. Roosevelt early in the decade of 1870, and here the family entertained during the summer months, dispensing the hospitality so intimately associated with that era. The frontage is on Ridgewood road and the western boundary is at Wyoming avenue. Colonel Theodore Roosevelt, nephew of the owner, and President of the United States in after years, spent many of his vacation days at the estate. W. Emelyn Roosevelt, executor, sold it to William H. Curtis, of South Orange, in March, 1902, who held title till June, 1905, when T. B. Ackerson, of New York, became the owner. He immediately opened streets, restricting the property and finding ready purchasers, several of whom required the inhibition of Sunday games being played on any of the property. The name of Roosevelt was memorialized by naming one of the roads in honor of the Colonel, and another for Sagamore, his estate at Oyster Bay. The property is now well occupied by modern homes.

The Maplewood Field Club which had been sustaining a great deal of interest among the citizens fond of outdoor sports for fifteen years, branched out recently into the Maplewood Country Club. Its original holding of sixteen acres was increased to fifty acres, occupying the land bounded by the Lackawanna railroad, Baker street, Valley road and Oakley road. It is a fine rolling tract and will contribute to the prestige of Maplewood in many ways. The finance committee, of which Arthur T. Muir is chairman, has worked out a plan for the building of a club house which will cost $150,000, and the place selected for it, a high plot of ground, commands an extensive view of the golf course and the tennis courts. The officers in 1920 are Louis E. Freeman, president; George Salmon, vice-president; John Low, secretary; Walter Becker, treasurer. The membership is open to families and there are about 450 names enrolled on the roster.

The Maplewood Improvement Society, organized June 21, 1908, has recently changed its name to the Maplewood Civic Society. It assists in beautifying the town and guards it from harmful influences. The officers are: President, Hart Darlington; vice-presidents, Corwin Howell and Charles L. Griffin; secretary, F. T. Albert; treasurer, Charles L. Moody.

Maplewood Woman's Club, one of the most active in the entire State, having a membership in 1920 of seven hundred, is engaged in nine distinct departmental activities. The club was organized on January 5, 1917, and was particularly active during the World War in various patriotic missions. The officers are: President, Mrs. M. Caswell Heine; vice-presidents, Mrs. Benjamin Jones and Mrs. Frederick R. Brown; corresponding secretary, Miss Bertha Hackman; recording secretary, Mrs. W. I. Auten; treasurer, Miss Viola Dobbins; Federation secretary, Miss Florence Baker.

The Maplewood Library Association was instituted in 1913, and has found quarters in the school building, where a library of 6,500 volumes is at the disposal of the people. The officers in 1920 were: President, Mrs. Henry P. Rogers; vice-president, Mrs. Samuel G. Memory; treasurer, Mrs. F. F. Durand.

Rev. George W. Clark, great-grandson of Timothy Ball, compiled interesting data relating to the house which he built in the early part of the Eighteenth Century, and which is still standing, and known as Ye Old Washington Inn. The clergyman noted:

The house is on the Ridge-wood or mountainside road, between Orange and Springfield, about three miles from either place and a short distance from either the South Orange or the Maplewood railroad station. In the front chimney, above the peak of the roof, is a stone inscribed "T. & E. B. 1743" (Timothy and Esther Ball), the date of the building. Another interesting feature is a small square aperture in the front wall of the house which leads to an old fashioned built-in bed which for purposes of warmth adjoins the huge chimney.

Timothy Ball, grandson of Edward Ball, of Newark, and son of Thomas Ball, near "Tuscan Hall," was born in 1711, was married to Esther Bruen about 1743. They are said to have lived in a house (log, probably) a few rods to the northeast, just over the brook that divided Orange from Springfield. Wishing to dig a well, a diviner came along and by use of sticks pointed out where water could easily be found on the southwest side of the brook. This located the more permanent house, which Mr. Ball was about to build, on that side of the brook.

The new house was built largely of stone, and required much time and labor in quarrying and preparing the stone. It was a commodious and substantial house for those days, but Mr. Ball enjoyed it only fourteen years. In the winter of 1757-1758 the smallpox was prevalent in New Jersey, and Mr. Ball died of the disease in 1758. The house and farm were left to be managed by the wife and two daughters. Five children had been born in the new house, all then under twelve years of age, three of them boys, John, Uzal and David. The latter was the grandfather of the writer, and in due time located about fifty rods away, towards South Orange. John settled near Boonton and Usal occupied the homestead. Edward, grandfather of Timothy Ball, was one of the original settlers of Newark and was born about the year 1642 or 1643. He married Abigail Blatchley, of Connecticut, about the year 1664 and removed to Newark in the year 1667 and probably died there (the exact date of his death being unknown). He was a prominent man in Newark's affairs—Sheriff, Committeeman on boundaries in matter of settlement with Lord Proprietors, Indians, etc. Is supposed to have had six children, among whom was a son named Thomas.

Thomas Ball was born about 1687-1688 and died on or about December 18, 1744. Married Sarah Davis about the year 1710. Was a blacksmith and constable of Newark between 1715-1716 and removed, between 1718-1720, to a tract between Hilton and Jefferson Village, New Jersey, where he died near the site of "Tuscan Hall," built by his son Ezekiel. Thomas Ball is said to have had twelve children, among whom was a son named Timothy.

Timothy Ball was born October 26, 1711, and died January 9, 1758. Was a farmer on the mountainside, west of Maplewood Station, near South Orange, N. J. Married Esther Bruen, December, 1734, and is said to have had eleven children, among whom was a son named Uzal Ball.

Uzal Ball was born March 20, 1748, and died April 9, 1799. Was a farmer, his homestead being situate near South Orange, N. J. Married Abigail Burnet and died leaving seven children.

There is a tradition in the Ball family that Edward Ball (grandfather of Timothy) was related to Mary, the mother of Washington; his father perhaps being the grandfather of Mary Washington. During the Revolutionary War, while Washington had his troops stationed at Morristown, he frequently came to the top of the mountain to witness the movements of the British troops near Elizabethtown and Staten Island, which could be seen in the distance. On these occasions he used to visit Usal Ball who lived on the homestead of Timothy Ball, his father. There he passed nights, and on more than one occasion, as a precaution, stabled his horse in their kitchen. Washington recognized the Balls as distant relatives, calling them cousins. John, David and Usal Ball, sons of Timothy, served with the New Jersey troops in the Revolution.

Timothy Ball made his will in 1752, and which was recorded February 8, 1758, as follows:

In the name of God Amen the first day of June 1752 I Timothy Ball of Newark in the County of Essex and Province of New Jersey being in good health in Body and perfect mind & memory thanks be given to Almighty God therefore calling unto mind the mortality of my Body and knowing that it is appointed for all men once to die do make and ordain this my last will & Testament that is to say Principally and first of all I give and recommend my soul into the hands of Almighty God that gave it and my Body I recommend to the Earth to be Buried in decent Christian Burial at the discretion of my Executors nothing doubting but at the General resurrection I shall receive the same again by the Power of God and as touching such worldly Estate wherewith it hath pleased God to bless me with in this life I Give Demise and dispose of the same in the following manner and form My will is that all my just Debts as shall hapen at my decease shall be paid by my Executors hereafter named and appointed out of my moveable Estate.

Item I Give and bequeath unto my loving and beloved wife Esther the use of all my Lands Tenements and Hereditaments during the time she shall remain my widow and no longer my will also is that my sd wife shall have fifty Pounds out of my moveables such things as she shall chuse out of the Invitary at her disposal forever.

Item I Give and bequeath unto my beloved sons namely John & Uzal and all other sons that my said wife shall have within nine months after my decease all my Lands or meadows eqaly to be Divided amongst them except I shold be in Debt at my Deceas so that there should not be moveables anough to pay them and the Legacies before & hereafter mentioned

SETH BOYDEN SCHOOL, SOUTH ORANGE

COLUMBIA SCHOOL, SOUTH ORANGE

then my will is that my Executors shall have power to sell Land at any time when they see fit and pay my debts and my will is that my Executors or any Persons under or from or by them or their orders or by my sons orders at any time may Devide my Land equaly amongs my sons, and my will is that if my Executors hereafter appointed shall see that I have Land inconveniant for my Sons and that there is Land more conveniant for them and for ther benefit that then they may sell some & buy others for my sons and my will is that if I should have any Land in pardonship with any Body that then my Executors may Devide it at any time and my will is that if there should be any more moveables then to pay the Legacys that my sons should have it.

Item I Give & bequeath unto my beloved Daughters Sarah Charity Rachel and to all other daughters as shall be Born of my said wife within nine months after my Decease they shall have fifty pounds apeace to be paid by my Executors when they are eighteen years old or before if they are married.

Item I do make ordain constitute and appoint my beloved wife Esther and my beloved Brother Aaron Ball and Nathaniel Ball the Sole Executrix and Execrs of this my last will and Testament and I do revoke nullifie and make void all former wills & Testaments by me in any manner of ways heretofore maid & declared hereby ratifying & confirming this to be my last will & testament and none other In Testimony whereof I have to this my last will & Testament set my hand and affixed seal the day and year above written.

Signed sealed published TIMOTHY BALL (Seal)
and declared by the
Testator to be his last will
and Testament in presence of
witnesses
Jonatha Tompkins,
Jedidiah Hedden,
William Green

Be it remembered that on the third day of February in the year of Our Lord one thousand seven hundred and fifty eight Jonathan Thompkins and Jedidiah Hedden two of the witnesses personally appeared before me Uzal Ogden duly authorized to Prove wills & qualify Executors in the Eastern Division of New Jersey & they being duly sworn on the Holy Evangelists did Depose that they were present and saw Timothy Ball the Testator within named sign & seal the within written Instrument and heard him publish pronounce & declare the same to be his last will and testament and that at the doing thereof the said Testator was of sound mind & memory to the best of their knowledge & understanding and at the same time William Green was present and signed as did they each sign as a witness in the Testators presence.

UZAL OGDEN

Be it also Remembered that at the same time Esther Ball & Nathaniel Ball two of the Executors within named personally came before me and were sworn to the due execution and performance of the within will & testament according to Law. UZAL OGDEN

Probate Granted by John Reading Esqr President &c in the usual form Dated the same 3d feby 1758

Recorded in Liber F of wills page 487 &c.

Remotely located on the extreme southern boundary of the township, the settlement of Hilton has its identification more with the city of Newark than with South Orange, being connected with former by trolley. The name of Hilton was chosen because of the hills featuring the contour of the land. Hither came Seth Boyden, the inventor, from his Newark home, seeking the quiet of the country in the early days of the Nineteenth Century, for further investigations into the fields of science. The house in which he lived is still standing on Boyden avenue, named in his honor. Henry Joralemon, famous as grower of strawberries, was also a resident of Hilton, where he cultivated a large acreage of the summer fruit.

CHAPTER LXXXIV
SOUTH ORANGE VILLAGE

Residents of the metropolis were attracted in growing numbers following the close of the Civil War, to the wide, rolling country of the South Orange township, where for the greater part of the year the outdoor life was freely enjoyed. The wide range of vacant land from which a choice could be made for the erection of homes, the clear and bracing atmosphere and the freedom from the commotion of the city life, were considerations inducing a speedy settlement in the vicinity of the station of the Lackawanna railroad. In a few years the colony had increased so rapidly and the desire for more extensive privileges in the conduct of public affairs so often expressed, that the movement for the erection of a separate municipality from the township took tangible form in 1869. The majority of the land owners in the southern part of the township were contented with their pastoral life, and it was not thought wise to disturb them in the suggested idea. Application was accordingly made to the New Jersey Legislature in the session of 1869 to allow the citizens of the South Orange township within a certain described district to establish a new government for the purpose of introducing conveniences not permitted by the existing arrangement and laws. There was no opposition, practically, and on March 25, 1869, an "Act to Incorporate the Village of South Orange in the county of Essex" was duly placed upon the statute books. The boundaries were described as follows:

Beginning at a point in the southeasterly line of Center street, where the same is intersected by the northerly boundary line of the township of South Orange; thence in a direct line to a point in the middle of South Orange avenue, one hundred feet southerly from the southerly corner of Seton Hall College farm house; thence in a direct line to a point in the middle of Irvington avenue, one hundred feet easterly from the easterly corner of the dwelling house formerly of Mary Clark, deceased; thence in a direct line to the southerly corner of lands of Catherine M. Hexton, in the center line of Prospect street; thence in a direct line to a point where the northeasterly point of land of Henry Fenner intersects a stone wall running along the brow of the mountain; thence in a direct line along the brow of the mountain to a monument stone in an angle of the northerly boundary line of the township of South Orange; thence along the said boundary line to the place of beginning.

The charter was ratified by the voters of the village of South Orange (its official title) at a special election held on May 18, 1869, when L. L. Coudert was chosen the first president, and the five trustees were elected as follows: William J. Beebe, Abijah F. Tillou, Theodore Blume, Thomas Fenner, James W. C. Gardner and William Redmond. Messrs. Beebe and

Redmond resigned during the year, and their places were taken by George B. Turrell and Eugene Plunkett.

Mr. Turrell was elected president of the village in the spring of 1871, but was compelled to resign in the autumn on account of failing health. During his travels abroad he made study of road making, which he described as "construction by repairs," and which was adopted in the repairing of the village streets. Re-elected village president in 1873, he met with strong opposition in the practice of the new method, but when it was demonstrated that an annual saving of several thousand dollars of the public money resulted from its trial the opponents ceased their criticism. Mr. Turrell was keenly alive to every possible improvement which would redound to the health and credit of the community.

The act incorporating the village, after a trial, was found deficient, and an amended charter was drawn by John L. Blake, counsel for Orange, which passed the Legislature on April 4, 1872. It was permitted to become a law without the signature of Governor Parker, who refused his signature because it provided for the appointment of the police justice by the Governor, which, in his opinion, was usurping the rights of the people, who, he declared, should elect their own officials.

Moses P. Smith, the first tax collector, served from 1869 to 1875; F. L. B. Mayhew, first treasurer, from 1869 to 1872, also the first clerk, serving in this capacity till 1872; Theodore Blume, the first police justice, was in office from 1872 to 1876. Henry Trenchard, who was appointed constable August 10, 1871, served as marshal from 1872 till 1882 and from 1883 to 1906.

John Gorham Vose, a New York lawyer, had been spending the summer months since 1859 in Orange Valley, near the South Orange line. Deeply impressed with the increasing possibilities of the surrounding land in the village limits as sites for suburban residences, he began the purchase of several farms in July, 1867, lying wholly or partly therein. An acquisition of seventy acres, known as the Jotham Quinby farm, but which had passed into other hands before possessed by him, was situated in the vicinity of Scotland road and extended to Ridgewood road. Montrose avenue, connecting these two thoroughfares, was laid out and the building lots restricted, were placed in the market at attractive prices. Henry A. Page was also interested in this real estate venture, and the influence of these two men upon this section of the village gave it a distinctive, abiding character. The attention of home seekers from New York and elsewhere was turned to this most eligible place of residence, named Montrose, and an exodus was soon in full force. In a comparatively brief time a colony arose in the former farm land, adding to the population of the village and sustaining it as a high class residence section. The Mountain House, formerly the Water Cure, fronting on Ridgewood road, near Montrose avenue, was accommodating during the sum-

FIELDING SCHOOL, SOUTH ORANGE

mer months a large number of out-of-town guests, and the charm of an exclusive summer resort was given the vicinity for many years. It was at the Mountain House that the New England Society of Orange observed Forefathers' Day for the first time on December 21, 1870, the 250th anniversary of the landing of the Pilgrims at Plymouth Rock.

Mr. Vose was a lover of the outdoor life and fascinated with the environment of the part of the village which he was so instrumental in improving. Forest trees abounded everywhere and liberal opportunity given for the display of æstheticism in laying out the plots. Mr. Vose, ably seconded in his landscape treatment by those settling in Montrose, had the satisfaction of seeing the surrounding acreage "blossom as the rose" in the seasons of foliage and flowers. A total of one hundred and seventy-five acres was purchased, his operations extending easterly to Center street and southerly to South Orange avenue. Montrose, Sterling, Warwick, Haxtun, Raymond and Ralston avenues, Randolph place, Grove road and other thoroughfares were opened, upon which a number of handsome residences were built. Nearly all the property was secured at prices ranging from $500 to $700 per acre.

Mr. Vose was an intensely public-spirited man and a benefactor in many ways. His desire to limit building to large areas was quite in accord with the ideas of the decade of 1870, but not of 1920. In the latter year it became necessary to secure consents of surrounding property owners to permit improvements of large parcels. Mr. Vose did not long enjoy his activities. He died on March 17, 1874.

Thomas S. Kingman formed a syndicate in 1891 for the improvement of land east of Center street. Montrose Park was the name given the one hundred and fifty acres acquired by the capitalists. New streets were laid out running at right angles with Center street, and the old roads and lanes connecting with the thoroughfare were utilized in developing one of the most picturesque sections of the Oranges. Among the new roads were Hartford road, Stanley road (named in honor of Henry M. Stanley, the noted African explorer), and Kingman road (named for Mr. Kingman, the promoter). Every care was exercised in surveying the lots, which averaged 100x200 feet in dimensions, and with ample restrictions, the property holders could without fear of nuisance erect costly residences, which are now so ornamental to the village. All public buildings except houses of worship were excluded, and a standard was created for each dwelling, below which none were now allowed to build.

Expressing their faith religiously, the members of the syndicate presented the lot on which St. Andrew's Episcopal Church now stands at the corner of Sterling avenue and Center street, to the parish in perpetuity. Mr. Kingman erected a number of handsome dwellings, all of which he disposed of at a good profit.

The territory embraced in Montrose Park was annexed to the village by the legislative act, approved February 10, 1891, entitled "An act to annex to the Village of South Orange, in the county of Essex, a part of the present township of South Orange." The boundaries were described as follows:

Beginning at a point in the northwesterly line of Center street where the same is intersected by the northerly boundary line of the said township of South Orange, which point is also the now easterly corner of said village of South Orange; from thence in an easterly direction along the division line between the townships of East Orange and South Orange to that point in said last mentioned line where the same will intersect with a line drawn parallel with the easterly line of Holland road and one hundred and fifty feet distant easterly therefrom when produced to said division line between the townships of East Orange and South Orange; thence in a southerly direction and parallel with said easterly line of Holland road and one hundred and fifty feet distant easterly therefrom to the southerly side of South Orange avenue; thence in a straight line southwesterly to a point in the middle of Irvington avenue, which is an angle in the present boundary line of the said village of South Orange; and thence along the southeasterly boundary line of said village of South Orange to the place of beginning.

For a long time the east branch of the Rahway river had been a menace, more or less, to the adjacent property, overflowing the banks in time of freshets and flooding the lowlands. The Court of Common Pleas was authorized by the law to appoint a Drainage Commission, and in 1881 the members devised plans for draining the stream. It was completed in two years, and not only afforded the relief needed by people living in the vicinity, but reclaimed a large area of swamp land.

Foreseeing the possibility of intrusion by manufacturing interests into the valley through which the east branch of the Rahway river runs, a number of citizens formed the Meadow Land Society in 1889, and their purchase of twenty-three acres from Edwin H. Mead included much of this valuable land lying between the Lackawanna railroad and Ridgewood road. It was all restricted, part being incorporated in the property of the South Orange Field Club, which became active a few months later. By deed and contract with Reune H. Martin, who then owned a large acreage on the eastern slope of the Orange Mountain, restriction was also there obtained by the Meadow Land Society against undesirable building. Among its members were William F. Allen, Robert Ward, Eugene V. Connett, Edwin S. Allen, Carl E. Billquist, L. P. Farmer, Cyrus F. Loutrel, Dr. Henry A. Mandeville, F. A. Wright, B. B. Schneider, Bleecker Van Wagenen, George B. Farrell and M. W. Ferris. The village of South Orange, from its very beginning, has been fortunate in the number of its public-spirited citizens, the results of their interest and labors of over half a century being seen in the character of this suburban community of 1920, which is one of the best governed in the country.

The most noticeable effect of the Meadow Land Society's timely move is seen in the park-like treatment given the reservation and also the surrounding property, including the well-kept grounds of the South Orange Field Club. Another step in the saving of a tract for adornment purposes was taken by several wide-awake citizens in 1908, when they purchased five acres of unimproved land, bounded by Grove road, South Orange avenue and Parker place, situated in the heart of the village. The attention of these citizens was attracted to the proposed sale of the property, and noting the absence of a park within the corporate limits, they quickly closed the deal, which involved the sum of $8,000. The village authorities were given the privilege of ownership, at the same price, which was accepted, and at an outlay of about $2,000 additional, converted the "wild land" into the beautiful "breathing place" which was named Grove Park. While no games are played there, it loses none of its attractiveness by the winding roadways and paths over which the people pass in large numbers in season. The annual June walk of the Sunday schools of South Orange is always held in Grove Park.

Humanity in general owes a debt of gratitude to a group of residents of the village of South Orange for the crusade begun in 1901 against the mosquito, and which after a campaign relentlessly carried on for a period of twenty years, has nearly banished it from the territory covered by Essex county, at least. From the very beginning of settlement when the Puritans built their homes on the west bank of the Passaic river they were invaded regularly every summer with swarms of the insect which bred in the adjacent salt water marshes and in local pools of water. The annoyance was endured year after year, and generation after generation, and it is a wonder that the people did not strike sooner at so insidious an undermining of their health. In the summer, when the singing, stinging creatures were abroad, sleep at night was quite impossible. Protection was in part afforded by placing screens at the windows and doors of homes, but even these precautions did not wholly eliminate the nuisance. Canopies and other coverings were necessary in the sleeping rooms. The Village Improvement Society numbered among its members several who were very active in matters pertaining to the public welfare, and the idea was conceived by Spencer Miller, one of the leaders, in 1901 that the mosquito having been unusually vicious in recent years could be successfully attacked in the village, which, in common with other communities, possessed a number of breeding places. He secured the aid of Professor L. O. Howard, Chief Entomologist of the United States Agricultural Department, who appeared at the Village Hall, on May 16, 1901, and lectured on "Mosquitoes and the Possibility of their Extermination." Mr. Miller operated the lantern while the pictures were thrown upon the screen. The lucid address of the speaker made most forcible the determination of the Society to begin forthwith a movement to exterminate the

insect from the village. It was shown that the genus culex was its com-
monest form, that the male was harmless, but the female had needle-like
organs with which they punctured the skin of human beings and animals,
not only extracting vitality but injecting poisonous germs. The speaker
explained that the female laid four thousand eggs in one mass on standing water, from which wrigglers were hatched to continue the annoyance
of man and beast. There were over thirty species; some were domestic,
breeding in fresh water, flying long distances, and seldom invading homes.
All mosquitoes were bred in stagnant water and from one to three weeks
were required to transform from eggs to winged mosquitoes. The Anopheles or malarial variety, never traveled over six hundred yards from
their breeding place, but they caused a woeful amount of suffering to
human kind by the poison they carried. A mosquito a day old was full
grown and the female three days old could lay eggs.

The Drainage Committee of the Village Improvement Society immediately became active, its members being Mr. Miller, chairman; Edwin S.
Allen, Eugene V. Connett and Robert S. Sinclair. Dr. Howard visited a
number of the breeding places in the village and pointed out just how the
larvæ could be wiped out by the use of kerosene oil judiciously spread
upon the surface of the stagnant water. During the summer every pool
in the village was visited, and after constant oiling the mosquitoes were
greatly reduced in numbers. The committee was then satisfied that they
were of local origin. In the autumn especially, it was noticed that the
pest was very scarce in the homes. About $1,000 was spent in the work.
In 1902, under the direction of the committee, draining of bog land, filling of holes and oiling the stagnant water which could not be abolished,
cost $1,200, one-half of which was for permanent work. During the third
season, in 1903, more than half of the wet places in the village were removed and the Board of Health looked after the oiling. There were eighteen days of continuous rainfall in June and twelve days of rainfall in
August. Mosquitoes then appeared in very large numbers, but the committee was not discouraged in its crusade. The village, though suffering
from the visit, it proved to be of short duration, compared with the experiences of other places. The net amount expended in 1903, mostly all
for permanent improvements, was $1,500. Oil was generously used
throughout the summer wherever a mosquito was expected to find a
breeding place. The village authorities were watching carefully for any
accumulated water on vacant lots, the township authorities were cleaning
the East Branch of the Rahway river and the improved appearance of the
village and township was most noticeable as the spots here and there
where water had in former years been allowed to stand, were entirely
removed.

Mr. Miller, who is considered the father of the New Jersey mosquito
extermination crusade, was made the subject of innumerable newspaper

comments and also giving wide publicity to the village. The "New York Sun" editorially said "that the man who substitutes one mosquito for two is a benefactor of the commonwealth, while he who replaces forty or fifty of these beasts of prey by two or three deserves a monument. Hurrah for Spencer Miller, of South Orange Improvement Society!"

An article appearing in the "Washington Post" at the end of the campaign in 1902 was copied in many other newspapers, in which it was said: "Mr. Spencer Miller says that during the past two years he has cut down the mosquito population seventy-five per cent. He has worked a territory about two miles square. All he wants now is to have the rest of the State treated with equal diligence. The trouble with mosquitoes is that they can be carried several miles on the bosom of a good strong breeze. Mr. Miller sees the point of this and frankly admits that it is hardly worth while to exterminate mosquitoes on a 2,400-acre lot if the pest from a mile away can visit you with the first zephyr. . . . Let us hope that Mr. Miller will go on."

One of the direct and beneficial results of the 1903. activities was the clearing of underbrush from the woods along Grove road, which greatly improved that section of the village, opening up long vistas of shady woodland in a former swamp, overgrown with brambles and impassable both from the nature of the soil and from the swarms of mosquitoes which infested it. Professor John B. Smith, chief entomologist of New Jersey, inspected the committee's work and about which he wrote as follows: "Your work within the limits of the village, as far as you have attempted it, is almost perfect. The few mosquitoes that have escaped would hardly count in the course of a season. In the first place you have destroyed the possibility of breeding culex pungens and anopheles. The chances of malaria have been reduced almost to a vanishing point and you will without any question gain the benefit of your work in the smaller number of insects that will appear in your houses later on."

Edward D. Duffield, of South Orange, member of the House of Assembly of the New Jersey Legislature in 1904, introduced a bill, at the request of Mr. Miller and his associates, which became a law on March 24, providing that owners of property where mosquito larvæ breed be compelled by Boards of Health to abate the nuisance as being detrimental to public health. The work in the village continued.

The Essex County Mosquito Extermination Commission was created by the act of the New Jersey Legislature, approved March 21, 1912. Its organization became effective as soon as the commissioners could prepare the necessary plans. Dr. Ralph H. Hunt, of East Orange, was chosen president, which position he has held ever since, giving unlimitedly of his time to the study of and working out of problems brought to his attention. Thorough inspection of the entire county was made possible by an appropriation of $75,000 by the Board of Freeholders, and at the end of the summer of 1913 the warmest commendations were elicited from those who had previously suffered from the attacks of the pests. There was a continued application of the rules laid down, which had also the most welcome relief in removal of many unsightly places.

The Mosquito Extermination Commission was still active in 1920 and the pest was becoming less bothersome till in the late summer of this year it was possible for residents in the areas where it formerly flourished to sit on piazzas and lawns without disturbance. This is without doubt the most valuable local enterprise conducted for the welfare of the people, for it has been the means of reducing the malarial infections and allowing more comfort in the home during long summer months.

Dissatisfaction with the service of the Commonwealth Water and Gas Company, of Summit which was supplying the village with water, formed the principal subject of discussion in the board of trustees during 1910. Ira A. Kip, Jr., was president, and Louis F. Blanchet chairman of the water committee. The corporation, when introducing its water in the village in 1890, offered to lay the pipe in the streets, thus saving the taxpayers a large sum of money for construction. With prudent foresight the trustees decided to provide the distributing system and to purchase the water which was delivered at Ridgewood road boundary, at the rate of $75.00 per million gallons. The arrangement continued till the plant at Summit was unable to supply the municipalities their full allowance, and the village, among others, suffered greatly. There was lack of pressure for fire purposes and the faucet supply became so diminished as to cause frequent appeals by the consumers to the Water Department for relief from the inadequacy of service.

The trustees employed John J. Boyd, of Hudson county, an engineer of extensive experience, to ascertain the possibilities of securing a water source within the village territory. He reported in June, 1911, that in his opinion a plentiful supply could be found by driving wells. Options were then secured upon the Henry Fenner estate, west of the Lackawanna round house. Tests were made during the summer of 1911 and water was found at a depth of two hundred and seventy-four feet. Four days of continuous pumping revealed an undiminished flow at the rate of 350,000 gallons per day. The chemical and bacterial examination of the water indicated it to be of good quality and free from any surface contamination. Another well driven about one hundred yards north of the one opened yielded 300,000 gallons per day. Two consulting engineers, Nicholas Hill, Jr., formerly engineer of the Water Department of New York City, and Cornelius C. Vermeule, of East Orange, one of the best known water supply engineers of the State, were requested to report upon the source of supply and the general plan of erecting a Water Works. Mr. Boyd's estimates were readily endorsed and an act of the New Jersey Legislature in 1912 gave the Village Trustees power to proceed with the construction. This was the first effort of the people toward municipal ownership and the interest in the outcome was keenly manifested by every taxpayer of the village. Approval was given the scheme at a meeting of citizens called for the purpose of testing public opinion.

Under the law, the State is the custodian of all waters within its boundaries and no municipality or corporation is permitted to supply water without consent of the Water Commission. After careful inquiry its consent was given to the Village Trustees to proceed with the work. The State Board of Health was also consulted and gave its approval of the potability of the water. One year after Mr. Boyd made his report all the obstacles were removed, and in July, 1912, the contracts were awarded and the building of the plant proceeded rapidly.

Seven wells were opened, the greatest depth being four hundred feet, and the dimensions of each one about eight inches. The method of raising the water from the wells is an approved device known as the air lift. Within this and extending down below the surface of the water about one hundred and forty feet, is a five-inch pipe and inside this is a four-inch pipe reaching to about the same distance. Air from the compressors in the pumping station is forced down the space between these two inner pipes to the bottom of the four-inch pipe, through which it rises in a series of bubbles, which lighten the water in the inside tube so that it is pressed upward by the weight of the solid water outside, and is driven out at the top in aerated jets. At the top of each four-inch pipe a deflector turns the water into pipes through which it flows by gravity to a basin.

The pumping plant having a capacity of 1,300,000 gallons per day of twenty-four hours was housed in a brick building of pleasing architecture. A reservoir was built on the mountain, near South Orange avenue, in the shape of a truncated triangle, two hundred and fifty-five feet in length, ninety feet wide at one end and twenty feet wide at the other. The depth is twenty-three feet nine inches, giving a capacity of two million gallons of water. There are two compartments, thus providing for any possible repairs and also permitting necessary cleaning. The water collected at the basin near the pumping station is forced up the mountainside to the reservoir and has given most excellent service for eight years. Twenty-seven acres of land adjacent to the pumping station and also on the high ground extending up to Walton road and to Hilldale avenue were acquired to prevent future encroachment. The tract on the top of the mountain where the reservoir is located extends back from South Orange avenue beyond the crest of the mountain and consists of about nine acres. The entire cost of the operation was $221,749.50. This also included the purchase of the land.

Formal opening and inspection of the plant occurred on November 29, 1913, and since then the village has been in possession of a water system which has met every demand made upon it. About one-third of the floor space at the pumping station was left vacant for the possible installation of an electric lighting plant. But this has not yet materialized.

Efforts of the Village Board of Trustees to erect a sewage disposal plant in the township of Millburn were thwarted by an injunction secured by a taxpayer and, after a contest, aggressively waged, it was permanently enjoined from carrying out its project. The Supreme Court held that one municipality could not purchase lands outside of its own limits for sewerage disposal purposes without first obtaining the consent of the municipality within whose boundaries the proposed disposal area would lie. Millburn township refused to grant its consent and the plan was therefore abandoned. Engineer Frederick T. Crane, of Orange, upon invitation, then proposed a gravity line to Newark Bay, tunneling under Headleytown. The estimated cost of ten and a-half miles of outlet sewer was $79,500. Mr. Crane's report was accepted by the Village Board of Trustees, and he was directed to proceed with the plans. Engineers Rudolph Hering and James Owen endorsed the suggestion that Headleytown be tunneled. Proceedings were encountered by the village authorities, however, in the unexpected opposition of property owners who threatened to interpose legal obstructions should any attempt be made to carry out the project. The proposed outlet was then changed and it was decided to discharge the sewage on the meadows at a point three hundred feet from Woodruff's creek, which empties into Bound Brook creek, its outlet finally being in the shoal waters of Newark Bay. Just at this time, early in May, 1898, Robert F. Sinclair, who had been deeply interested in the sewering of the village, called a conference of various municipalities at the Village Hall, as a member of the Board of Trustees, and chairman of the Sewer Committee, for the purpose of considering a joint participation in an outlet sewer direct to the waters of Newark Bay. After expressing favorable opinions of the plan the representatives attending from West Orange, Irvington, Vailsburgh, Newark and South Orange Village, authorized Engineer Alexander Potter to make a preliminary survey. At the next meeting on September 29, 1898, delegates were present from Millburn and South Orange township. Mr. Potter made his report upon the building of the sewer from Irvington junction to tidewater and the next two and a-half years were occupied in preparing the way for the cities and towns to enter into the joint contract, securing rights of way and allowing the engineer opportunity to draw plans and specifications for construction. The contract to join in the union sewer was duly signed on March 15, 1901, by commissioners representing Irvington, Vailsburgh, Newark, Millburn, Summit, South Orange Village and West Orange. Officials elected on March 27 were Edward D. Tuttle, of Irvington, chairman; William Rollinson, West Orange, secretary; Francis Phraner, Summit, treasurer; Adrian Riker, of Newark, counsel, and Alexander Potter, engineer.

Francis Speir, of South Orange, was chosen chairman of the executive committee, which position he held till the end of the construction of the great trunk sewer. Engineer Potter, having prepared his plans for the building of the first section which was to pass through Elizabeth, negotiations were opened by Mr. Speir with the Special Sewer Commission representing that city. It was most important that a speedy settlement be made, as it was correctly adjudged that if the outlet to tidewater was secured the right of way through the remaining territory would not be so difficult to obtain; intimations were made that a large sum of money would be required to secure an agreement permitting the laying of the sewer. Mr. Speir and Engineer Potter so clearly pointed the necessity of immediate action, however, and offering use of the sewer to the city of Elizabeth, that all other demands were waived, and on August 27, 1901, the agreement was duly made between the joint meeting and the municipal officials. In return for the privilege of laying the pipe line, the city was permitted to drain 100,000 cubic feet of house sewage into it every day. This most notable concesssion assured the success of the entire scheme, for with the right of way in the section leading directly to tidewater, there could be little opposition in securing permission to cross property through the balance of the territory. As in this negotiation, so it was in all the proceedings of the joint meeting for three years, harmonious action marking every step of the proceedings. Not once did a discordant note enter into the deliberations of the commissioners.

Section one, the most important part of the sewer, from its entrance into the city of Elizabeth, at the town of Union line to Woodbridge avenue, in diameter is forty-two inches; from there to Princeton avenue, sixty-six inches, and the balance of the distance to Staten Island Sound, at the outlet, it is seventy-two inches, the point of emptying into the water being within two hundred feet of the town of Linden. The sewer extended westerly to Summit, and its entire length, at completion, was twenty-three miles. making it one of the largest sewerage enterprises ever carried on in New Jersey. The idea was suggested by a resident of the village of South Orange and the results obtained were well worth all the labor and financial outlay. Seven inland towns were thus given for all time sewer facilities which under any other arrangement would have been less sanitary, at least. Mr. Speir, as chairman of the Executive Committee, reported at the joint meeting, held on June 16, 1904, that "the Joint Trunk Sewer having been constructed, the life of the joint body ceases tonight, and the new body for maintenance takes its place. We trust that the labors of the new body will be marked by the same unanimity of action as has been shown in the joint body." The items involved in the mass of detail handled by the Executive Committee, varied from the value of three and one-half miles right of way through Bayway in Elizabeth to the damage done to an apple tree. Private rights of way for about one hundred separate plots were purchased.

The Village of South Orange paid $150,000 as its share of the plant. While it was being constructed, sewers were also being laid in the village streets, the cost of which was $253,500. The total cost of building the trunk sewer was $813,000, and the mileage of all sewers laid is 159, involving the expenditure of $1,775,000.

"The one factor standing out pre-eminently and making for the success of the enterprise," said Engineer Potter, in his final report, "was the untiring and intelligent interest taken by Mr. Francis Speir, of South Orange Village, from the inception of the work till its entire completion. While there seems to exist among the members of the Commission a keen rivalry to promote and advance the best interests of the joint project in every way in their power, no one will begrudge this special acknowledgment of the invaluable services of Mr. Speir to secure this end. The fair and impartial manner in which he approached all matters, great or small, won the admiration of all."

Through the tactfulness of Francis Speir, president of the Village Board of Trustees, the Lackawanna railroad officials quickly arrived at an arrangement with the village officials for the elimination of the grade crossings within their jurisdiction. Work was begun in 1914 and finished in the early autumn of the following year. The quaint little wooden building used as the Montrose station seemed a fixture in this picturesque community till the workmen arrived one day and began altering the landscape. The station, the Lyons greenhouses adjoining on the east and everything movable within a certain radius, gave way to the well-prepared plans of the Lackawanna engineers. About December 1, 1914, the public was given an idea of just what was to be accomplished in placing above grade the span of the railroad passing through the village. The new station was just receiving its finishing touches, and instead of having the one approach through Montrose avenue, it was also in line with Vose avenue, the removal of the greenhouses having made this a possible improvement. The new station, built of red tapestry brick, inlaid with block brick, was located on the east side of the track, but the most striking feature of the change aside from the elevation of the tracks was the park effect given the approach from the east. The vehicular paths were paved with amiesite, and a wide walk extended from the corner of Vose avenue and Montrose avenue to the main station. Shrubbery growing in the summer further added to the ornamentation. On the west side of the track a shelter house of the same material as the main station was erected, and there was a wide approach provided by the acquirement of the land at the corner of Meeker street and Montrose avenue. The dwelling standing there was removed further west on Meeker street; the line of Montrose avenue was changed about fifty feet to the west of the former course, between Vose avenue and Meeker street, and the entire work about the Montrose station is in relation to the natural beauty of the surrounding property.

Equally important changes were made at the South Orange station which in no wise interfered with the appearance of abutting property, but in a very great measure added to the values. The abolishing of a dangerous crossing was sufficient reason to permit of any form of grade crossing elimination, but the Lackawanna officials practically spared no money nor time in making the section of their holding through the village as artistic as modern invention could devise. The South Orange station was elevated and the series of pillars used in supporting the tracks about the plaza were all built of concrete and of an imposing style of architecture. The station, erected of the same material as that used at the Montrose depot, extended from a point east of South Orange avenue to Second street. It was found necessary to lower the roadbed of the avenue about two feet to provide the required height of fifteen feet for the tracks. Entrances to the station are from First and Second streets and South Orange avenue. The contribution of the village to the improvement was $23,000, while the Lackawanna Company spent about one million dollars.

President Francis Speir was honored with a banquet by his fellow citizens, served in the new South Orange station on November 15, 1915, as a tribute to his excellent service in bringing about such a laudable and lasting benefit to the village.

Official recognition of the beginning of Columbia School dates from 1814, when the records are first available. A special meeting was held on Wednesday evening, July 22, of that year by "the proprietors and asso-, ciates of the school in South Orange," when "it was agreed that the said associates should exercise the privileges allowed them by law and use the means to become an incorporated body." Seventy-three citizens were enrolled, and on August 3 following the name "Columbian School of South Orange" was formally adopted and the following trustees elected: Moses N. Combs, Nathan Squier, Jotham Quinby, Amos Freeman, Joseph Pierson, Joseph B. Ball and Jeptha Baldwin. Messrs. Squier and Combs were chosen president and secretary respectively, and the school was incorporated on September 9. South Orange was a farming center, the majority of its people living in the same rustic manner as had their forebears for several generations, attending the Sabbath Day services at the meeting house now the First Presbyterian Church of Orange, with the same degree of regularity. The Newark and Morristown turnpike (South Orange avenue) was very much traveled by drovers and teamsters, on their way to or returning from market at Newark.

"It was unanimously resolved," reads a resolution of December 31, 1814, "First, that the trustees of the said school do proceed in arrangements for building; second, that the said building be built on what is commonly called the school house common; third, that the said building be built of wood, two stories high, forty-five feet in length by thirty-five feet in breadth." The funds, $1,716.83, were raised by subscription under the management of the trustees. At a meeting on October 26, 1815, the building having been completed, it was resolved "that the price of tuition be fixed at $1.75 per quarter, for spelling, reading and writing;" for arithmetic, in addition to these branches, twenty-five cents extra was charged. It was also decided to purchase firewood, and divide the cost at the end of each quarter equally among the pupils except such as the trustees deemed expedient to be exempt on account of inability to pay. Isaac Combs, engaged as the first teacher, served only one year. The number of children carried on the roll on March 9, 1818, was forty-five, this being the number guaranteed Aaron McConnell, employed as teacher at the rate of seventy-five dollars per quarter, the school being open the entire year. Henry D. Hedden, who took charge on April 2, 1827, was voted the sum of ninety-six dollars for six months' supervision and teaching, and forty-eight dollars was allowed a woman teacher for the same time. Teachers seldom remained longer than a year. Thus the school continued till after the Civil War. Jacob Maxwell served very acceptably as principal from 1866 to 1886. The brick building, two stories in height, was occupied in place of the one of wood in 1880, at a cost of $16,000, the upper floor, however, not being completed till three years later. Classes were first graded by Mr. Maxwell in 1867, and later the school district was changed from No. 6 Clinton to No. 28 South Orange township, which also included Vailsburg, now part of Newark. During the term of Dr. Elmer E. Sherman, principal, 1887-1893, free text books and supplies were introduced and the High School was established. The first graduating class consisted of one student, Miss Etta Kilburn. Manual training was added to the system in 1890, and in 1891 the High School course was made one of four years. Dr. George J. McAndrew, who succeeded Dr. Sherman, continued as principal from 1893 to 1900. In 1894 the township plan of administration was adopted by the State. The township of South Orange then consisted of three school districts—Hilton, Maplewood and the village, each having a board of trustees of three members. The new system brought all the schools under one control, and a Board of Education of nine members, three to be elected each year, from the district at large, to have entire charge of the schools. In 1898 a brick addition was built on the Columbian School, for which $25,000 was expended.

Henry W. Foster became the superintendent in 1900, and in November another addition of brick and devoted to elementary training was placed on the Columbia building. The cost of construction was $30,000. A special meeting of the taxpayers of Hilton was held on January 9, 1912, when it was voted to spend $12,000 for a lot and at a subsequent meeting on March 5 the sum of $60,000 was authorized for the construction of the school building and $5,000 for the furnishings. The new school first occupied on September 18, 1913, when State Commissioner Calvin N.

RICALTON SCHOOL, SOUTH ORANGE

Kendall delivered the dedicatory address, was named in honor of Seth Boyden, the noted inventor. The rapid increase in population in Maplewood made necessary the enlargement of its school and at a special election on June 10, 1913, the sum of $45,000 to provide a suitable addition was sanctioned by the voters. An allowance of $67,000 was also voted for a school to be erected on Academy street, near Roland avenue. This was dedicated in the following year and named in honor of Charles Gale Fielding, president of the Board of Education for several years. Mr. Fielding died in 1916 and on October 15 of that year a memorial service was held for him at the Columbian School, Hon. John Franklin Fort, former Governor of New Jersey, presiding.

In 1920 the Board of Education authorized the construction of another building at the corner of Grove road and Turrell avenue, and named it in honor of James Marshal, president of the Board during the years 1916-1919, inclusive. This will involve an outlay of $250,000, including the land, building and equipment.

The total enrolment at the end of the school year in June, 1920, was 2,536. All the buildings are taxed for space. The Columbian School arranged for the accommodation of 750 pupils, in 1920 had an enrolment of 1,089. The general plan of the immediate future in administering the affairs of the South Orange schools is to erect elementary school buildings containing the grades of kindergarten and through the sixth at the proper point throughout the district, so that there will be one not far from the home of every young child; to change the Maplewood building in course of time to a junior school, then enrolling the seventh, eighth and ninth grades; to develop the Columbian, first, through a period of six years in the High School, the seventh, eighth and ninth grades forming a junior unit, and the sophomores, juniors and seniors forming a senior unit. After a few years the plan is to erect a Senior High School in the center of the district, but the first thought will be for a series of schools for children not yet adolescent, then the schools at which the young adolescents will be concentrated and one for the older youth.

"The general indication which should be gathered by those who are interested in the efficiency of the schools," comments Superintendent Foster, in his annual report for 1920, "is that there is a tremendous variation in the mental capability of the children. There are as many as seven or eight different ages in a single grade . . . yet there is a curious belief on the part of most people that the schools fail if they do not train every child to become a good penman, a fine speller, an accurate arithmetician and able to read anything intelligently. The truth is that two per cent. of children are actually sub-normal, ten per cent. so mentally low that they find great difficulty in getting and retaining any academic training, and at least thirty per cent. of all pupils decidedly below average mentality. A decidedly important conclusion to be drawn from such facts is that when it is apparent that a child is incapable of mastering academic instruction he should be given in place of that part which he cannot master a practical training that will fit him for being useful in life. . . . It is becoming plainer every day that the assumption of privilege on the part of the few to be a more and more dangerous attitude in this world. The safety of our democracy will depend upon the maintenance of clear avenues of opportunity for those who have mental capability to rise from any locality and any circumstance of birth to become a part of that minority who have the vision and judgment to govern, and the prevention of class privilege of every name and nature. The proper functioning of the schools is vital from this point of view. Americanism stands for equal opportunity for each to make the best of himself, so that he can render the best service of which he is personally capable, looking to the service first, and not to the reward alone: It will be some time before the schools will fully meet the demand that each child shall receive the kind of training to which his type of mentality is adapted—not so long as purely academic training is regarded as the only training worth while and the same sort demanded of every child."

The Board of Education in 1920 is composed of Robert S. Sinclair, president; Harvey I. Underhill, vice-president; Matthew W. Galbraith, William B. Sayer, Harold M. Beattie, Louis V. Blanchet, E. Morgan Barradale, Orrin G. Cocks and George E. Low. Henry W. Foster is superintendent. John H. Bosshart is principal of Columbian School; Miss Juliaette Stewart, principal of the Fielding School; Ross O. Runnels, principal of the Maplewood School, and Miss Mabel F. Starck, principal of the Seth Boyden School, at Hilton. The budget for 1920-1921 is $289,419.48.

"A few years ago the members of the Grand Army of the Republic living in South Orange requested the Board of Education to assume for them the responsibility for the observance of Memorial Day, upon the ground that their purpose was to educate the youth of each succeeding generation through commemoration of the sacrifices that have been made for our national ideals into veneration for the flag and all it stands for, and to inspire them with devotion to our country. The duty was gladly accepted. The flag of the post, the records, the insignia and the little fund that had been accumulated were all received, and since that time the Board has been responsible. On each Memorial Day two processions form, one from Maplewood and one from the Village, which march to the center of the district, at the Fielding School, not far from the cemetery, and there in a most beautiful and adequate setting have joined in inspiring exercises such as cannot fail to train all who attend in true patriotism."—From a report of Superintendent Foster.

The South Orange Library Association held its first meeting in 1864 at the rooms of the Republican Club, the members first enrolled being William J. Beebe, Charles J. Beebe, F. L. B. Mayhew, George Waite, Rev.

FREE PUBLIC LIBRARY, SOUTH ORANGE

D. G. Sprague, Rev. J. Allen Maxwell, Lewis B. Henry, Edwin H. Mead, Joseph L. Taintor, Phineas Bartlett, Eugene H. Durand, Joseph W. Taylor and Moses A. Peck. Stephen Ballard was appointed librarian in 1865 at an annual salary of $150, and from which he was expected to pay an assistant. At the close of the first year there were 139 members on the roster, and 567 volumes on the shelves. The library was incorporated under the general laws of the State on October 25, 1886, the incorporators being Carl Edward Billquist, president; Bella C. Morrow, vice-president; Henry F. Hitch, treasurer; Margaret Howard White, secretary, and Annie Redmond Cross, Lily Page Ely, Bella C. Brown, Sophia Rutan Connett, Henry Lilly, Frank A. Wright. An offer of Eugene V. Connett, on November 28, 1894, to furnish a lot on the west side of Scotland road, at Taylor place, for the erection of a stone or brick building to be used for library purposes, was conditioned upon the raising of $7,500, the estimated amount of the construction. This was raised, and Mr. Connett increased the size of the lot by an addition of twenty-five feet. Formal opening was on May 8, 1896, the address being made by Edward Self, a longtime resident of the village; James McC. Morrow reported that $7,743.98 was contributed and expended in the enterprise and that the association was free of debt; Mrs. Edwin H. Mead contributed a beautiful clock in memory of her husband; T. O'Conor Sloane was given credit as the one securing the first subscription to the building fund; appreciation was expressed to Mr. Connett for his generous gift of the land, and Harmon H. Hart, president of the Village Board of Trustees, also expressed the appreciation of the village officially. The total number of books in the library was 4,571. In May, 1920, the number had increased to 10,796. The officers are: President, H. J. Schnell; vice-president, James Marshall; secretary, Irwin Berry; treasurer, A. T. Brainard. Miss Julia Schneider is the librarian.

For the purpose of encouraging outdoor sports and for the promotion of social intercourse, a group of athletes and others meeting at the home of William Frederick Allen, on June 14, 1889, decided to form an organization in which these two features would have a wide scope. An agreement was signed by forty-four tentative members to become identified with it under by-laws to be "hereafter adopted, the initiation fee to be five dollars." This was the creation of the South Orange Field Club, one of the most widely known athletic organizations in northern New Jersey, and which has for a third of a century sustained the true spirit of the sportsman who loved a good game in the great outdoors. The first officers chosen were: President, Reune Martin; vice-president, William H. Curtis; treasurer, Henry W. Freeman; secretary, Robert Speer. During the summer of 1889 baseball and tennis were played on Dr. Fenner's field, and in the autumn a five-year lease was effected with the Meadow Land Society for use of the field north of South Orange avenue and between the Lackawanna railroad and the East Branch of the Rahway river, the society practically agreeing to grade the land and bring it to a condition needed by the club. Edwin H. Mead presented the barn occupying part of the premises, to be used as the club house, which, after being remodeled and otherwise improved, served well its purpose. A bowling alley was added and part of the field was flooded in the winter months and skating enjoyed. Tennis courts and baseball were played in the summer and other games were introduced as the demand was created for them. In January, 1895, the club house was destroyed by fire. Arrangements were at once made for the erection of a specially designed building, costing about $11,000.

When golf became a popular outdoor sport a course was opened in the immediate vicinity, in line with the progressive ideas of the founders, that games tending to prove the mettle of true sportsmen should be fostered by the club. The membership in 1920 was 475, and the officers were: President, Arthur A. Kreuter; vice-president and secretary, Harold Milbank; treasurer, Charles W. Hodson.

Rev. Louis Cameron, rector of the Church of the Holy Communion, and one of the best known men of the village, was seized with a serious illness in the autumn of 1909, and a flood of sympathy poured into the rectory from every direction. The beloved minister, the faithful guardian of the parish since November 1, 1895, had also served several local organizations, notably Century Lodge, Free and Accepted Masons, as its Master. There was but one thought in the public mind when his spirit took flight into the other world—that a memorial should be erected to his name and kindly offices. Subscriptions were quickly forthcoming and the five-acre tract situated on the east branch of the Rahway river was purchased and turned over to the village authorities as the playground for the children and in memory of Rev. Mr. Cameron. It was dedicated in 1912 as the Cameron Field. A walk was laid from South Orange avenue to the entrance of the ground, and there the boys and girls find ample space and apparatus to play to their hearts' content.

William Frederick Allen, who came to South Orange in 1880 and settled on Ralston avenue, was the inventor of the Standard Time, now used in every part of the world. In 1875 he was elected permanent secretary of the Railway Time Convention, in which all the railway companies of the country were members. Mr. Allen presented to the association at their meeting in April, 1883, a report advocating the adoption of a complete system of standardizing time which he had devised, providing for an elastic instead of a rigid boundary line between the hour sections, designated every point on the boundary lines where the change from one hour section to the other was to be made, arranged a method of passing from the use of one hour standard to another without danger of interference or mistake, and proposed nothing that could not be adopted in practice. By this change, at the stroke of the hour at high noon on November 18, 1883, fifty different standards of time resolved themselves simultaneously into four, while the minute hands of watches were reset at all points to the same minute mark on the dial. One of the most effective changes was noticed on a certain railroad running from New York to Boston which used three distinct standards of time. Thus the recording of the hours as we have it today was the invention of Mr. Allen, who later, in 1884, was appointed by President Arthur a delegate to represent the United States at the International Meridian Conference, which met by invitation of the Government at Washington in October of that year. The Meridian of Greenwich was there chosen as the international prime meridian and standard of time reckoning. This was Mr. Allen's system, and it has worked out most successfully the world over.

Seton Hall College, near South Orange avenue, and opposite Center street, occupies a commanding position on a plot of land formerly known as Chestnut Ridge, and was built about 1860. The college was founded at Madison in 1856, as a Catholic institution, and incorporated under the laws of New Jersey in 1861. The buildings are commodious and provided with all the modern equipment. Fire has visited the college upon several occasions but each time the restoration has been immediate. The college was named for Mother Seton, who introduced the Sisters of Charity into the United States. She was the aunt of Rev. J. Roosevelt Bayley, who attributed the conversion of his faith to the prayers offered by her.

Fifty years have passed since the village form of government was adopted for this section of South Orange, and the one prevailing idea of the founders that it should ever be the home of people of culture and refinement has been well sustained. There are twenty-five miles of streets, nearly all paved with modern treatment, and the area of the village is 1,575 acres. The center of affairs is in the Village Hall, at the corner of South Orange avenue and Scotland road, where all the departments are housed. The oldest official in point of service is the clerk, M. F. Fitzsimmons, who has held the position twenty years. A total population of 7,274 was given by the census of 1920. The net assessed valuations are $14,863,526; the local budget raised by taxation amounts to $174.310, for county purposes $92,584.90 and for schools, $128,985.67. There are sufficient fire and police departments, a Shade Tree Commission, and a Board of Health is continually alert in its special work. There are six churches—the First Presbyterian Church, Trinity Presbyterian Church, Church of Our Lady of Sorrows, First Methodist Episcopal Church, Church of the Holy Communion and the Colored Baptist Church. The free postal delivery has been in operation since December 1, 1900.

EAST ORANGE FREE PUBLIC LIBRARY

CHAPTER LXXXV

EAST ORANGE

Though the country was passing through a costly Civil War and the critical stage of it had not yet been reached, the leaders of the eastern part of Orange were not awed in their demands made upon the Legislature during the sesssion of 1863 that a new municipality for them and their fellow citizens be created. They wanted separation from Orange, and their wishes were granted. After the excitement had calmed a little following the passage and approval of the measure the people began taking their bearings. Some were living in East Orange, the name of the new town, who desired residence in Orange, and *vice versa.* Unique distinction was given several families of having their sleeping rooms in one town and their dining room in another. The boundaries had been made as freely as possible that those citizens who so desired could be free of incorporated Orange. It was the wish of the people living in East Orange to enjoy the simple life, free of the frills and influences of a town assuming "city airs." If Orange had not sought its enlarged powers in 1860, when the charter was granted, it is a grave question if East Orange would ever have existed. The boundaries as laid down in the act approved March 4, 1863, are:

Beginning at a point on the line between the town of Orange and the township of South Orange, where the center of Center street in said town of Orange would intersect said line; thence in a northerly or northeasterly direction to a point on the north side of Main street, in the said town of Orange where the line between the lands of Caleb G. Harrison and Nathan W. Pierson, near the corner of Baldwin street and said Main street would intersect the north side of Main street; thence in a northerly or northeasterly direction to a large oak tree on the lands of and near the residence of William Patterson; thence in a northerly or northeasterly direction to a point on the east side of Park street, in said town of Orange, where the angle in said street, near the residence of Aaron Williams would intersect said point; thence on in the direction of the last mentioned line to the west side of Park street; thence in a northerly or northeasterly direction to a point in the center of the bridge over the Nishuyne Brook, where the south side of Dodd street (or the street running from David Riker's store to the Orange Cemetery) would intersect said point; thence in a northerly or northeasterly direction to a point in the center of the north side of the bridge near the residence of Henry Stucky, and thence in the line of the last mentioned line to the line between the town of Orange and the township of Bloomfield; thence along the line between the said town of Orange and the said township of Bloomfield to the line between the town of Orange and the city of Newark; thence along the line between the said town of Orange and the said city of Newark to the line between the town of Orange and the township of

South Orange; thence along the line between the said town of Orange and the said township of South Orange to the place of beginning.

About two thousand four hundred acres, or less than four square miles, were included in the area, the larger part of it being unimproved except for farming purposes. The act provided for the election of a township committee and other officials on the second Monday in April. This was held at Timothy W. Mulford's wheelwright shop, on the south side of Main street, east of Burnet street. Mr. Mulford was a man of affairs, for a score of years conducting a successful business in the manufacture of wagons. The total number of votes cast at the election was only 112. The disparity between them and the population of 3,000 was caused by the large number of men being absent from town and enrolled in the Federal army and navy fighting for the maintenance of the Constitution in the Civil War.

There were three school districts—Ashland, Franklin and Eastern—which were managed by boards of trustees. The election was for officials to govern the city, Aaron Harrison being the judge of election and Charles Crane clerk. The following were chosen members of the Township Committee: William King, John M. Randall, Aaron B. Harrison, Charles Crane and Elias O. Doremus; Assessor, Moses H. Williams; Receiver of Taxes, George Condit; Overseer of Roads, Stephen M. Peck; Overseer of Poor, Henry Pierson; members of Board of Chosen Freeholders, James Peck and Calvin Dodd.

The Township Committee's meetings were held at the office of Moses H. Williams, 251 Main street. William King, who had been most active in securing the passage of the act creating East Orange, was chosen chairman on April 16; Joseph L. Munn, clerk, and Amzi Dodd, counsel. In the settlement with Orange the town received one-third of the Poor Farm, thirty-three and one-third acres, fronting on South Orange avenue. Then the committee proceeded to fix the budget for the year, which amounted to $8,488.60. The ratables were placed at $1,042,350.

The Second Presbyterian Church of Orange (Brick Presbyterian), at the corner of Prospect and Main streets, did not at once change its name. For a third of a century the families of that denomination living in the territory east of Park street, Orange, and extending to the great Meadow brook, the boundary line at Newark, were as a rule regular attendants at the church services on the Sabbath and at the mid-week prayer meeting.

The boundaries of the town produced an awkward effect upon the parish. The parsonage, at the corner of Hillyer and William streets, was placed in Orange and the church in East Orange. Rev. James H. Taylor, who succeeded Rev. John Crowell as pastor, November 18, 1863, was a militant minister of the Gospel, and kindly hearted. He was soon the central figure of the community, and upon him the critical eye was cast by

HOUSE BUILT BY DAVID RIKER ABOUT 1846; FOR MANY YEARS THE ONLY STORE OF ITS KIND BETWEEN MONTCLAIR AND ORANGE; A MEN'S GATHERING PLACE FOR SEVERAL GENERATIONS, AT CORNER OF DODD AND NORTH PARK STREETS, EAST ORANGE.

those who did not favor the aggressive and patriotic manner he assumed as he went on his daily missions, traveling about the parish on horseback and relieving distress, regardless of the church membership of the family in need. The minister became more popular than ever. But an opposition developed, and on January 24, 1868, he resigned, while the parish was at its greatest height of prosperity. Before leaving, he and Mrs. Taylor were laden with gifts, resolutions and other expressions of good will of the large majority who wanted him to remain.

There was another church in East Orange in 1863—the First Baptist, instituted on June 16, 1837. The edifice in which the congregation worshiped was erected at the corner of Mechanic street (North Maple avenue) and a lane leading to Grove street running alongside the Lackawanna tracks. Elder John Beetham was called as the first pastor, and served about a year. Rev. Willim D. Hedden, a native of Orange, who married Miss Rachel Hatt, daughter of John Hatt, a founder of the church, was the pastor in 1863. He had served one year, from May 13, 1855, to June 22, 1856, when he resigned. Recalled in 1858, Mr. Hedden, who later received the degree of Doctor of Divinity, continued as pastor till 1882. He was a native of Orange, and beloved by a large circle of townspeople. The Munn Avenue Presbyterian Church was taking form in this period, its organization meeting being held on June 24, 1863, in the Eastern District school house, situated on the southerly side of Main street, opposite the Eastern School of a later date. The first pastor was Rev. Fergus Lafayette Kenyon, a recent seminarian, who served till 1867. Henry Pierson, Jotham Hedden and Samuel C. Jones were elected elders, and plans were at once devised for the erection of the edifice at the corner of Munn avenue and Main street.

Improvement of the roadways began in 1869, the Township Committee having awarded the contract for the macadamizing of two sections of Main street, one extending from Prospect street to the Orange line, and the other from Grove street to the Newark line. The remainder of the roadway was completed in 1870. During the next two years other streets were attended to, most important of all being Washington street, which was nearly ten feet below grade, at Main street. Cherry street, Munn avenue, Prospect street, North Park street, Dodd street, Grove street and Harrison street were also macadamized. Gas lamps were first lighted in Cherry, Harrison and Washington streets, on October 7, 1872. In 1873, on the tenth anniversary of the town government, the population, in keeping with the improvements, was of slow growth. The Federal census of 1870 showed the total number of persons living in East Orange to be 4,115, so that there could not have been more than 5,000 in residence on March 4, 1873. Ridges and valleys were topographical features of the landscape, and brooks and partly inundated lands existed in every part of the town. South of the Lackawanna tracks and east of Harrison street, Halsted's woods and bog land (owned by Matthias

Ogden Halsted), extended a long distance. They were very popular with young people, who enjoyed picnics there in summer and skating in winter. A brook, having its source in the lots west of Harrison street, near the Lackawanna tracks, flowed northeasterly, crossing Main and Washington streets and then on to the brook which ran by the eastern edge of Cat Swamp, in a northerly direction. The latter began at the point on Main street, opposite the First Reformed Church. The Elizabeth river's source was in a spring, afterward part of the High School site on Winans street. The water has continued its flow for time immemorial and showed no signs of abating in the second decade of the Twentieth Century. The stream takes a southerly course across Main street and parallels South Arlington avenue. In Doddtown a chain of ponds, enclosed on the course of the Second river, were furnishing power for the Dodd sawmill on Glenwood avenue, near the Bloomfield line, then operated by Israel Dodd, who became a town official, and the grist mill run by Reuben Dodd, at the point where Midland avenue now crosses the stream. Half a mile further west, Matthias Soverel, the first ice man of the community, impounded the water principally for use in the winter months, when its frozen surface furnished skating for the devotees of this healthful pastime and also sundry harvests of the ice crop for the following season's supply. Matthias Dodd was a prosperous farmer, whose home was on Grove street, and Aaron P. Mitchell, his home on Main street, near Mechanic street (now Maple avenue), was specializing in the dairy products for which this part of the town had become popular. Park avenue and Central avenues had not been opened, and the only direct route from East Orange to Newark was over the Main street.

Some day a wise man will tell us why the site of the present City Hall was named "The Promise Land" in the hazy period antedating the beginning of East Orange. Other familiar places were "Crow Hill," at the apex of Harrison street, about where the Orphan Home is situated; "Pecktown," in the vicinity of Main street and Maple avenue and Cherry street (North Arlington avenue) ; a few of the older residents were still speaking of "Whiskey Lane" (now Grove street), and Bull Spring, sending forth a never-failing supply of excellent water from the quicksands in the valley between Prospect street and Glenwood avenue, was so named because a fine animal was said to have disappeared in the uncertain soil about the spot.

Boot and shoe making was the chief industry of the town, and the men-folk gathered at the stores at night on week days, just as they do now in the back settlements, and discussed the questions of the day. David Riker's store, at the corner of North Park and Dodd streets, in Doddtown, was a favorite resting place for travelers on their way to and from Cranestown, a few years later named Montclair, and there the gossip of the day was dispensed. The horse-car passed along Main street at irregular intervals, and the Morris & Essex railroad was the only medium for reaching New York by direct route.

Streets were not lighted at night; there were no improved roadways, nor sidewalks; the post office was in Orange; the water for domestic purposes was drawn from wells or springs; gardening in the summer months was fashionable, and neighborly calls in the evening at all seasons were in vogue. Guided by the uncertain rays of a lighted lantern, men and women picked their way over the uneven way till they reached the desired location. The life of the town was primitive but enjoyed nevertheless and proved a very substantial foundation for the great city expected in the distant future.

During the first ten years improvements were slowly and steadily made. George W. Thorpe, who opened Glenwood avenue, from Washington street to Springdale avenue, in 1867, had purchased the Samuel Condit farm, the homestead of which was at the corner of East Park and Washington streets. Mr. Thorpe built his handsome home on Glenwood avenue, opposite East Park street, and also erected other houses in the vicinity. On March 14, 1868, Halsted street was being opened from Main street to Central avenue, and on March 4 a supplement to the East Orange act passed the Legislature, giving the Township Committee power to provide gas lamps and other improvements. A contract was awarded for the laying of a plank sidewalk on Main street on September 19 of this year. Charles H. Sleight announced on November 28 that he had opened two hundred acres of skating pond at Mulberry (now North Clinton) street and William street. This was a section of the Cat Swamp. Work on Central avenue was completed on July 4, 1868, and one year later, on September 18, 1869, an article appeared in the newspapers stating that some one had fenced in the section between Grove street and the Newark line and planted Indian corn thereon.

East Orange was then the seventeenth municipality in the State in point of population. The total value of taxable property reported by Assessor James E. Reynolds in 1873 was $4,829,400, and there were less than eight hundred houses in the town. No street ran west from Harrison street between the railroad and Central avenue, and no street, except Harrison street, in the section known in later years as the Third Ward had been in use ten years. Amherst street ran only from Central avenue to Harvard street; Burnett street extended from Main street to Beech street; South Walnut street ended at a fence line a hundred yards south of the railroad; South Arlington avenue, then known as South Cherry street, had just been opened from Lenox avenue (then Orange street) to Central avenue; Shepard avenue, Carnegie avenue and Oak street north of Central avenue were unknown, and Orange, Chestnut and Beech streets had just been laid out and were entirely unoccupied save for two small houses on the westerly end of Beech street. In the entire section of the

Third Ward, bounded by Evergreen place, South Cherry street, Central avenue and the Lackawanna railroad, there were only thirty-eight houses.

South of Central avenue and west of Clinton street, Williamsville had been laid out by Moses H. Williams, who was a member of the House of Assembly, and a well-known operator in real estate. East of this tract the Elmwood Home Association, incorporated May 11, 1853, had laid out thirteen streets, but the houses were few in number. The tract was bounded by Elmwood avenue, Rhode Island avenue, Oak street, and Park street (now Freeman street). The incorporators were Daniel T. Clark, president; Isaac M. Tucker, secretary; James Williams, Leonard Lewis, William Burnet, B. F. Harrison, S. W. Mulford, David Thompson, W. M. Wyckoff, George T. Smith and C. O. Jessup.

Munn avenue, Maple avenue and Grove street were the only ones opened from Main street to Central avenue, east of South Cherry street. Hawthorne avenue had not been projected nor had Mitchell place, Winthrop terrace and Pulaski street (now Hollywood avenue). Steuben and Sterling streets ran only from Main street a short distance south of Sussex avenue, and ended at the Mitchell farm. The extension of these streets through this tract and also the opening of Ninth avenue, from the Newark line to Grove street, placed in the market a large tract of land which was quickly disposed of to homeseekers. South of Central avenue the Cemetery of the Holy Sepulchre occupied a large tract extending from Grove street west, and from Munn avenue east was the farm and homestead of James Peck, one of the best known men of the period, who served as a member of the House of Assembly and of the Essex County Board of Freeholders for a series of years. The farm was afterward divided and sub-divided, streets laid out and the tract named Hyde Park, where a large population was to find a home in later years.

Mulberry street (now North Clinton street) ran north from Main street, and merged into Summit street, the latter continuing to Cherry street. Lloyd avenue (Ashland avenue) began at William street and ran north across the line of Carleton street, which from that point extended to Prospect street. The extension of Carleton street, from Ashland avenue to North Clinton street; of Ashland avenue, from Main street to William street, and from Carleton to Summit streets, with the extension of the latter street intersecting Ashland avenue, and the opening of Prospect terrace, north of Carleton street, from Prospect street to Ashland avenue brought a large and valuable tract into the market. Walnut street, which had just been extended from Park avenue to Springdale avenue, also made available a number of building lots upon which high grade residences were to be erected.

Doddtown, which had been very much agitated in recent years over an effort to change its name to that of Orange Dale, was feeling the impetus of a real estate boom, which suddenly came to a climax in the panic

PALMER HOUSE, EAST ORANGE

of September in 1873.   Charles A. Lighthipe, Michael Mohor, David N.
Ropes and other dealers in real estate were opening farms and converting
them into building lots, and of course, laying out many miles of streets.
Dodd street was the principal artery of travel through Doddtown, the
outlet being through Prospect street on the east, and North Park street
on the west.   Midland avenue only extended from the Bloomfield line to
Dodd street, but a lane connected the main thoroughfare with a grist mill
built at the foot of the hill, on the Second river.

The northeastern section had not begun to feel the real estate boom.
The opening of Park avenue from the Newark line to Llewellyn Park did
not result in a demand for building lots, and the entire line of the avenue
was marked by vacant lots and few houses.

Hope Lodge, No. 124, Free and Accepted Masons, was the first fraternal body organized in East Orange.   Thomas W. Topham, who became
the first master, and Nelson G. Baldwin, called the Masons living in the
town to a meeting held in the Eastern School House, on the south side of
Main street, near Maplewood avenue, on July 22, 1871.   It was there
decided to proceed with the enrolment, and then apply to the Grand Lodge
for a charter.   The lodge was regularly constituted on February 5, 1872,
with the following officers: Thomas W. Topham, master; Nelson G.
Baldwin, senior warden; Charles F. R. Moore, junior warden; George
Booth, treasurer; John D. Topham, secretary; Charles B. Day, senior
deacon; A. E. Hedden, junior deacon; John G. Truesdell and Henry A.
Hottenroth, masters of ceremonies, and Joseph C. Wills, tyler.

Gardner R. Colby, George W. Fortmeyer, Samuel C. Burdick and
others equally as well known, organized the East Orange Improvement
Society in 1880, for the purpose of discussing public affairs, suppressing
any nuisance which might creep into the town, and to guard it against
any objectionable enterprises.   The membership numbered nearly three
hundred, and among the many accomplishments of the town which found
a ready sponsor in the Improvement Society was the abolishment of the
Sewerage Disposal Works and the direct connection with tidewater
through the Newark sewers; the improvement of the roadways, and improved train service on the Lackawanna railroad.   The object in view
of the Association was to make the town one of select residence and to
provide for the comfort of the people.   Its Committee on Public Welfare
was ever active in regard to these matters.   The society continued till
about 1900, when its need was no longer felt and the governing body was
giving the very best possible service to the taxpayers.

The "East Orange Gazette," established in 1873, and published on
Thursdays, was the one local organ, official and otherwise.   In the issue
of January 10, 1878, it was announced that "a pleasant company recently
assembled in the lecture room of the Junction Church to listen to a telephone.   A wire connected the room with Joseph L. Munn's house, and
the words spoken and pieces sung were heard very distinctly."

Residents in the vicinity of the Brick Church station of the Lackawanna railroad were developing public sentiment at this time favorable
to its improvement. Washington place had no outlet at the southerly end,
it being blocked by the wooden building erected in 1864. The population
was increasing and the commuting element was demanding better accommodations about the station. Agreeing to erect a brick building in
place of the one now considered useless, the company was true to its word
when the citizens became active in securing the necessary land. The support of N. B. Taylor, who owned the property on the west side of Washington place, was enlisted, and he offered to give twenty-five feet of a plot
100x80, if he was allowed $2,000 for the balance. The money was ad-
vanced by Gardner Colby, of Harrison street, till it was raised by public
subscription. Mr. Taylor also gave a strip of land thirty-five feet front
on the north side of the railroad, and which provided an outlet to Harrison street. Other purchases of property and the removal of a few old
buildings completely transformed the "dead-end" street and its surroundings. The depot, well adapted in every way for the accommodation of the
public and having a wide plaza, was opened on December 1, 1880. Three
years later the East Orange station, of similar type and surrounding, was
erected.

A strong tendency toward a more efficient government was manifested by those citizens familiar with the city affairs as the decade of
1880 merged into the last one of the Nineteenth Century. The three
school districts—Franklin, Ashland and Eastern—had been recognized
for some time in the annual election for members of the Township Committee, two representatives being elected from each and one at large to
serve thereon. In 1886 the town was laid out in four wards, but the
school districts remained a few years longer. Each of the wards was
represented in the governing body by two members, and one selected at
large, making nine in all. In 1892 the creation of the Fifth Ward added
two more, and thus the membership remained till 1895, when an act of
the Legislature gave authority to the town to elect a president, possessing
all the powers of a presiding officer and those of a mayor. Joseph P.
Thompson was first elected to the office, being succeeded by Colonel
Abraham Ryan in 1897, and he by Edward E. Bruen.

It was very apparent in, the latter part of the closing decade of the
Nineteenth Century that the township form of government would no
longer answer the purposes of a municipality so highly organized as East
Orange. One legislator characterized the situation as similar to that of
a man endeavoring to array himself in boy's clothing. The population
was about 30,000, and embarrassing situations arose at unexpected mo-
ments. At a special election on December 9, 1899, the voters accepted
the law incorporating the town as a city. Anticipating the assumption
of a new government, the Township Committee decided on January 29,

1898, to erect a new City Hall on the Main street line and in front of the brick building used ten years or more, partly by the city officials and partly by the police department, the latter, however, now demanding all the space. The corner-stone of the new building was laid on July 29, 1898, and its occupation on December 11, 1899, marked also the institution of the city government. President Edward E. Bruen was sworn into office as the first mayor, and the name of the East Orange Township Committee was changed to the East Orange City Council. Edward R. Crippen was selected the first chairman, and Judge John Franklin Fort, serving as counsel, was continued in that office. During the evening the judge and others made addresses of felicitation upon the auspicious event, and all spoke optimistically of the future. Since then the city has taken a position as a model municipality, an economic and efficient administration marking the passing years.

Three years later the City Council was nevertheless struggling with one of its greatest problems. Certain citizens wanted Park and Central avenues transferred to the care, custody and control of the Essex County Park Commission, and others were equally insistent that trolley lines should be operated along them. The application of the Public Service Corporation to the City Council for a franchise to operate a trolley line on Central avenue created a furore in the city. Notwithstanding strong opposition, the ordinance passed the Council on May 2, 1902, at one of the stormiest meetings in the town and city history. A group of citizens, well known for their determination to carry out a purpose, declared as they left the hall that the councilmen would regret the step they had taken. One irate citizen announced that he would organize a movement which would drive every man who voted for the ordinance out of the City Hall.

Three months later the Citizens' Union was organized at the home of George H. Austin, corner of Washington and Hillyer streets. Archer Brown was named president, Samuel H. Dodd treasurer, and Alden Freeman secretary. The platform adopted, which proclaimed the organization to be non-partisan, recommended certain improvements in the administration of city affairs and, of course, inveighed against the trolley line on Central avenue. Edward K. Sumerwell was nominated for mayor, and a complete ticket was placed in every ward to be voted upon at the November election in 1902.

The campaign became exciting as the Union's orators went through the city proclaiming the need of a change in the city government. Telling arguments were used in the speechmaking, and literature was sent broadcast explaining why there should be a change in the City Hall management. The Republicans, being in power, were required to respond to the criticisms, but the situation was unique in that it was the first time that they had ever been called upon to contest for the city or township offices. Overwhelming in numbers, the Republicans had practically elected their ticket at the primary, and the general election was merely a formal affair in so far as it related to the election of local officials. But now all the peaceful ways were changed to a whirlwind pre-election contest, savoring more of the years when a President of the United States was chosen. The Democrats, lured to the Citizens' Union fold by its proclamation of non-partisanship, were enjoying their novel relation of being actually engaged in a contest for local officials, which seemed productive of success.

When the announcement was made of the contest at the November polls, it gave the Citizens' Union officials encouragement to go on in their fight, though they had only elected two members to the City Council and also a representation on the Board of Education. Farnham Yardley, of the Second Ward, and Willis L. Brownell, of the Fifth Ward, were the councilmen elected, and Julian Arthur Gregory, a Democrat of the Fifth Ward, was elected a school commissioner. Mr. Gregory, becoming popular, was elected mayor in 1911, and the first and only one of that party so honored. He served several terms and gave a very satisfactory administration.

Again mustering courage, the Citizens' Union entered the campaign of 1903 and continued its crusade against the City Hall officials. The contest was continued another year or so, and the Central avenue ordinance, having been shunted back and forth between the City Council and the courts, was finally passed on June 10, 1904. The contest may well be considered as the most aggressive ever waged in the city for the introduction of an improvement. Trolley cars running along Central avenue were the open sesame, as it were, for the development of unoccupied land, bringing homesteaders and adding to the taxable valuations of the city. The Elmwood section, in its highly populous state of 1920, justifies the City Council's action, but since the ordinance granting the franchise became of record the automobile and jitney have come into general use, and the transportation problem is no longer confined to the steam and trolley cars.

Under the direction of the City Council, Jerome D. Gedney, city counsel, and Edward M. Colie, engaged as associate, a charter designed to meet the special needs of East Orange was prepared and submitted to a committee of citizens representing the various civic and political organizations. After it had been thoroughly digested, a bill was prepared incorporating the charter, for introduction in the Legislature of the winter of 1908. It became Chapter 250 of the public laws, and effective January 1, 1909, if the voters affirmed at a special or general election. One of the provisions was for the recall of the mayor for nonfeasance or malfeasance in office, and ample power given the department officials to conduct their affairs in the most expeditious manner and without hampering the

HOUSE FORMERLY STANDING ON NORTH PARK STREET, NEARLY OPPOSITE HIL-
TON STREET, EAST ORANGE; PROBABLY BUILT ABOUT 1800, BY ELIAS O. MEEKER

interests of the city. The charter was adopted by the voters at the November election in 1908. The taxable valuations in 1920 are $64,536,554, and the total levy is $1,873,650.62. The budget for local needs is $967,-398.84.

Charles H. Martens is mayor of the city, and the members of the City Council are: First Ward, William B. Dailey and J. Wallace Winslow; Second Ward, Augustus Roche, Jr., and Frank Bliss Colton (chairman); Third Ward, Milton W. Chalmers and William E. Wilson; Fourth Ward, George M. Thornton and Nathaniel P. Gardner; Fifth Ward, Joseph M. Brown and Burton E. Emory.

East Orange had a population in 1920 of 50,710, and though electric light had been used by municipalities generally throughout the country, even those of one-half of the population of the city, the authorities have held on to the gas flame for illuminating the streets at night. In another year, it is hoped, there will be a change and Main street, at least, furnished with a light at night which will eliminate the shadows settling down upon the thoroughfare after sunset. The City Hall has failed for several years to meet the requirements of the growing city, and it has become necessary to secure quarters elsewhere for the Board of Health and the Water Department. There are about seventy-two miles of streets in the city, all but seven miles of which are paved. Keeping pace with the modern-day road building, the Engineering Department has introduced many of the systems in use in other cities, and which have given general satisfaction. Washington street is paved with wood block, and being an artery of travel has well stood the wear for several years. Main street, which has been sustaining the weight of heavy traffic upon its concrete pavement, is to be disturbed, according to present indications, during the coming year, when the sidewalks are to be reduced in size several feet and the space thrown into the roadway. This will mean the removal of fine shade trees and resetting many of the pipes laid under the surface.

The city spent $13,000 during the year, in round numbers, in maintaining and planting shade trees about the city. This is one of the most useful departments and the work of preserving the thousands of specimens to be seen about the streets engage the time of a corps of experts and assistants. Superintendent Ernest H. Bennett has been a faithful official for many years.

A perfect drainage system, involving over thirteen miles of piping, clears the valleys of surface water immediately after rainfall, and is quite in contrast with the condition noted only a few years ago in certain parts of the city where standing water made it quite impossible for pedestrians and others to pass along. The health of the city has increased proportionately by the building of these drains and it has been well worth the money spent upon them. Ever since the mosquito extermination became a county propaganda through the establishment of the Essex County

Mosquito Extermination Commission, and of which Dr. Ralph H. Hunt, of East Orange, is the president, the Board of Health has coöperated in every way to drive the pest out of the community. Waste water no longer collects at any time of the year, and the running brooks passing through the city carry away the surface water not taken care of by the drains.

East Orange has branched out into a city famed for its high-grade features—schools, water, its government and other agencies. The fire and police departments are well regulated and entirely free from political influence, and so it can be said of the entire local government that there is absolute freedom of any power aside from the regularly constituted officials having charge of the public affairs. This comment is not made as a reflection upon any other community or municipality, but it is a condition that the progressive citizens pride themselves upon, and rightly so.

Ampere, which includes the larger part of the Fifth Ward, is practically a city by itself, its interest being quite local, though its loyalty to the city as a whole is as consistent as those living in other sections. It has a branch post office named Ampere, and its residents fully appreciate the perils of grade crossing on the Montclair branch of the Lackawanna railroad which passes through that part of the city. Elevation of the tracks is now forecasted in 1922. Main street, in the vicinity of Grove street, is also a distinct part of the town. The brick building standing at the south corner of the two thoroughfares, was known for many years as National Hall, and used for a time in the early days of the incorporated town as a public library. Public celebrations of Independence Day were held in the auditorium of this building in the decade of 1870.

Hyde Park, extending south from Central avenue and east of Munn avenue, has grown up on the farm of James Peck, and is well laid out with streets, fronting on which are the comfortable homes of a goodly number of people. Elmwood, the section south of Central avenue, and from Freeman street, on the east to Sanford street, on the west, is also a section having its own peculiar characteristics. The beautiful Elmwood Park is a valuable asset, and for a number of years the neighborhood interest centered about the chapel which Richard Purdue was instrumental in starting soon after the beginning of the town, and now the Elmwood Presbyterian Church. Long stretches of vacant land of a quarter of a century ago are now occupied by homes and other buildings. Central avenue, in this vicinity, has become a business center which adds to the exclusive character of the environment. Brick Church is named for the edifice standing at the corner of Prospect and Main streets. A large volume of business is there transacted daily. Though it has no local official standing, Brick Church is the name of the principal Lackawanna station in the Oranges and is familiar through the country to the traveling public. At Arlington avenue and Main street, another business section was early developed, and here the post office has always been located. During the first two decades the locality was known as the "Junction," because the horse cars crossed the steam railroad tracks at this point.

Doddtown, of the olden days, is no more, but the First Ward, the name now applied to the northern section of the city, includes all the original territory. It is believed that there are more owners of homes in the First Ward than in any other part of the city, and under the banner of the First Ward Local Interest Club there is a live, intensive interest in its welfare.

One of the hoped for achievements in the line of æsthetics is the outcome of the City Planning Commission's efforts, which involves a plan of rounding out awkward corners, straightening streets, making beauty spots and performing other acts toward making the city symmetrical and beautiful.

There are thirty-three churches in East Orange—five Presbyterian, four Methodist, three Congregational, four Episcopal, four Roman Catholic, two Baptist, one Evangelical Lutheran, one Disciples of Christ, two Dutch Reformed, one Swedish Methodist, one Independent Methodist, one Independent Christian Brethren, three Colored Baptist and one Christian Science.

Of the fraternal and benevolent societies the Free and Accepted Masons have four—Hope Lodge, Ophir Lodge and East Orange Lodge, and Jersey Commandery, Knights Templar. All meet in the Lyceum, which was opened in 1910, except Ophir Lodge, which holds its communications in the Essex County Trust Company building, where the East Orange Lodge of Elks is also housed. The American Legion, the Knights of Columbus, Knights of Pythias, Royal Arcanum, Odd Fellows, are all represented in the city.

Among the hoped for improvements in the near future none will be more welcome than the grade crossing elimination on the Lackawanna railroad. East Orange is the last of all the municipalities along the Morris and Essex division from Morristown to Hoboken to receive the great benefit of this relief. Fifteen years of constant negotiation are at last resulting in some tangible progress and the city will no doubt be called upon to spend a large sum of money as its contribution to the work, which if it was done ten years ago would have been less burdensome to both corporations—railroad and city.

East Orange will continue to be a residential city, and its proximity to New York makes it most available for those engaged in business there to provide for their families in the well arranged and well ordered neighborhoods so characteristic of it.

Postal facilities were first granted East Orange in 1869, when through the efforts of John M. Randall and William King the post office was established on February 15, 1869. This would not have been possible, however, without the assistance of United States Senator Frederick T. Frelinghuysen, of Newark, who used his influence to bring the desired relief to East Orange. Hitherto all mail matter for its people was delivered and dispatched from Orange, and it was decidedly inconvenient for those families living at a distance to make the trip of several miles to and from the office. But the two faithful citizens who were largely instrumental in producing this betterment could not agree upon its exact location. Mr. King wanted it near his residence on Grove street and Mr. Randall was equally insistent that it should be at Cherry street. Mr. Randall won in the contention and Isaac C. Beach opened the office for business on a February morning in the railroad station, known as "the Junction," so named because the horse car tracks crossed the Lackawanna tracks. The postmaster was also the station agent and general information man. He held the commission for six years, when declining health compelled him to resign. Stephen M. Long continued as the postmaster from January 6, 1875, till 1886, when a political change in the presidential office brought an innovation in the postal affairs of the Oranges, and for the first time in its annals a woman was given the appointment. Miss Mary E. Simonson received her commission on January 13, 1886, and on February 20 the postmistress was at the helm of affairs in the East Orange office. Post offices more accessible to the geographical centers were being demanded by the rapidly growing population in 1880. In this year the Watsessing office was opened on Dodd street, near Meadow street, for the accommodation of the Doddtown (First Ward) residents. In May, 1882, William H. Allen was made the Brick Church postmaster, the office being opened in his stationery store on Main street, opposite Washington street, and on July 1, 1886, it was raised to a second class office. Grovestend was the name of the fourth post office opened in the city, in the drug store of William Kean, on Main street, near Grove street, in October, 1883.

Miss Simonson established her office in the Doan building, near the corner of Arlington avenue and Railroad place, where she gave an excellent administration. A plan of house numbering prepared by the Orange Water Company was officially adopted by the Township Committee in the spring of 1887, and the numbers were placed on the buildings throughout the town so rapidly that the entire work was completed in the early summer. Miss Simonson immediately made application for the installation of the carrier system, stating that the requirement of the postal authorities that the houses and other buildings have suitable numbers was complied with. Her request was duly investigated and the credit for the introduction of the first free delivery of mail matter in the county outside of Newark rests upon the East Orange office. With the new order of affairs taking effect on July 1, 1887, the post offices at Watsessing,

Brick Church and Grovestend were abolished, and, larger accommodations being needed by the one office, quarters were secured in the Commonwealth building on Main street, corner of North Arlington avenue, where they have since remained.

Miss Simonson was deposed on account of another political change at the White House, and Benjamin Harrison, President, appointed William H. Baldwin postmaster on February 19, 1890. Miss Simonson left a good record of the administration of four years. Mr. Baldwin served tilll July 2, 1892, when he died. Louis McCloud then took hold and served till December 13, 1894. Grover Cleveland having been re-elected President, he appointed Benjamin Hilton, a well known and popular Democrat. A new fourth class office was opened by Postmaster Hilton at the eastern boundary of the town and named Ampere. Marcus Mitchell was the next postmaster, taking office at the expiration of Mr. Hilton's commission. Mr. Mitchell was commissioned February 8, 1899, and served till September 2, 1912, when his death created widespread sorrow. He had administered the postal affairs of the city with marked fidelity and for a longer term than any other postmaster, retaining the confidence and respect of the government authorities and the people. E. Tracey Lanterman, who next became postmaster, was appointed by President Wilson and is in office in 1920.

There are now sixty-nine carriers and clerks engaged in the daily work of receiving and dispatching the mail at the East Orange office, which enjoys the distinction of handling more incoming mail per capita than any other municipality in the country. Over fifteen hundred pieces of parcel post alone are handled every week day, and the special delivery letters are abnormal in their volume. The hope of the immediate future is a new office, the present quarters in the Commonwealth building answering inadequately the purposes of ordinary routine.

East Orange was the first of the group of the Oranges to enjoy running water in the homes and other buildings, due to the farsightedness and public spirit of Frederick M. Shepard, who associated others with him in forming the Orange Water Company, under authority of the act of the New Jersey Legislature of April 5, 1865. The charter, which specially empowered the company to conduct the business pertaining thereto, remained unused till 1880, when the Citizens' Health Association, composed of members representing all the Oranges, began a movement for supplying the entire district with a wholesome water service. Meeting with no encouragement, a coterie of interested citizens led by Mr. Shepard then formed the organization and decided to act independent of any official action. Stock of one thousand shares, six hundred of which were held by the officers, found ready purchasers. Frederick M. Shepard, East Orange, was president; David N. Ropes, Orange, vice-president; Joseph A. Minott, East Orange, treasurer; George P. Kingsley, Orange, secretary, and with the following composed the board of directors: John M. Randall, East Orange; Charles A. Lighthipe, Orange; Dr. William Piersen, Orange, and Joseph L. Munn, East Orange.

After explorations for a source of supply, the engineers finally decided upon the Boiling Spring, situated on Grove street, near the Bloomfield line, where borings had revealed a large underground current of water suitable for domestic and other purposes. A contract entered into with East Orange, through the Township Committee, on December 11, 1881, guaranteed the necessary fire hydrants and water and the company was given the privilege of selling its product to private consumers. Three artesian wells were drilled and an open well twenty-four feet in diameter was excavated, another fifty feet in diameter, another of one hundred feet in diameter, then two wells of twenty-seven feet and one of fifty feet in diameter, all connected by an underground water gallery 700 feet long, ten feet wide and twenty feet deep, also five additional artesian wells.

Five months were required to build the plant, work being started in the spring of 1882. A public exhibition on November 1, at the corner of Prospect and Main streets, revealed a pressure sufficient to throw a stream over the steeple of Brick Presbyterian Church, which showed no weakening as the water poured steadily out of the hose. The power house at the intake provided for three pumps, having a total capacity of seven million gallons each day of twenty-four hours, supplied with steam from five boilers all of which were operated in mass or separately. Ten miles of street mains were laid in 1882. Over 100 acres of land were acquired for protection and production of the water supply, which Professor George H. Cook, State Geologist, pronounced "good, wholesome waters, fit for all household purposes and free from all organic matter."

The company's equipment was enlarged from time to time as the demands increased, until in 1902 about 22,000 people were being supplied with water. The system then consisted of 140 acres of water land, yielding approximately 1,400,000 gallons per day, a pumping plant with good reserve pumping capacity, about fifty-five miles of distributing mains twelve inches or less in diameter, 340 fire hydrants, 4,400 service connections and about sixty meters. Several years previous the company had been forced to purchase water from the city of Newark in order to meet the demand in East Orange, the open wells not yielding sufficient water to supply the growing municipality. In 1902 the average use was practically 2,250,000 gallons per day.

The quality of water furnished by the company wells was excellent. The usual pressure maintained throughout the municipality was ample for all ordinary domestic purposes, the demand being met by increasing the pumping rate and raising the pressure to the proper point for good fire-fighting conditions, the pumping station being notified by special signal in case of fire.

COLUMBIAN SCHOOL, EAST ORANGE

ASHLAND SCHOOL, EAST ORANGE

Prior to 1900 the question of municipal ownership of the public water system had been quietly discussed and in that year the agitation assumed definite shape, events occurring in rapid sequence. The fact that the development of the city trended eastward meant that the water lands of the private company would soon be reached, and contamination of the water was feared. The question of water rates also lent power to the growing feeling that the city should own and operate the public water supply. An appraisal of the system was undertaken by the City Council, and the facts obtained were used in argument for erecting a municipal plant. Other possible supplies were investigated, and in February, 1901, the Water Company, sensing the trend of public opinion, offered to sell its entire plant, except the real estate and pumping station, for $800,000, a second offer in June, 1901, being for the same amount, but including the property and pumps. The City Council rejected the offers, and on December 17, 1901, at a special election, the citizens voted by the overwhelming proportion of 25 to 1 to establish a municipal supply. Early in 1902 the city decided to condemn the system of street mains, hydrants and connections and the franchise of the private company. The condemnation commission reported a value of $425,000, but the City Council rejected this price also on December 8, 1902. On December 20, 1902, the City Council offered $250,000 for the system, the Orange Water Company rejecting the offer, and replying on December 27, 1902, with an offer to sell for $425,000. The office of the Water Company was in the Commonwealth building and President Shepard went about his daily affairs apparently unmoved by the attitude of the city officials toward him.

On the afternoon of December 27, 1902, at a special meeting of the City Council, the following resolution was adopted:

Resolved, That the City Council make a final offer to the Orange Water Company of $350,000, payable at the option of the city, in thirty-year 3½ per cent. bonds, for the property and franchises applied for in condemnation proceedings, together with the use of the springs, engineers' and firemen's houses, pumping equipment and switch west of Grove street; the Water Company to sell the coal and pipe on hand to the city at cost.

Three days after the adoption of the above resolution, on December 30, 1902, at another special meeting of the City Council, the following letter was read:

East Orange, N. J., December 30, 1902.

The City Council,
    East Orange.
Sirs:
    Your offer of December 27 is accepted.
        Respectfully,
            THE ORANGE WATER COMPANY,
                FREDERICK M. SHEPARD, President.

The East Orange Water Department began business on January 1, 1903. Having determined upon a new source for the water supply, the City Council engaged Cornelius C. Vermeule, civil engineer, a resident of East Orange, and an authority on the underground currents of the State, to prepare plans. Borings were first made along the Passaic river, near Singac, but these were not satisfactory. Then the line of the Passaic Valley was tried in the vicinity of White Oak Ridge, near Millburn, west of the Second Mountain and along the Canoe brook and Slough brook branches. The first well tapped sent forth a large stream with such force as to justify further investigation. Satisfied that the right place had been tapped, the City Council purchased several farms in the vicinity and the work of drilling the first group of wells was started in the late summer of 1903, the plans prepared by Mr. Vermeule being accepted on August 28. On November 16, also of this year, the first pipe for the large main to connect the city with its new supply was laid at the corner of South Clinton street and Central avenue, and on January 13, 1905, the work on the plant had advanced far enough to permit of turning off the old water and supplying the people with the more desirable commodity secured at White Oak Ridge. A twenty-four inch pipe ran from the pumping plant to the storage reservoir erected on the Mountain, in the Village of South Orange, having a capacity of five million gallons. From this altitude the water was sent rushing down to the city distributing system consisting of eighty miles of mains from four inches to eighteen inches in diameter. There were also seven hundred and thirty fire hydrants at the disposal of the Fire Department. The quality of water was vastly superior to that secured at the Boiling Spring, which had become highly charged with lime.

Exercises in celebration of the completion of the water works were held at White Oak Ridge on Saturday afternoon, June 2, 1906, when the public was given an opportunity to inspect the administration building and the wells supplying the city with water. Stephen W. Ougheltree, chairman of the City Council, presided, and after the unveiling of the tablet and the raising of the flag to the top of the new pole, he announced the speakers as follows: "The Past," Edward E. Bruen, former mayor; "East Orange, a Pearl in a Suburban Setting," Mayor William Cardwell; "Municipal Ownership as a Civic Force," Philemon Woodruff, former City Council; "The Present," Farnham Yardley, chairman of the Water Committee; "Patriotic Coöperation the Precedent of Success," Jerome D. Gedney, City Counsel; "Engineering Features of the New System," Cornelius C. Vermeule, the designer of the system; "The Future," Arthur A. Reimer, Superintendent of the Water Department.

A water reserve of 1,854 acres, partly in Millburn and partly in Livingston townships, give assurance with water rights in 175 additional acres, in 1920 of an ample supply to the city for all time. The artesian

STOCKTON SCHOOL, EAST ORANGE

wells are in two groups of twenty each, yielding about four millions per days and the pumping plant and appurtenances are all in excellent condition. The water is now metered and the daily consumption is about three million gallons. Under the provisions of a new charter a special election was held on May 4, 1909, when the voters decided upon the establishing of a Board of Water Commissioners. The first members appointed were Samuel Whinery, president; Colonel Oscar H. Condit and Nelson H. Genung. An appraised value of the water system in 1920 places it at $1,857,120.89. There are 921 hydrants in the city and one hundred and two miles of water mains.

Sentiment was centering about a most desired public improvement in the late winter of 1885—the building of a sewerage system, the climax of the agitation being reached at a mass meeting held in National Hall, Grove and Main streets, on the evening of March 2. Resolutions were then adopted unanimously favoring the taking of initial steps to properly sewerage the town, which was growing at such a rate as to make further delay dangerous to the health of the people. Three forms of referendum were prepared for the voters by direction of the Township Committee, to be balloted upon at the spring election. One was for installing sewers at once, another in favor of the plan, and a third opposed to the sewers. There were 428 votes cast favorably on the first proposition, 158 on the second and 490 on the third. An analysis of the vote showed that those sections of the town most in need of the improvement and in which the greater part of the expense of construction and maintenance would be borne, were overwhelmingly in favor of proceeding at once with the work of installation. Methods of obtaining an outlet for the sewage were suggested from time to time during the year, and it was finally decided that there were but two ways of disposing of the city waste, first by constructing a costly outlet to Newark Bay, and, second, to erect a chemical disposal works in the township and treat the sewage in accordance with modern methods, claimed to be in successful operation in cities and towns similarly situated. Carroll P. Bassett, of Newark, was employed as engineer, and Rudolph Hering, of Chicago, as the consulting engineer. Their plans and surveys included a recommendation submitted at the meeting of the Township Committee on August 9, 1896, that the disposal works treatment of sewage be adopted and the city laid with small iron pipes in the general receiving system.

Property in the vicinity of Dodd street and Glenwood avenue was purchased for the site of the station, it having been determined that the flow would be by gravity to that point, the only logical place in the town for its location. Notwithstanding the vehement protests by citizens of the First Ward—Doddtown of the old days—the Township Committee ordered the engineers to advertise for proposals for prosecuting the work. The land secured had been owned by the Dodd family for over two hundred years, and the saw mill, a landmark of very delightful memories, was formally abandoned on September 18, 1886, when the Township Committee and others observed this beginning of the town's sewerage and drainage by a celebration, in which well laden tables of sundry articles of food, set in the open, proved one of the magnets of attraction. The hum of the saw was now hushed forever, the water was drawn off the lake and raceway and operations for installing the disposal plant were changing the appearance of the surroundings.

B. J. Coyle secured the contract for the construction of the street mains on September 1, 1886, but the building of the disposal works and the preparation of the ground were retained by the engineers. The contractor failed in April, 1887, and the unfinished work was also assumed by them. About thirty miles of streets were laid in 1888; in May of this year the first use of the sewers was permitted, and in October the entire township was enjoying the service. All except the section lying north of the railroad and east of Grove street, was operated by gravity. In this section a small pumping station built under the roadway of Park avenue, near Seventeenth street, was provided for pumping the sewage into the Grove street mains. Later the station was abandoned and a larger pumping plant placed in a brick building at Springdale avenue and the railroad crossing gave the service desired.

Residents of the First Ward did not become reconciled to the placing of the disposal works in their neighborhood nor did they relinquish their efforts to secure the abolition of the chemical treatment and filtration system of disposal.

From the very beginning, obstacles appeared in the way of a continuance of the plant. The solid mass, chemically treated, which it was believed would be eagerly seized by farmers for fertilizing purposes, did not find many patrons. The flow of waste water, supposed to be pure, into the Second river was not altogether satisfactory to the health officials of Bloomfield. Complaints were being lodged with the Township Committee at nearly every meeting in 1893, and on August 23, injunction proceedings were begun by the township of Bloomfield against a continuance of the nuisance. A rule was therefore granted by the Supreme Court to show cause why East Orange should not be permanently restrained from operating the disposal works. Newark had now changed its source of water supply from the Passaic river to the Pequannock watershed, and the opportune moment arrived for an arrangement with that city for a way out of the embarrassment when it sought permission for a right of way for one of her sewers through East Orange. An agreement was entered into and then by contract whereby the town could empty its sewage into the Millbrook sewer. James A. Owen, county engineer, laid out the plans, and Thomas A. Nevins was given the contract to complete the piping with all expedition at a cost of $240,000, so that

ELMWOOD SCHOOL, EAST ORANGE

WASHINGTON SCHOOL, EAST ORANGE

relief could be given the First Ward residents and also those of Bloomfield. The pumping station ceased on June 4, 1895, and on December 4, six months later, the sewage was diverted from the disposal works to the tidewater outlet by gravity. The entire amount involved in the construction of the sewers, was $800,000. This also involved the acquirement of land and the erection of buildings. The one used about five years for the collection and treatment of sewage was allowed to remain idle. While the filtration plant may have been successfully operated in other communities the fact remains that there was scarcely an hour after its general use that a nuisance was not created. The building, constructed of trap rock, was later diverted to other purposes when the tract became a part of Watsessing Park.

Occasional fires in homes and other buildings about the middle of the decade of 1870 suggested the institution of a Fire Department to certain citizens who petitioned the Township Committee on November 9, 1874, that action be taken to bring about the much needed protection. There the matter rested till mid-winter in 1877-1878, when the stables owned by Benjamin Cairns, on the east side of Washington street, near Main street, and other buildings, were destroyed by a fire which occurred at 1 o'clock in the morning on February 1, 1878. The loss, $18,000, was the most serious the town had sustained and the people and officials were alarmed and ready to participate in any plan for a better safeguarding of the lives and property. The deficiency in the law under which the Township Committee conducted the public affairs, was overcome by a legislative act of March 28, 1878, permitting townships to appropriate $1,000 each year for fire purposes. Then came the disaster on December 28, 1878, when Charles Thatcher and Milton Thatcher, brothers, lost their lives in a fire which destroyed the barn of W. F. Kidder, at the corner of Grove and William streets. Spurred to renewed action the officials secured the passage of another bill by the Legislature in the session of 1879, giving townships authority to raise $5,000 for the purchase and maintenance of fire equipment. Brick Church residents were now active in securing subscriptions toward the payment of a fire truck and on January 25, 1879, Ashland Hook and Ladder Truck Company was duly organized by twenty-five members. Peter Y. Everett was chosen foreman; John F. Walsh, assistant foreman; Stephen M. Long, secretary, and E. S. Atwood, treasurer.

A second-hand truck, equipped with ladders, pikes and buckets, was received on February 5, 1879, and stored in the carpenter shop owned by Philip C. Williams, and situated on Main street, directly opposite the First Reformed Church. Alarms of fires, it was agreed, should be sounded by the bell of that edifice. The first run of the Ashland Company was on March 28, the next month, when fire was discovered in the home of C. C. Beers, on Orange street, near Burnett street. The buckets were rapidly passed from wells to the burning building and everything possible was done to prevent its destruction, but the efforts were futile. The loss was $12,000.

The truck was man-drawn and fires were often raging when the volunteers arrived, some of them fatigued by the exertion of the run through the streets and in no physical condition for the work ahead of them. But the spirit was in that first company of fire fighters of East Orange, and they responded with promptness whenever there was cause for their service. Business men, commuters and others well known were enrolled in the membership. On a very warm summer day Ashland Hook and Ladder Company was called to extinguish a fire in the Orange Orphan Home on Harrison street. Though the temperature was exceedingly trying the firemen replaced their straw hats with the leathern headgear of the fire fighter and bravely walked and ran along Main and Harrison streets, their minds filled with the possibility of large loss of life. Urged on by the exigency of the alarm, the men struggled to the very limit of their ability to quickly reach the conflagration. At last, after covering a mile of roadway, the objective was brought to their view, only to find that the fire had been extinguished some time before. Within three years water was introduced into the city and the erection of fire hydrants caused the Ashland Hose Company to be organized and it was attached to the one first instituted. On October 1, 1882, 1,000 feet of hose and a carriage were purchased and a public exhibition was given when the Water Works were completed by the Orange Water Company, just one month later, on November 1, 1882.

One of the best stopped fires by the East Orange Fire Department in its volunteer days occurred at night on March 20, 1884, in Ashland School, now occupied by the parish of Our Lady Help of Christians, on North Clinton street. With a steady water pressure it was possible to confine the loss to the assembly hall, amounting to only $6,000.

The roller skating rink on the west side of Harrison street, near the Lackawanna tracks, was the scene of many brilliant assemblages during the few years of its existence, beginning in 1883, but the annual banquet of the East Orange firemen annually held there was a complete symposium of civic interest. Annually in the autumn the firemen's parade, in which the Township Committee rode in open barouches, called the people from their homes to look upon the men who were guarding and administering the town affairs. These customs have been absorbed in the rapid pace of the years, but the days of the volunteer firemen are among the most pleasant in the early history of the community.

The two companies were accepted by the Township Committee on June 11, 1883, when the East Orange Fire Department was given an official standing. A fire committee for general supervision of the department, created on April 23, 1883, consisted of Israel L. Dodd, Richard

FRANKLIN HOSE COMPANY HOUSE, EAST ORANGE, 1884

Coyne and Samuel C. Jones. Eastern Hose Company No. 2 was organized December 11, 1883. Franklin Hose Company No. 3 was accepted by the Township Committee on April 14, 1884, and Prospect Hose Company No. 4 on May 24, 1886, but existed only nine years, being disbanded on April 1, 1895. Elmwood Company was the last one created, on September 12, 1887.

Henry Mills, the first chief of the department, served from 1883, till 1892, when he was succeeded by Joseph D. Burchan, and he in turn by Samuel J. Blair. The bell tower from which the alarms were sounded by hand power, was erected in the rear of the Police Station, under contract awarded June 15, 1885. In October, 1887, the provincial method gave way to the Gamewell fire alarm system, which was then set up in the township. The City Council on November 11, 1901, adopted the call system. Under its provisions the volunteer firemen were replaced with twenty-one call men and in March, 1907, the paid department was installed. All the fire apparatus had been horse-drawn for a number of years.

There are five engine companies and two truck companies included in the Fire Department in 1920. The training school for the firemen at the fire headquarters in the Ashland headquarters, one hour each afternoon, has been of great assistance in the fighting of fires. All the apparatus is motor driven and the fire alarm system keeps Chief George L. Mitchell in constant communication with every part of the city.

Policing East Orange was not a difficult matter during the early years of the separation from Orange. One or two constables looked after the safety of the people and their homes and uniformed policemen were not seen upon the streets till twenty-three years after the local government had begun to function. George Snow and Henry Blaurock were the principal guardians of the peace during the decade of 1870 and till the police department was organized in 1885. No lock-up was provided for infractors of the law and all apprehended were immediately transferred to the county jail in Newark. Excepting an occasional outbreak of burglaries, the town was free of any menace to its orderliness. But the population steadily increased and in 1884 the creation of a police department was forcing itself upon the Township Committee. Duly appointed Chief of Police, Constable Blaurock assumed charge of the force of six men placed at his disposal, in April, 1885. George Snow and William R. Huff were the sergeants. A frame structure used as the station house was erected on the city-owned lot, known as the "Promise Land," and a few months later the fire alarm tower was also placed there. The first floor, a room 10x12 feet, and heated by a pot stove in the winter months, was the station house, and also used by the court. Three cells were built directly in the rear. Alfred F. Munn, appointed the first police justice in 1888, found his time only partly employed in looking after the cases brought to his attention. The frame structure gave way to one of brick, the first floor being used as a city hall and the second floor by the police department.

William H. O'Neill is the chief in 1920, the department occupying the entire brick building in the rear of the present city hall. The force consists, besides the chief, of seventy-three individuals, including lieutenants, sergeants, etc. Constant watchfulness is maintained every hour of the day and night for the appearance of evil-doers. Patrolmen are in communication with headquarters by a separate telephone system and an alarm service can be heard in all parts of the city in an instant, if emergency requires. Every possible agency has been added to the department for its effective policing the city. Colonel Oscar H. Condit is president; William J. Harnisch, secretary, and Henry Lippincott is the third member of the Police Commission, which has entire supervision of the Police Department.

The Orange Riding and Driving Club had its inception in a riding class for ladies and gentlemen which met for two seasons in the old riding academy, later the Gatling Gun Company A Armory, on North Clinton street. It was incorporated in June, 1892, by nineteen well known gentlemen of the Oranges. Its first corporate name was the Riding Club of Orange, but in June, 1895, it was changed to the Riding and Driving Club of Orange. The first officers were Charles Hathaway, president; William C. Horn, vice-president; Henry G. Atwater, secretary; Edward P. Alling, treasurer. The club at first rented the old riding academy, and met there regularly for practice riding for three years. In the meantime a lot was purchased on Halsted street, immediately adjoining the Orange Athletic Club house, having a frontage of one hundred feet on Halsted street, with an L running through to Prospect place. On this lot commodious, attractive and convenient buildings were erected, affording accommodations for a fine riding room, stables, club and reception rooms, and auditorium. A value of $50,000 was placed upon the property. In December, 1895, the club began its annual autumn horse shows, which were brilliant social events, the enthusiasm of the members continuing till the automobile came into general use. The last notable affair given at the academy was the circus, in the autumn of 1918, for the benefit of the War Relief Fund.

The Board of Health was organized in 1885. For a number of years the township physician and the chief of police looked after the nuisances and other matters brought to the attention of the Board, and at one time the Building Inspector lent a hand in looking after the health of the town. William T. Bowman, who had been acting in the dual capacity of building inspector and health officer, finally took up the latter duties independent of the other office. The work of the Board broadened out and now includes the issuing of licenses to plumbers and the inspection of all plumbing work done in the city; the issuing of licenses to icemen and the inspection of the source from which they receive their supply, and the oversight and fumigation of all contagious and infectious diseases, and of general sanitary conditions.

Inspection of dairies from which milk is supplied to the city is carried on under the joint commission. Fifty years ago the milkman drove up to the door of his customer, in a vehicle not always free of dirt and stain, rang a bell and then waited for the woman of the home to appear with a pail or pitcher. A long handled dipper was filled with milk, withdrawn from a milk can and no care whatever was given to the cleanliness of hands of the purveyor, who always poured in "good measure." The bottom of the milk cans, at the end of the trip frequently disclosed sundry collections of debris. Under the care of the Boards of Health this disease-producing custom has been forever eliminated from our community and the milk bottle, carefully filled and made air-tight, is now left at the door without the formality of announcing the presence of the carrier by ringing a bell.

Dr. Charles D. Moulton is president of the Board of Health in 1920, the other commissioners being Colonel Charles A. Andrews, Stephen V. B. Brewster, Dr. George A. McLellan, and William J. Snow. T. Dudley Ballinger is the secretary and health officer.

Noted for its fine growth of trees, East Orange authorities had paid very little attention to their care in the public thoroughfares till the idea was advanced in December, 1903, that a Shade Tree Commission be established. Duly appointed in January, the members did not organize till the following April. Ellis Apgar, first superintendent, was a born naturalist. He spent much of his time while not occupied in examining and planting trees, in the fields, searching for remnants of the flowers which grew so profusely in the early days. The moist soil in the low-lying lands produce many varieties even at this late day. The work of the Commission begun in the spring of 1904 included planting, pruning, treatment of trees for insects, removal of dead trees and the repair of those injured.

During the sixteen years that the Commission has been organized, many miles of the city streets have been improved by uniform planting. The insect pests have been successfully combatted, and since 1906 the repair of old and injured trees, by filling cavities with cement, has been carried on. The Commission conducts a nursery at White Oak Ridge, where at one time over four thousand trees were under cultivation. The present commissioners are Edward M. Colie, president; Charles Bradley, William E. Wallace and Ernest H. Bennett, secretary and superintendent.

While the jurisdiction of the Shade Tree Commission does not extend to the trees on private property, advice regarding the treatment of trees may always be obtained freely from the Superintendent, whose office is in the City Hall.

Governor Fort appointed Worrall F. Mountain judge of the new East Orange District Court in June, 1909. He also named Noah M. Baldwin as the clerk and Abram S. Overmiller sergeant-at-arms. The court sits on Tuesdays and Thursdays and has jurisdiction over cases up to $500 all over the county. The first court room was on the second floor of the old City Hall, over the police station, but these quarters soon became too crowded, and court is now held in the council room in the City Hall. Through the prompt and courteous attention of those in charge, and the wise and equitable settlement of all cases brought before it, the local court has gained a high position among the courts of the county. Michael F. Judge is the judge in 1920.

Cultivation of the voice musically, prompted a group of twenty young women of the town to meet at the home of Mrs. George F. Seward, Hawthorne avenue, in 1887, and there mutually agree to begin the study of the most pleasing art. Arthur D. Woodruff was invited to instruct the class, the arrangement continuing till 1896, when the group branched out into the Musical Art Society, and officers who have been reëlected each year were chosen as follows: President, Mrs. Alexander King; vice-president, Mrs. William P. Thorpe; secretary, Mrs. Charles A. Trowbridge; treasurer, Mrs. John K. Gore. The first concert was given in Music Hall, Orange, in January, 1897. Regularly every year since then, in January and in June, the Society has been heard in programs of very high musical character, the sustaining funds being provided by an associate membership numbering two hundred and fifteen citizens. Mr. Woodruff has been the only conductor and the highly finished concerts arranged for the entertainment of the patrons is answer enough for the harmonious spirit prevailing within the organization and also the leader's fine sense of coöperation. There were one hundred and ten well known women enrolled in the society in 1920.

The Republican Club of East Orange was the outgrowth of an informal organization of gentlemen, who, under the name of "The East Orange Republican Club," and at the suggestion of Frank W. Coolbaugh and others, made an excursion to Washington to attend the inauguration of President Harrison, March 4, 1889. The party numbered about two hundred and fifty, and the trip lasted from Saturday afternoon until Tuesday night, a Washington hotel being chartered for the accommodation of the party while at the National Capitol. The party traveled in both directions in a special train of Pullman vestibuled parlor cars. Interest in the club was most apparent, and it has been a strong and prosperous one ever since. For several years it occupied a suite of rooms on the second floor of the Randall building, corner of Main street and South Arlington avenue, with an assembly hall on the third floor, and on the completion of the East Orange National Bank (now the Essex County Trust Company) building, the entire second floor was rented by the club

EASTERN SCHOOL, EAST ORANGE

LINCOLN SCHOOL, EAST ORANGE

and handsomely fitted up for its uses. For twenty years or more the club observed the anniversary of Lincoln's Birthday with a banquet, at which distinguished speakers made the occasions ever to be remembered by the high, patriotic tone injected into them.

Residents of the First Ward were very happy indeed when they learned that one of their representatives, Councilman William Cardwell, had presented an ordinance in 1899 to the City Council, turning over to the Essex County Park Commission the unused land near the corner of Dodd street and Glenwood avenue, and which was abandoned when the city changed its method of sewerage direct to tide water. The Park Commission accepted the offer on February 26, 1900, and an act by the Legislature empowered the commission to add the abutting property thus extending the proposed park to Dodd street and also to the Franklin Bluff. These properties were secured for about $27,000. Blessings frequently come in disguise, and so it appears that the beautiful park soon laid out in the First Ward was ample compensation for the trial and inconvenience caused by the existence of the sewerage disposal works. The name Watsessing was given the reservation, and under skilful landscape treatment it became one of the most attractive in the entire chain in the county.

"The work at Watsessing Park," reported the Essex County Park Commissioners for the year 1914, "was practically completed last season, and in the summer of 1915, the entire area will be thrown open to the use of the public." This park had its beginning in the generous gift by the city of East Orange of the old Disposal Works, about six acres in extent. This area was increased from time to time by legislative appropriation, and by the generosity of the town of Bloomfield, which bonded itself to the amount of $30,000 in order to secure further park area. It is intersected by Glenwood avenue and the Delaware, Lackawanna & Western railroad, but its total area is about seventy acres. In the older part lying chiefly in East Orange, are play field and tennis courts. The Second river runs through the park, and a wooded knoll on the western boundary adds greatly to its picturesqueness. The cost of the improvements was about $168,265.00.

Three-fourths of an acre of Orange Park is also in East Orange. An improvement which eliminated a large area of bog land was the laying of the Black Brook Valley drain in the last decade of the Nineteenth Century, through the valley between North Munn avenue and North Maple avenue. The work cost only $61,748.04, but it involved a great deal of time in adjustments and labor. Through the tract thus drained the section of the Parkway, from Main street to William street was opened in 1900 and afterward extended to Park avenue. The part on the south side of Main street, extending to Central avenue, connected the two fine avenues which the City Council on April 12, 1897, turned over to the

Essex County Park Commission for their care, custody and control. Park avenue was saved for a pleasure driveway. From the Newark line to the entrance of Llewellyn Park, in West Orange, there is an undulating surface of roadway, with shrubbery planted in the center, relieving the view of the traveler and ornamenting the thoroughfare, which with the well-kept grounds of the premises along the four-mile stretch, fulfill the expectations of officials of half a century ago that Park avenue would in a distant day be a pleasure drive and a fine residential section of the county. Traffic of all kinds except vehicles for passenger transit are ruled off the avenue and the result is seen in the well preserved roadway.

Mayor William Cardwell, in his special message to the City Council on June 10, 1907, recommended the immediate laying out of playgrounds for use by the children of the city, thereby starting a movement which proved in a few years to be one of its best assets. It was proposed that the reservation known as Elmwood Park, in the Third Ward, which had been used as an ash dump, be converted to the use of the children in that part of the city. It was also suggested that the Orange Oval, laid out in a field near Grove street by the Orange Athletic Club, now defunct, be secured as a general playground for the entire city, if it could be purchased at a reasonable price. Councilman Edward S. Pierson, at the City Council meeting on June 24, offered a resolution, which was unanimously adopted, recommending that the Mayor appoint three Playground Commissioners, under the law known as the Playground Act, and that the proposed purchase of the Orange Oval be referred to the commissioners, who were named by the Mayor on the same evening as follows: Paltiel R. Bomeisler, one year; Horace A. Bonnell, two years, and Thomas R. Creede, three years. Mr. Creede was chosen president, and Lincoln E. Rowley secretary. On July 1 the commission was authorized by the City Council to purchase the Oval, the sum of $45,000 having been appropriated for that purpose. In October a tract in the rear was added to the main field and an entrance twenty-five feet wide from Grove place also purchased. Improvements were made as found necessary, and on September 7, 1908, the ground was dedicated with imposing ceremonies and in which the raising of the Stars and Stripes to the top of the Liberty Pole was a feature. Thomas R. Creede, president of the Commission, presided and the addresses were delivered by Mayor Willliam Cardwell and Rev. Dr. Fred Clare Baldwin, pastor of Calvary Methodist Episcopal Church. The latter declared that play was one of the inalienable rights of childhood.

The Elmwood Park was completely filled with ashes, and the city authorities spent $35,000 in building a seven-foot concrete pipe drain 1,600 feet in length, enclosing the flow of the Elizabeth river and which reclaimed soil more or less "spongy." Nine acres are within the enclosure and Alden Freeman has announced that he will spend $150,000 in beau-

ALTAR OF DEMOCRACY AND COURT OF HISTORY
ELMWOOD PARK PLAYGROUND, EAST ORANGE, N. J.

tifying them and adding necessary fixtures. His offer to the City Council of a group of statuary to be placed there as a memorial to his father, Joel Francis Freeman, has been accepted, and the setting will take place some time during the coming year. There will be a group entitled "The Shrine of Human Rights," executed by Ulric H. Ellerhuson. The figures are eight feet in height, set upon a base seven feet high. The group will form part of the lighting system, as electric lamps will be placed in the liberty torch and in the shrine. There will be four pedestals for busts of types of individuals representing America, Europe, Asia and Africa, they being Pocahontas, Columbus, Confucius and Fred Douglass.

An athletic field is in use at the Ashland School ground, on Park avenue, opposite North Clinton street, it having been purchased by the Board of Education in 1905 for $8,000. A contribution of $1,800 was tendered by interested citizens for use in the erection of bleacheries, and here on this field, in the rear of the school, were played many exciting games of baseball and football. In 1920 the sum of $100,000 was raised by the sale of bonds, which is to be applied to the building of a concrete stadium in the near future. Accommodation will be provided for seating 8,000 persons.

In 1919 four and a half acres of land adjoining the Columbian building, at the corner of Springdale avenue and Grove street, were secured upon payment of $28,000. During the coming year it is to be graded and equipped as a modern playground.

The Board of Recreation Commissioners consisted in 1920 of Thomas A. Barrett, president; W. Nelson Knapp and Francis N. Lord. The amount placed in the budget for the maintenance of the playground work for the year 1920 is $10,600.

Through the friendship of Alexander King, an East Orange citizen, and Andrew Carnegie, the steel magnate, the city was enabled to draw upon the latter in the sum of $50,000 for the building of a Free Public Library. Mr. Carnegie had during the decade of 1890 provided the means for erecting libraries in municipalities where assurances were given for their maintenance, in his announced plan of disposing of his fortune while in the flesh. An agreement was entered into between the city authorities and representatives of Mr. Carnegie wherein the former was obligated each year to raise a certain sum by taxation. A lot was also secured by the city at the corner of Main street and Munn avenue, and upon it the library was erected and informally opened on January 22, 1903. The first board of trustees had been in existence three years, however, and was composed of Frederick M. Shepard, president; Edward O. Stanley, secretary; David S. Walton, treasurer, and Judge John Franklin Fort, Alexander King, Charles A. Sterling, Harry T. Ambrose, John C. Lyon, Robert W. Hawkesworth and James B. Dill. In 1905 a State law reduced the size of the board to five members. An addition to the library being very much needed the trustees of the Carnegie Library fund granted $40,000 in 1914, making $90,000 in all provided for the main library. The completed building, designed by Hobart A. Walker, was opened in 1915, and more than doubled the space. The books in circulation when the Library opened in 1903 numbered about nine thousand. In 1920 it had increased to 61,423 volumes of almost every character and description.

Further requests of the Trustees of the Carnegie fund for two more allotments of $13,000 each with which to erect the branch libraries in the First Ward and Third Ward, were also granted. The building, at the corner of Dodd and Fulton streets, was opened on August 1, 1909, and named the Franklin Library. There are 8,085 books at the disposal of the people in that section of the city, and a very commodious reading room. The library in the Third Ward was built on the site at the corner of South Clinton street and Elmwood avenue, and was opened on January 11, 1912. Its 7,861 volumes find ready readers in the populous section known as Elmwood. Another branch library was instituted in 1915 at 215 North Eighteenth street, in the Ampere section, and some day it is hoped to arrange for a building of the general style of the other branches of the main library, thus making a chain circling the entire city.

Miss Sarah Slater Oddie was the first librarian. Miss Louise G. Hinsdale, the present holder of the office, is completing her tenth year in that capacity and under her supervision the library is enjoying a widening use among a people who appreciate the most excellent advantages offered for their mental stimulus. The board of trustees in 1920 is composed of Edward O. Stanley, president, who has served for twenty years as a member; George W. King, William F. Etherington, Wilbur S. Johnson and Charles A. Trowbridge. Dr. Edwin C. Broome, superintendent of the schools, acts as secretary of the board.

LINCOLN STATUE AT PARKWAY AND NEW STREET, EAST ORANGE

CHAPTER LXXXVI

EAST ORANGE—CONTINUED

In nearly every part of the country the people were preparing at the end of the year 1908 to remember the centennial of the birthday of Abraham Lincoln, the Emancipator and Martyr. East Orange was one of the first municipalities taking steps toward erecting a permanent memorial to this great life which had been welded so completely into the American ideals. David L. Pierson appeared before the City Council on October 26, 1908, and suggested that as one of the features of the local Lincoln celebration, a bronze statue of the President be erected in the triangular plot in front of the Commonwealth Building. Chairman Edward S. Pierson, in accordance with the wishes of the council, appointed Councilman John Lenord Merrill and Frederick Saxelby, Dr. William D. Robinson, Robert A. Travis, Captain John H. Palmer, Captain Oscar H. Condit, Colonel George P. Olcott, David L. Pierson and Edward H. Dutcher, with Mayor Cardwell as chairman, to arrange for the exercises on the anniversary day, February 12, 1909, and to proceed also with the suggested memorial bronze tribute. The committee organized on November 16, Mayor Cardwell presiding. Dr. Robinson was chosen secretary and Captain Condit treasurer.

The exercises were held in Commonwealth Hall on the afternoon of February 12, 1909, Governor John Franklin Fort presiding. The oration was pronounced by Rev. Dr. Fred Clare Baldwin, pastor of Calvary Methodist Episcopal Church, prayer offered by Rev. David O. Irving, pastor of Bethel Presbyterian Church, and the Lincoln Gettysburg address was read by Vernon L. Davey, Superintendent of the public schools. The committee having charge of the celebration consisted of Colonel Olcott, Dr. Robinson and Councilman Saxelby.

Messrs. Pierson, Dutcher and Palmer were appointed a committee on statue, and the commission was awarded to Francis Edwin Elwell, of Weehawken, to execute the bronze of Lincoln, at a cost of $8,000. The site selected was at the North Parkway, where New street crosses. Ground was broken for the placing of the granite base on Saturday, November 19, 1910. Though the cold winds swept through the valley, a company of patriots proceeded with the simple ceremony. Rev. Dr. Baldwin delivered a brief address, the Gettysburg classic, the day marking its anniversary of delivery, was read by David L. Pierson, and Mayor Cardwell turned the first sod.

Dedicatory exercises of the completed statue were held on Flag Day, June 14, 1911, and several thousand men, women and children attended. Captain John H. Palmer was master of ceremonies, and the exercises were opened by former Mayor William Cardwell and chairman of the Lincoln Centenary Committee, who introduced Mayor Julian A. Gregory as the presiding officer. Rev. David O. Irving offered prayer and the oration was by Rev. Dr. Baldwin. Dr. Robinson unveiled the statue and a copper box, the contents of which were announced by David L. Pierson, was placed in the base. The cost of the memorial was $8,000 and was raised by subscription from among the people.

On November 27, 1911, over three years following its appointment, the Lincoln Centenary Committee made its final report to the City Council. Adjournment was made to a neighboring banquet hall, where Thomas R. Creede, one of the most thoughtful of citizens regarding the bestowal of credit for faithful services performed, was master of ceremonies. Under his direction de luxe copies of Lincoln's life were presented to four members of the committee. They were Captain John H. Palmer, Captain Oscar H. Condit, Dr. William D. Robinson and David L. Pierson. This was the first statuary erected in East Orange, and on the anniversary of Lincoln's Birthday, in 1912, President William H. Taft placed a wreath upon the statue in the presence of several thousand spectators, while Battery A fired a salute in honor of the distinguished guest. A self-constituted committee, consisting of David L. Pierson, Lincoln E. Rowley and Fred Danby, has with the aid of the Boy Scouts, remembered the anniversary of Lincoln's Birthday each year, by assembling in the City Hall, holding brief exercises and then proceeding to the Parkway and placing the tribute at the memorial.

Citizens of the Second and Fifth wards met at the Columbian School, corner of Springdale avenue and Grove street, on November 18, 1908, and discussed plans for the organization of a civic and social club. Several other meetings were held and on January 14, 1909, the name Columbian Club was adopted and officers chosen as follows: President, George R. Howe; first vice-president, Joseph Froggatt; second vice-president, William Hampson; treasurer, R. S. Suiter; secretary, F. R. Serles; trustees, J. G. Ward, Edward S. Pierson, Duane E. Minard. Excavation was begun for the foundation walls of the club house on June 22, 1909, in a lot at the corner of Grant and Roosevelt avenues, and the building was completed on January 15, 1910. This was the center of the neighborhood known as Ampere for several years, and the expositions on local and other matters of public concern interspersed with the social affairs gave the club house the prominence due it and the enthusiasm has not waned with the passing years. There are one hundred and fifty members on the roll, and the club is in a sound financial condition and worthily reflects the best spirit of the community life. The officers at present are: President, J. P. Quinlan; first vice-president, J. W. Scott; second vice-president, L. B. Haigh; secretary, R. C. Lawless; treasurer, E. J. Voorhis; trustees, G. P. Williams, F. S. Downs, M. W. Blackmar, F. R. Serles, James Froggatt, Sr., Louis Stotz, Eugene Boggs.

UNVEILING OF LINCOLN STATUE, PARKWAY AND NEW STREET, EAST ORANGE, JUNE 14, 1911

On an April evening in 1909, a few citizens of the First Ward met at the home of Thomas G. Schriver, on Boyden street, and listened to an overture made by David L. Pierson for the observance of Independence Day at Watsessing Park. It was the Lincoln Centenary year, and it was suggested that in commemoration of the event that a Liberty Pole be dedicated in Watsessing Park, and the occasion made one for rallying the residents of the vicinity patriotically. The speaker spent many of his boyhood days in the ward and for this reason he and Mr. Schriver endeavored to stimulate interest in the proposed permanent patriotic expression. Enthusiastically about fifty of the middle-aged and younger men of the ward set about the task of collecting the funds and arranging the program. In a few weeks the community was stirred as it had never been before by the personal appeals made to the residents and the park was the mecca to which nearly every family traveled on Monday, July 5. The pole was dedicated and the flag, gift of the Junior Order of United American Mechanics, was duly displayed therefrom. The entire affair moved along with ease and the enthusiasm augured well for the future of Doddtown, now the First Ward of East Orange. The Park Commissioners were present, and the utility of adding to the park the Franklin Bluff overlooking the Second river, which flows on the westerly edge of the reservation, was pointed out to them. Within a year this was annexed just in time to escape purchase by the syndicate bent upon placing it in the market for home sites. Athletic games played in the afternoon and the fireworks displayed at night set the pace for future celebrations and activities along ward improvement lines.

In September the leaders in the celebration formed a permanent organization and named it the First Ward Local Interest Club. John W. Coulston was elected the first president, and during the following years Independence Day celebrations were not once adjourned on account of weather but each one had its individual merit and in a few years were designated the official celebration of East Orange.

The club lent its influence to the widening of North Park street, from Dodd street to the Orange road, and thus provided a medium for trolley connections between Montclair and the Oranges. Then followed an addition to the Franklin School, improved service on the Crosstown trolley line, increased mail delivery, better lighting of streets, guarding the Second river from pollution, saving the ward from a garbage crematory, and other betterments.

On Tuesday, February 3, 1920, the long hoped for possession of a permanent home for the club was realized, when title was taken by the Franklin Realty Company to the Amzi Dodd property at the corner of Dodd street and Fulton avenue and the formal opening occurred on Saturday evening, February 14. President Samuel H. Quackenbush announced that $17,000 had been subscribed for stock to be used in financing the venture. The patriotic and civic work of the ward is now centered in this most accessible home, and at the end of eleven years there is no abating of the enthusiasm so ardently displayed on the first Independence Day celebration.

The officers of the First Ward Local Interest Club in 1920 were: James A. Skinner, president; George A. Shelley and Mortimer W. Sargeant, vice-presidents; Hamilton A. Gordon, recording secretary; George H. Schroeder, corresponding secretary; J. Wallace Winslow, treasurer; Rev. David O. Irving, historian; W. A. Bearmore, auditor; Louis McDavit, George S. Dates, Jr., Andrew J. Whinery, M. DeForrest Soverel, Henry L. Cadmus, Frank H. Taylor and Samuel H. Quackenbush, trustees.

Membership in the Woman's Club of Orange had grown so rapidly and the interest in its welfare was so deeply seated that its managers decided to build a home which would be the center of the social and civic life of the community early in the Twentieth Century. A lot was secured at the corner of William and Prospect streets, and there, under the direction of the Woman's Realty Company, incorporated especially for carrying on the building operations, the structure was erected which is prominently in the public eye today. Mrs. Henry P. Bailey, chairman of the building committee, acquitted herself with a great deal of credit by dismissing the architect and practically superintending the finishing of the work herself. The formal opening was on Wednesday, April 18, 1906. A musical was the feature of the evening. The interior of the house has an admirable arrangement. A large reception hall leads at the west end to the large auditorium, and at the eastern end to the library, roomy and cheerful. One of the first notable events held in the home was the Centennial banquet on the night of June 14, 1907, and after a use of fourteen years the club house still retains its popularity, the income from rentals financing the project without drawing upon the club treasury.

In 1920 there is a paid up membership of one thousand, and a waiting list of nearly three hundred. The club has taken a leading position in the public questions of the day. Its public forum proved such a great success that it became necessary to adjourn to the High School auditorium to accommodate the increasing attendance. Ranking fourth in point of longevity of the 20,000 Woman's Clubs in existence in the country today, the organization also has after forty-eight years one of the charter members, Mrs. Clara Ropes Prescott, on the roster, and who has been present at most of the meetings. The officers in 1920 are: President, Mrs. Winthrop E. Scarritt; vice-presidents, Mrs. Charles H. Clark, Mrs. Charles W. Evans, Miss Margaret R. Mason; corresponding secretary, Mrs. Foster Debevoise; recording secretary, Mrs. Edward F. Chamberlain; federation secretary, Mrs. Howard Marshall; treasurer, Mrs. G. LaRue Masters; assistant treasurer, Miss Jessie G. King; chairman of legislative committee, Mrs. Louis G. Peloubet.

Calling attention of the City Council on the second Monday in March, 1912, to the fact that the fiftieth anniversary of the corporate life of the municipality would be attained on March 4, 1913, David L. Pierson suggested that an official committee be appointed to arrange for its celebration. The idea, meeting with the approval of the members, Frederick Saxelby, chairman, announced that he would act as its head and appointed Councilmen T. McCurdy Marsh and P. H. Lawless as his associates. Conferring with Mr. Pierson, who had prepared the preliminary plans, the committee decided to invite each councilman to name five citizens from his district from among whom committees were to be selected for arranging the details of the birthday party. The anniversary day, it was planned to observe with a banquet, and on the evening of March 4, a representative company of men and women of every section of the city attended this affair which was held at the Woman's Club. Mayor Julian A. Gregory presided, and the speakers were Governor John Franklin Fort, Judge Frederic Adams, Rev. Dr. Fred Clare Baldwin and Thomas R. Creede. The remainder of the program, it was planned to defer till the week in which Flag Day would occur in June, because of the probability of more propitious weather conditions.

Special services held in the churches on Sunday, June 8, began the second part of the celebration, followed on Monday by the opening of the historical exhibit at the East Orange Free Library. An automobile tour of the city was made by the general committee on Thursday night, June 12, starting from the City Hall, which was brilliantly illuminated for the occasion. Stops were made at the High School, where an exhibit of pupils' handiwork was viewed; Watsessing Park, Elmwood Park, and ending at the Library. Addresses were made at each of the places, where large crowds of people had gathered, and the evening ended with an inspection of the various local historical articles collected at the Library. Fifteen hundred boys and girls of the public schools engaged in a series of folk dances and other movements at the Orange Oval on Friday, June 13. Miss Loretta Seger, directress, and Miss Geneva Baldwin, her assistant, led in a very pretty parade of the participants, preceding the exercises. When the dancing was finished all the flagbearers from the schools gathered in the center of the field with the children massed about them, singing "The Star Spangled Banner," in which the audience of several thousand joined. The day's celebration ended with a display of fireworks on the Parkway near the Armory of Battery A.

Notwithstanding the very high temperature the street parade, the principal event of the golden jubilee anniversary, held in the afternoon of Flag Day, June 14, was a success from every viewpoint. Colonel George P. Olcott was marshal, and the line starting from the corner of Harrison street and Central avenue in the early afternoon, made a circle of the city center, passing over Central avenue to the Parkway and thence to Park avenue, to Prospect street, to William street, North Harrison street, and Main street to the City Hall, where Mayor Julian A. Gregory and city officials reviewed the procession.

The display of Seabury & Johnson, whose pharmaceutical plant is on Glenwood avenue, near the Erie railroad, was very elaborate. The products of the company shown in a glass case, mounted high on a float, was guarded by six trained nurses, in uniform. White was the prevailing color and bales of snowy cotton were placed at the rear of the float, giving a most beautiful effect. In large letters at the side were these words: "Thanks to the East Orange Fire Department we are still in it." The plant narrowly escaped destruction one week previously, which caused a damage of $50,000, but was admirably handled by the firemen. The Crocker-Wheeler Company displayed about six tons of machinery—motors, dynamos, transformers and electric fans, and there were many other floats showing various phases of the business life of the city. In the military division the First Regiment, of Newark, the First Battalion, Fifth Regiment, of Orange, and Battery A, of East Orange, made a most excellent appearance and the police and fire departments and civic and fraternal societies all added to the demonstration which was the largest ever held in East Orange.

A dinner served in the armory of Battery A in honor of the first voters, was a fitting climax to the week's celebration. Mayor Julian A. Gregory acted as toastmaster, and the guests included Richard Coyne, Viner J. Hedden, J. Cook Culberson, Bethuel Smith Williams, Winfield Smith Williams, Jeremiah P. Ball, Joseph L. Munn, first township clerk, William P. Condit, Abram M. Baldwin, John Thatcher, Philip Harrison, Viner Van Zandt Dodd, Cyrus Harrison, Joel W. Hatt and C. Milton Harrison. Besides the special committee of the City Council, the following were also active in preparing and carrying out the details of the celebration:

Plan and Scope Committee—David L. Pierson, Chairman; Mrs. Charles W. Steele, Mrs. Frank B. Colton, Mrs. Charles B. Yardley, Mrs. William L. Smith, Mrs. W. Clive Crosby, Mrs. A. J. Baldwin, Mrs. E. O. Stanley, Mrs. Joseph Frogatt, Mrs. Edward F. Chamberlain, Oscar H. Condit, DeWitt Cook, Bloomfield Littell, Roland Wiggins, Edward S. Pierson, Henry B. Gombers, John C. Lyons, Charles P. Titus.

Citizens' Committee Semi-Centennial—First Ward: Frank H. Taylor, Joseph F. Kelly, George Kelly, Louis A. Eger, Bloomfield Littell, Amzi Dodd, William Cardwell, Roland Wiggins, Howard Marshall, Charles Ferguson.

Second Ward: J. S. Henry, Edward S. Pierson, E. F. Anderson, Stuart Bingham, E. H. Walker, George H. Austin, E. E. Clapp, W. H. Aborn, John L. Merrill, Franklin Webster.

Third Ward: Ogden H. Bowers, Henry B. Gombers, Henry P. Baldwin, William B. Harris, Lincoln E. Rowley, Fred Germain, J. W. Chase, Oscar H. Condit, Edward L. Kent, Fred Moritz.

Fourth Ward: W. G. Thomas, W. D. Mitchell, M. D.; DeWitt Cook,

ENTRANCE TO HIGH SCHOOL, EAST ORANGE

Russell Palmer, Chester W. Drummon, William J. Harnish, James L. Garabrandt, Henry W. Landau, Charles S. Orben, Louis Hedden.

Fifth Ward: Willis L. Brownell, DeWitt C. Reynolds, James Shanks, Charles P. Titus, J. C. Lyon, E. Tracy Lanterman, George P. Hedden, Frank R. Serles, A. N. Messer, C. L. Waterbury.

Chairmen of Committees—Finance and Accounts, Colonel O. H. Condit; Exploitation (Badges, Postals, Stamps, Co-öperation of Business Men), Frederick Germain; Souvenir Program, Charles S. Orben; Printing, Chester W. Drummon; Decorations, Frederick Moritz; Co-öperation of Civic Organizations, Frank R. Serles; Church Services, Charles P. Titus; Music, C. L. Waterbury; Entertainment of Guests, Bloomfield Littell; Historical Exhibits, David L. Pierson; Transportation, James L. Garabrant; Public Safety, A. N. Messer; Adjustments, Willis L. Brownell; Banquet, E. Tracy Lanterman; Athletic Tournaments, John C. Lyon; Concessions, Henry P. Baldwin; Grandstand, William Cardwell; Fireworks, William B. Harris; Fraternal Societies, William J. Harnisch; School Participation, Rev. F. Q. Blanchard; Parade, Colonel George P. Olcott; Coöperation of Boys' Uniformed Organizations, Thomas R. Creede; Invitation of ex-Residents of East Orange, Henry W. Landau; Publicity, Raymond H. Doremus; Business Men, A. Seldon Stalker.

Battery A, Field Artillery, marched out of its Armory on North Clinton street, near Carleton street, which it had occupied for sixteen years, for the last time on June 23, 1912. Through the influence of Governor John Franklin Fort, aided by Colonel Austen Colgate, State Senator, and Colonel Oscar H. Condit, at one time commandant of the battery, an appropriation of over $100,000 was made by the Legislature, providing for the building of a new Armory on the North Parkway in East Orange. It was constructed of brick and so far completed that Battery A Veteran Association held its annual dinner there on April 27, 1912. A short parade was held on the day of formal opening on June 23, and the exercises at the Armory were limited to a few brief addresses. There is a large tan bark enclosure for drilling purposes and a large gallery running around three sides. Necessary rooms are arranged on the first and second floors for the accommodation of the militia. The Armory is maintained v the State Military Department. Batteries A and C marched ou. of there for duty on the Mexican border in the summer of 1916, and again in 1917 for service in the World War. Captain Claude E. Lanterman and Captain Edward C. James, commandants of Batteries A and C respectively, were promoted lieutenant-colonels before the departure for overseas, and consequently were relieved of their commands.

East Orange was divided into three school districts many years before it became a separate municipality. Residents of Doddtown, having a very high regard for the public life of Benjamin Franklin, officially named its district in his memory on March 13, 1825, at a meeting held in the home of Zebina Dodd, when these resolutions were adopted:

Resolved, That we, the subscribers, build a school house twenty-five feet deep by thirty-four feet in length and two stories high.

Resolved, That there be seven trustees appointed to take charge of said house for the present year.

Resolved, That the house be known by the name of Franklin School of North Orange.

Building operations did not begin till May, the site chosen being on Dodd street, near Girard avenue of a later day, and when completed the frame structure represented an outlay of $233.93. The room on the upper floor was not finished till 1833, when it was used for the neighborhood prayer meetings and for the Sunday school already established. The seal used by the trustees was a United States ten-cent piece. Meagre was the equipment of the class-room, the pupils sitting two in a seat at a stationary slanting board serving the purpose of a desk, under which the books were kept. The slate was in use and so was the quill pen. Eleazer Monroe Dodd, a native of Orange and a prominent citizen of the county, was one of the first schoolmasters. While serving later as health officer of Newark, he succumbed during the cholera outbreak in that city in 1854. The brick structure, erected on the south side of Dodd street, was dedicated April 24, 1874. The lot purchased of Josiah Dodd cost $4,808.33, and the building $14,447.00. Four rooms were added ten years later, thereby doubling its capacity. In 1892 the school, becoming overcrowded, the assembly hall was partitioned into two rooms. One, devoted to kindergarten work, which had its beginning at this time, was under the supervision of Miss Mary I. Dodd. Another addition, made in 1898, cost $45,000, and other improvements have been made till today the ground, building and equipment represent an outlay of $117,217.29. Lincoln J. Roys is the principal. The enrolment of pupils in 1920 is 954. Franklin School has a most artistic setting. The Second river curves around the southern end and the entrance from Dodd street allows ample adornment of lawn with shade trees and shrubbery, giving an appearance seldom attained in laying out school grounds. There are approximately 250,000 square feet within the enclosure.

Mention has been made of the Ashland School in the main history. It stood on Prospect street, directly in the rear of Brick Presbyterian Church, and of the many interesting historical incidents connected therewith was the Independence Day celebration in 1861, for which the girl pupils made a bunting flag, eight by twelve feet in size, and it was raised to the top of the staff by thirteen of them, representing the original Thirteen Colonies. The Civil War was then beginning. Elias R. Pennoyer, whose name is revered by many men and women today, became the principal in 1869. The familiar title, "The White School House," clung tenaciously to the building for half a century, notwithstanding the bestowal of the name of Ashland. Arrangements were made by the trustees almost simultaneously with Mr. Pennoyer's engagement for the abandonment of the old house, it being sold with the lot to the Second Presbyterian Church, for $4,000, on July 30, 1870. A plot of ground

NASSAU SCHOOL, EAST ORANGE

PROGRESS OF FRANKLIN SCHOOL, EAST ORANGE

1. First School, built in 1825. 2. Second School built. 3. Third School, as it appears to-day.

225x200 feet in size was secured on Mulberry street (North Clinton street), and there on September 5, 1871, the new Ashland School was dedicated. John Lenord Merrill, president of the board of trustees, presided, and Rev. Dr. Henry F. Hickok, pastor of Brick Presbyterian Church, offered prayer. Rev. George A. Adams, pastor of the new Trinity Congregational Church, was the principal speaker. Three stories in height, the building, of brick, made an imposing appearance in its surrounding of frame dwellings, cottages predominating. Ten class rooms and an assembly room on the third floor, which by means of a rolling partition could be made into two class rooms, provided ample space for the school-age population for a long period. The investment amounted to $50,000. Four rooms were added in 1885. The school was attended by the boys and girls living south of Main street, the district extending to the South Orange line.

Ashland District, the largest in the town, now became overcrowded and the trustees planned for another building to accommodate the pupils living south of Central avenue. A lot was purchased on the east side of South Clinton street, near Elmwood avenue, and upon it a four-room brick school was built, which was named South Ashland. Primary grades only were taught there, the pupils of the higher classes attending the Ashland School till after the completion of the Nassau School, on February 20, 1899. Four teachers and 170 pupils were transferred from the Ashland to the Nassau School on this date. From the beginning of the school year in 1890, till March, 1892, the High School occupied temporary quarters in Ashland's assembly hall.

In the spring of 1891 Mr. Pennoyer presented his resignation as principal to the Board of Education, after faithful service of twenty-two years, to take effect at the end of June. Clarence E. Morse was engaged to fill the vacancy. Need of a larger and more modern building was most apparent in the beginning of the new century, and the parochial school of the Church of Our Lady Help of Christians, adjoining, being cramped for space, a happy solution was given the problem vexing each. The property was sold to the parish officials in 1906 and a new site secured on the north side of Park avenue, nearly opposite North Clinton street. Classes dismissed in the old Ashland building, at the beginning of the Christmas holiday season, resumed their studies in the new one on January 7, 1907. It has eighteen class rooms, a large auditorium and other rooms for special work. The cost was about $160,000. The school is in possession of many works of art—framed pictures, casts and statues, parting gifts of graduating classes. John Spargo is the principal.

Eastern is one of the original three school districts. The boundaries are thus described in an act of the Legislature, passed about 1835: "All the land lying east of the center of Cherry street (Arlington avenue), from the Bloomfield line to Main street, and from said point on Main street to the east side of the town farm on the South Orange line, shall be the Eastern District." A two-story frame school was built on the south side of Main sreet, opposite the present one and for at least two generations the boys and girls were there taught the foundation (if not all) of their education. During a part of the Civil War period John Burroughs, who later became an eminent naturalist, was the teacher. He graded and systematized the school with a great deal of success.

A lot 200x194 feet in size, on the north side of Main street, was purchased and a brick building corresponding in size and style of architecture to the Ashland School, was erected and dedicated on September 4, 1871. John M. Randall, chairman of the building committee, turned the keys over to Daniel C. Whitman, president of the board of trustees, prayer was offered by Rev. Charles A. Smith, pastor of the Munn Avenue Presbyterian Church, and Colonel Joel B. Baker, of Troy, New York, engaged as the principal, delivered an address. Miss Mary D. Baldwin and Miss Georgianna Stevenson, teachers in the old building, were transferred to the new one and remained there many years. Colonel Baker died in 1875, and Clarence F. Carroll served as principal for the next three years.

Vernon Llewellyn Davey, whose life and work was to be indissolubly associated with the educational system of East Orange, succeeded Mr. Carroll and for twelve years administered the affairs of the school so successfully that he was promoted to the superintendency, when the office was created in 1890. Miss Stevenson acted as principal for a year and then Edward H. Dutcher was appointed in 1891 and is now approaching his thirtieth year of consecutive administration.

The value of the Eastern School buildings, ground and equipment is $117,217.29. Several additions have been made, and 752 pupils are enrolled in 1920.

Elmwood School is an outgrowth of the South Ashland, and in 1890 Charles J. Majory was principal, and Miss Laura Lindsley, Miss Ida Tappan and Miss Ida Roos were the teachers. Enlargements to the building were made upon several occasions, meeting the growth of the vicinity, which was very rapid after the trolley line appeared on Central avenue. Albert H. Wilson became the principal in September, 1892, and four teachers were under his charge. His place was taken by Charles H. DeKroyft in 1899, he having assumed the principalship of the Nassau School. When William H. Smith came as the principal, there were eighteen teachers, but the number was reduced to fourteen at the opening of the Washington School. Mr. DeKroyft died at the beginning of the school year in 1908, and a tablet has been erected in his memory in the school, a tribute of teachers and pupils. The value of the Elmwood property in 1920 is placed at $236,697.58.

Meeting the demand for school facilities in the northeastern part of the town, known as Ampere, the Board of Education laid out a new dis-

ELMWOOD BRANCH OF FREE PUBLIC LIBRARY, EAST ORANGE

FRANKLIN BRANCH OF FREE PUBLIC LIBRARY, EAST ORANGE

trict in 1892, which extended from William street on the south, north by the Parkway to Park avenue, west to Clinton street, north to the Bloomfield line and east to the Newark line. The country was celebrating the 400th anniversary of the discovery of America by Christopher Columbus, and in his honor the building was named Columbian. It was built at the corner of Grove street and Springdale avenue, and was first occupied in the spring of 1893. There were eight rooms in the building. The plot measured 100 feet on the latter thoroughfare, 390 feet on the southerly side and 200 feet on Grove street. Dairy farms surrounded the school and only three houses were standing north of Springdale avenue. A pasture land extended southerly, including land between Fourth avenue and Nineteenth street, and open fields stretched westerly to Arlington avenue.

Completed at a cost of $30,000, the building was used by the kindergarten, first, second and third grades. One hundred pupils were enrolled on the opening day. But the population was increasing and in 1897, the first eighth grade class, consisting of sixteen pupils, was graduated to the High School. Then it became necessary to transfer the seventh and eighth grades to the Eastern School till 1902, when the school was again given the grammar standing. A portable building was used in 1912 for primary classes till the new addition on the southeast corner was occupied, and in April, 1913, three class rooms and the principal's office were completed on the first floor. Frank S. Coe has been the only principal since the school was organized. A custom established at the graduation to present a gift to the school, has added greatly to the collection of works of art. The value of the plant in 1920 is $210,050.25.

Better school accommodations were needed in the Fourth Ward near the end of the Nineteenth Century, but the Board of Education and the people could not agree upon a site, which was finally decided upon in 1898 at the corner of South Arlington and Central avenues. In February, 1899, the building was finished and named Nassau. Ten years later an addition provided fifteen class rooms in the entire school. Albert H. Wilson, principal of the Elmwood School, was transferred to Nassau and on February 20, 1899, 182 pupils from Ashland, 32 from Eastern, 63 from Elmwood School and 26 new pupils were enrolled in the new school. In 1901 thirty-one pupils of the first class were given certificates of promotion to the High School. The value of the plant in 1920 is $113,104.98.

Indication of the growth of Ampere (Fifth Ward) was the demand for another school in that vicinity early in the decade of 1900-1910. A lot was therefore purchased on William street, extending from Nineteenth street to Greenwood avenue, and the school house named in honor of Richard Stockton, the only martyr of the Signers of the Declaration of Independence and a Jerseyman, was opened for the reception of pupils on February 13, 1905. William H. Smith was placed in charge as the principal. The building contained twelve class rooms, an auditorium on the third floor and other necessary rooms. The Stockton coat of arms appears in the stained glass windows of the auditorium. Mr. Smith was transferred to the Elmwood School in 1908 and Charles J. Vrooman was chosen as his successor. The enrolment in 1920 is 614 and the value of the plant was $93,813.71.

That the Eastern and Nassau schools might be relieved of the crowding attendance, the Lincoln School, named in honor of the Martyred President, was built on a lot at the corner of Maple and Central avenues, and six grades enrolled at the opening in September, 1908. The eighth grade was added in 1911, thus giving it full grammar standing. W. F. Sargeant was the first principal and he was succeeded by J. H. Bosshart. Thomas L. Barnes is the principal in 1920. An addition was made to the school in 1914, providing a total of thirteen class rooms. The enrolment is 616 and the value of the plant is $128,383.50.

Washington School, named by Orange Chapter, New Jersey Society, Sons of the American Revolution, in honor of the Father of his Country, was ready for occupation in February, 1912, at the corner of Sanford street and Kenwood place. There were twelve class rooms and eight more added in 1920. The enrolment is 579 and the value of the plant is $169,654.59. The principal is William Brady.

In 1889, with scarcely a dissenting voice, the districts were consolidated and numbered forty-five of the county of Essex, and the County Superintendent of Schools appointed a Board of Education, composed of two members from each of the four wards. Joseph L. Munn was elected the first chairman, and Rev. Dr. John Crowell the district clerk. The first annual report was issued by the new board in 1890, when it was announced that the expenditures for that year were $40,760.67, and the value of the property $165,000. Vernon L. Davey, principal of the Eastern School, was elected superintendent in 1890, and he at once began the work of building up an organization which soon proved to be not only efficient but superior to many systems much longer in operation. At the time of consolidation there were High School Departments in Franklin, Eastern and Ashland schools, each of the latter two having a three-year course, while the former had one of only two years. Graduating exercises for the three schools were held in Commonwealth Hall in June, 1889, and in 1890, a four-year course having been adopted by the Board of Education, only three students were graduated. The exercises were held in the Ashland School auditorium.

One of the first acts of the Board of Education was the purchase of a lot on Winans street, and the erection of a brick building, costing $120,-000, for use as the High School, and occupied in December, 1891. It contained ten recitation rooms, two large study rooms, a drawing room, chemical laboratory and a gymnasium on the third floor. Two rooms in the basement were afterward equipped for manual training and mechanical drawing. Superintendent Davey was chosen principal, his staff consisting of seven assistants in the regular course and three in the preparatory classes. Lincoln E. Rowley, in 1896, was chosen vice-principal, holding the office for two years, when he became principal. In May, 1900, he retired, and Charlès W. Evans became his successor at the beginning of the new school year, in September. He served till 1912, when Ralph E. Files, the present principal, assumed charge of the office.

Enrolment in the High School became so largely out of proportion with its capacity that the Board of Education was compelled to consider plans for future and present-day needs, early in the decade of 1900-1910. As the outcome, the plant now so thoroughly equipped and giving such excellent service, was devised. Land extending from the High School lot on Winans street to Walnut street, was secured and the three-story brick structure was ready for occupancy in September, 1911. Connection was made with the old building and the students, and administrative forces found ample space for all their requirements. A large auditorium, capable of seating 1,200 persons, having an entrance on the ground floor, was a feature very much appreciated by the public patronizing concerts, lectures and other forms of entertainment. Space was provided also for complete departments in Domestic Science, Manual Training and Commercial work.

Superintendent Davey, whose health had been failing, was compelled to retire, his resignation being accepted by the Board of Education in June, 1913. He died on December 30, 1914, leaving the educational system of East Orange of that date as his monument. His exceptional judgment for the selection of teaching talent which enabled him to gather a remarkable corps of instructors about him, his comprehensive grasp of a multitude of details, his adequate scholarship, his unfailing courtesy, combined with a firmness of a strong executive, all coöperating through his long term of service, make his record one that has few equals in the country and one of which the city feels justly proud. On December 5, 1915, a bronze tablet, upon which Mr. Davey's portrait is strikingly illuminated, and placed on the northerly wall of the auditorium, was dedicated with an inspiring order of exercises. The inscription upon the tablet reads:

Vernon Llewellyn Davey,

1852..............1914.

Founder and Builder of

The Public School System of East Orange.

Principal of Eastern School 1878. First Superintendent

of Schools 1890. Retired 1913.

Leader in Education   Able Executive

Wise Counsellor.

Inspiring Teacher   Friend of Children.

This is the tribute of the pupils,

Teachers and other associates in education work.

Dr. Edwin C. Broome succeeded Mr. Davey as superintendent of the schools. In his report for 1919-1920, Dr. Broome speaks of the phenomenal growth of the High School, stating that the present building was filled to capacity eight years after its erection, demonstrating the need of a building program which looks many years ahead. The enrolment in 1920 is 1,654, an increase in ten years of 852, giving a percentage of 119.6. The total value of the High School plant is $538,410.19, and of the entire system $1,989,035.89. Out of a total enrolment of 8,907 in all the schools only 970 are reported as retarded, the low percentage of 10.8. Prizes of various character are awarded to successful students for essays upon studies of the year, and the general work throughout the schools in every department is of a very high order of merit.

Honors were taken by the High School teams in the Rutgers Interscholastic debates, New Jersey Interscholastic baseball games, and in New Jersey Tennis championship.

The Board of Education in 1920 consists of Edmund H. Walker, president; John W. Noble, vice-president; Blanche P. Durgin, Daniel A. McMillin and George W. Jackson. Dr. Edwin C. Broome is superintendent of the schools, and Fred T. Dugan is secretary of the Board of Education. Under the provision of the school law which makes it obligatory for a Board of School Estimate to be established each year by the City Council and the Board of Education, Burton E. Emory and George W. Thornton represent the former and Messrs. Noble and Walker the latter. The function of the Board is to decide upon the amount needed to carry on the work during the school year. The total disbursement for the year 1919-1920 is $737,607.38. A model in every respect, the East Orange schools occupy a leading place in the country's educational systems for general efficiency and high figure of merit. In its every department, from the kindergarten to the graduating class, there are employed the best equipped teachers obtainable and the results secured are the strongest commendation of their success.

CHAPTER LXXXVII

THE MOST NOTABLE MAN IN THE WORLD

One summer day an automobile, electrically propelled by an elderly man, with a lady seated by his side, passed along the streets of the Oranges and Newark, unobserved by the moving throng. If, instead, they had been riding over the thoroughfares of Tokio, Japan, the constabulary would doubtless have had a difficult task in preserving order, so eagerly would the populace have greeted the greatest inventive genius in the world today. Thomas Alva Edison was making a trip from his West Orange Laboratory to the Market street depot of the Pennsylvania railroad, in Newark, and few if any of the thousands of persons he and Mrs. Edison passed even turned to catch a glimpse of them. Indeed, the people have become accustomed to the presence of the distinguishd inventor and he can move about in public places without any harassment whatever, which is not always the case with eminent statesmen, soldiers and others who have become popular through their personal efforts or from other causes. But Mr. Edison does not depend upon public plaudits for a fixed place in popular estimation. In fact, he cares little for the "lime light." His achievements are known by men and there are millions of them today enjoying the products which his wonderful brain has extracted from the mystic realm.

Mr. and Mrs. Edison, after their marriage in February, 1886, became residents of Llewellyn Park. Glenmont, their home, is situated between Parkway and Honeysuckle avenue, and for a third of a century men prominent in the affairs of the world have there occasionally conferred with the great inventor over processes inaugurated or in a social gathering. Built of stone, brick and wood, the house, as Dixon, in his life of Edison, says is "refreshingly independent of architectural rules, yet it presents a wealth of fancy, which brings into view at every turn unguessed and delightful surprises. It abounds in gable roofs, picturesque nooks and angles, carved balconies and mellow sheets of stained glass, the whole set in a panorama of rare shrubs, floral arabesques and beds of emerald velvet, the brilliant coloring of which is thrown in broad relief by a background of sombre pines. The extensive grounds contain specimens of rare and beautiful plants and shrubbery. The hall after the fashion of English manors, is luxuriously furnished. Red mahogany, cunningly wrought, enters into the composition of the floors, walls and ceiling, affording an effective background for the glowing Eastern fabrics which abound. Mr. Edison's den contains the large collection of gifts from the crowned heads of Europe and other celebrities, and gold medals of merit from the various expositions in recognition of his wonderful achievements of electrical inventions." Into this environment Edison brings his tired body and brain at the end of long periods of constant application to problems which are conquered only by diligence and perseverance.

Edison, a self-made man, has risen to his supreme place upon the heights of inventive genius by his own efforts. He was born in Milan, Ohio, February 11, 1847, his father, John Edison, having fled from Canada, five years previous to escape from punishment for taking part in a revolt against the government. Thomas remembers a visit to Vienna when he was five years old. He was taken there to see his grandfather, then in the last year of his life—his one hundred and second. This grandfather's name was Samuel, whose father, Thomas, was a well-to-do banker of Manhattan in Revolutionary War days and who signed his name to Continental currency. The genealogy and much other information contained in this chapter is taken from "Edison, His Life and Inventions," a two-volume work of 500 pages each, written by Frank Lewis Dyer, general counsel for the Edison laboratory and allied interests, and Thomas Cummerford Martin, former president of the American Institute of Electrical Engineers, and sanctioned by the inventor. The volumes were published in 1910.

He did not have much schooling—in fact, only three months in a public school at Port Huron, Michigan—but his mother, we are told, was a highly educated woman, and did not neglect to lead his youthful steps along the paths of knowledge and wisdom. At the age of twelve he began as a bread winner, selling newspapers. While thus engaged he issued the "Grand Trunk Herald," on the Grand Trunk Railway running into Detroit. A station master whose child he had rescued from an onrushing train, taught him how to operate a telegraph instrument as a reward. While thus engaged he invented an automatic repeater, by means of which a message could be transferred from one wire to another without the aid of an operator. When he was seventeen he conceived the idea of sending two messages at once over the same wire, which led to his experiments in duplex telegraphy. Gradually rising from one position to another, in 1871 he became superintendent of the New York Gold and Stock Company, inventing the printing telegraph for gold and stock quotations. He was established in a Newark workshop at this time and from there, in 1876, moved to Menlo Park. His system of duplex telegraphy was developed into quadruplex and sextuple transmissions. The carbon telephone transmitter, used quite generally throughout the world, and the pyromagnetic generator, the object of which is to produce electricity direct from the heat energy of coal or other fuel without the intervention of a steam engine or other prime motor, were other inventions; but the most important of all was the production of the incandescent lamp. After perfecting a device having a platina burner, he adopted a filament of

THOMAS A. EDISON INDUSTRIES, WEST ORANGE

carbon of high resistance, enclosed in a glass chamber, from which the air was almost completely exhausted.

Till October 21, 1879, there was nothing in existence resembling our modern incandescent lamp. On that date the labors of Edison culminated in its invention which possesses all the essentials of the one in use today. With its bestowal upon the world a new gainful pursuit was opened, and thousands of operatives are now engaged in making lamps and accessories of this lighting system. The first public exhibition was given at Menlo Park, in December, 1879, and was also the first instance of sub-division of the electric light. A great deal of interest in it was created throughout the world, inasmuch as scientific experts had testified before a committee of the English House of Commons in the previous year that such a sub-division was impossible. While working out the problem Edison investigated nearly three thousand theories and series of experiments. Experts were sent to all parts of the globe in search of fibres that could be utilized for the manufacture of carbon filaments, and the exhaustless zeal with which the inventor pushed his researches day and night was finally crowned with the success he so eagerly sought and richly deserved.

The phonograph, now an indispensable article in the world home life, was invented by Edison in 1877, and the patent issued February 19, 1878. He was the very first to apply the induction of coil to the transmission of speech. The motograph receiver, generally known as the loud-speaking telephone, is an invention by which the voice from a telephone can be received with such power as to be readily heard by a large audience. The telephonograph, is as the name implies, an arrangement by which a telephone communication from a distance can be recorded on the phonograph and reproduced at will. By the megaphone, which was invented by Edison during his acoustic researches, conversation can be carried a long distance. The electric dynamo was to a certain extent, a completed invention, when Edison took up his work and its general principles and details of construction were well understood by experts, but the inventor began nevertheless his experiments that revolutionized the method of building dynamos. He was the first to design large steam dynamos, and in 1881 he built a dynamo weighing twenty-seven tons, and of which the armature was built of massive bars of copper instead of wires.

Desiring a laboratory nearer his home, Edison in 1887, purchased the property at the north corner of Valley road and Lakeside avenue, West Orange, there being a large unoccupied frontage on the former thoroughfare at that time. The site chosen for the laboratory was near Cook's pond, a small body of water, the delight of the boys living in the vicinity in the decade immediately preceding. The laboratory, built of brick three stories in height and 250 feet in length was soon erected, together with four other one-story brick buildings, each one hundred by twenty-five feet in size.

Surrounding the plant was a high picket fence, with an entrance gate on Valley road. The keeper was instructed to allow no one to enter if not possessed of a pass or having legitimate business with Edison or his assistants. A new attendant went on duty on a certain day, and the inventor found to his dismay that he was barred from his own laboratory because he could not satisfactorily identify himself to the one so truly following instructions. Several minutes elapsed before Edison was released from his predicament. Scores of people endeavor to visit him every day, and for his protection it has been necessary to guard him from the majority of these callers. Official parties of scientists, school teachers and students and others equally interested in the Edison products are received when the day's schedule permits.

On entering the main building, the first doorway from the ample passage leads the visitor into a handsome library, finished throughout in yellow pine, occupying the entire width of the building and almost as broad as it is long. The center of this spacious room is an open rectangular space about forty feet by twenty-five feet, rising clear forty feet or more from the main floor to the paneled ceiling. Around the side of the room run two tiers of galleries, divided as is the main floor beneath them, into alcoves. These alcoves are formed by racks extending from floor to ceiling, filled with shelves, except at two sides of the galleries, where they are formed by a series of glass painted cabinets, containing extensive collections of curios and beautiful mineralogical and geological specimens, among which is the notable Tiffany-Kunz collection of minerals acquired by Edison. Here and there in these cabinets may be found models which he has used at times in his studies of anatomy and physiology. Countless thousands of specimens of ores and minerals of every conceivable description, gathered from all parts of the world occupy many of the shelves, while others are used for filing the large number of periodicals read by Edison. Experimental rooms are in use on the second floor, where researches are made and on the third floor are, in glass cabinets, the experimental incandescent lamps and an immense variety of phonographs, telegraph and telephone instruments upon which Edison has spent his energies. Thousands of pages of notes are stored away in the archives, all written by the inventor. Over fifteen thousand pages were made on one point alone while solving a very difficult problem.

The first of the brick buildings adjoining the laboratory is known as the galvanometer room, the next as the chemical laboratory, the third as the pattern shop and store room and the fourth for "rough and ready" operations. In the stock room are skins of animals, hair, horns, hoofs, teeth of almost every known domestic and wild animal, tusks of elephants, hides of rhinoceros and hippopotamus, horns of antelopes, antlers of deer and others. Every known variety of grain and cereals, fishes

INTERIOR OF LIBRARY OF MR. EDISON'S LABORATORY, ORANGE

from all quarters of the globe, rare and costly drugs and chemicals, ore of gold, silver, copper, tin, iron and other metals, flour, sugar, silks, fabrics and innumerable other articles used by Edison in his experiments.

Perfecting his magnetic ore separator, Edison started on a prospecting tour for the metal early in the decade of 1890. The magnetic needle disclosed evidences of it in the hills of Sussex county and a large area of land was purchased in which the delving for rock-producing ore was soon begun. The separation was on a colossal scale. Gigantic rolls which by the force of momentum were capable of crushing rocks of vastly greater size than ever before attempted were installed in the mill, and for five years the work continued while a village of workers and others clustered about the scene of operations. It was given the name of Edison and here the inventor devoted nearly all his time to the perfecting of the plant. Over two million dollars were spent in the enterprise. Reluctantly the inventor abandoned his operations when he realized that they would not yield ample financial returns. His labors and money were practically all swept away. The plant at Edison was vacated and then, still retaining his pluck, the inventor began the manufacture of Portland cement at New Village, and which proved more successful and remunerative.

Of the better known Edison inventions none have given more employment to people, cheered tired humanity so completely and created a more definite place for itself than the motion picture. This was not made possible till after Edison had toiled for a long period over the problem of doing for the eye what the phonograph had done for the ear, and it was his hope to combine both so that motion and sound could be recorded simultaneously. But the idea did not materialize into a public commodity. Having at last obtained the proper material upon which to secure the photograph, the problem then remained to devise an apparatus by means of which from twenty to forty pictures per second could be taken, the film being stationary during the exposure, and upon the closing of the shutter being moved to present a fresh surface. Edison's solution of the problem involved the production of a kodak in which the pictures could be taken with the rapidity indicated, and with preciseness of adjustment that each should exactly coincide with its predecessors even when subjected to the balance of enlargement by perfection. This was accomplished, and in the summer of 1889 the first modern motion picture camera was made. More than this, the mechanism for operating the film was so constructed that its movement took place in one-tenth of the time required for the exposure, giving the film an opportunity to rest prior to the opening of the shutter. Edison gave the name of kinetoscope to the invention, but it is now known as the moving picture machine. The patent was granted January 31, 1891, and on March 7, 1892, an exhibition was given at the laboratory of the completed work.

An unpretentious wooden structure, erected in the yard of the laboratory, served as the first motion picture studio. It had a movable roof in the center which could be raised or lowered at will. The building was covered with black roofing paper and also painted black inside. There was no scenery to lighten the sombre environment, which was needed as the common background for the performers, throwing all their actions into high relief. The whole structure was set on a pivot, so that it could be swung around with the sun, and the movable roof was opened so that the accentuated sunlight would stream upon the actors whose gesticulations were being caught by the camera. From this crude beginning the paraphernalia used in the production of moving pictures is now most lavishly arranged with every medium possible at hand for obtaining the best results.

Edison says the secret of achievement is based on hard thinking and hard work, both of which he combined in the invention of the storage battery. He established a chemical plant at Silver Lake, where he worked out the problem. His biographers state that "sometimes when Mr. Edison had been working long hours he would want to have a short sleep. . . . . He would often crawl into an ordinary roll-top desk and curl up and take a nap, using several volumes of Watt's Dictionary of Chemistry for pillows. We fellows used to say that he absorbed the contents during his sleep, judging from the flow of new ideas he had on waking."

Cook's Pond, where ducks sported in the warm months, was at the back door of the laboratory, and meadow land stretched away in every direction. Edison, having decided to manufacture the phonographs near his workshop, purchased much of this acreage and erected thereon two large buildings, one for the making of instruments and the other for the construction of disk blanks. The third floor of the laboratory was then fitted up as a music room. In time the site became an industrial center, employing several thousands of men and women, and the output representing millions of dollars in value. Say the biographers of Edison:

Inventors of practical devices may be broadly divided into two classes—first, those who may be said to have made two blades of grass grow where only one grew before; and, second, great inventors, who have made grass grow plentifully on hitherto unproductive ground. The vast majority of practical inventors belong to and remain in the first of these divisions, but there have been, and probably always will be, a less number who, by reason of their greater achievements, are entitled to be included in both classes. Of these latter, Thomas Alva Edison is one, but in the pages of history he stands conspicuously pre-eminent—a commanding, towering figure, even among giants.

The activities of Edison have been of such great range, and his conquests in the domains of practical arts so extensive and varied, that it is somewhat difficult to estimate with any satisfactory degree of accuracy the money value of his inventions to the world of today, even after making due allowance for the work of other great inventors and the propulsive effects of large amounts of capital thrown into the enterprises which took root, wholly or in part, through the productions of his genius and energies.

This difficulty will be apparent, for instance, when we consider his telegraph and telephone inventions. They were absorbed in enterprises already existing, and were the means of assisting their rapid growth and expansion, particularly the telephone industry. Again, in considering the fact that Edison was one of the first in the field to design and perfect a practical and operative electric railway, the main features of which are used in all electric roads of today, we are confronted with the problem as to what proportion of their colossal investment and earnings should be ascribed to him.

Difficulties are multiplied when we pause for a moment to think of Edison's influence on collateral branches of business. In the public mind he is credited with the invention of the incandescent electric light, the phonograph and other widely known devices, but how few realize his actual influence on other trades that are not generally thought of in connection with these things. For instance, let us note what a prominent engine builder, the late Gardiner C. Sims, has said.

Mr. Sims is quoted as follows:

Watt, Corliss and Porter brought forward steam engines to a high state of proficiency, yet it remained for Mr. Edison to force better proportions, workmanship, designs, use of metals, regulation, the solving of the complex problems of high speed and endurance, and the successful development of the shaft governor. Mr. Edison is pre-eminent in the realm of engineering.

In this connection follows a list of some of the products for which the Edison inventions have tended to create a greatly increased demand: Copper, iron, steel, brass, zinc, nickel, platinum ($5 an ounce in 1878, now $26 an ounce), rubber, oils, wax, bitumen, various chemical compounds, belting, boilers, injectors, structural steel, iron tubing, glass, silk, cotton, porcelain, fine woods, slate, marble, electrical measuring instruments, miscellaneous machinery, coal, wire, paper, building materials, sapphires.

Just as the day's work was ending on Wednesday, December 9, 1914, fire was discovered at 5:17 o'clock, in the film testing department, a one-story frame structure, near the center of the block of buildings, over twenty-five in number. The Edison Fire Company, carefully trained and known as one of the best factory fire-fighting organizations in the country, was immediately called into action. But the inflammable celluloid with which the building was stored, soon made it a seething furnace. Alarms were then sent to the West Orange Fire Department, followed by calls for assistance from Orange, East Orange, Newark, Bloomfield and Montclair departments, all of which responded. There was a general spread of the flames, both northwest and southeast, the smaller one-story structures and the massive concrete buildings all being engulfed in the fiery progress. To the southeast the flames caught up freight cars on a siding piled with lumber, and then swept into the cabinet-making building, where thousands of phonograph cabinets and millions of feet of expensive wood were stored. The great concrete structures were six stories in height and extended the length of an ordinary city block along Lakeside avenue. Into them the fire penetrated with force enough to tear out the windows, pass through concrete partitions supposed to be fireproof and through solid reinforced concrete floors. The heat was intense, rolling in massive waves over the doomed plant.

To the northwest the fire ate its way into the amberole record building, a five-story reinforced concrete structure, where the cylinder type of phonograph records are made. The administration building and all of its records were destroyed early in the evening, despite the efforts of the firemen to save them. Tons and tons of water were thrown into the burning area, by well-manned streams connecting with hydrants in a radius of half a mile. Orange sent its water hurling at the burning mass; the West Orange supply and the one furnished by the plant did not fail in their pressure. Powerful pumpers threw streams of such force that they tore the hose out of the firemen's hands. Mr. Edison's desire to save the laboratory, where many precious records were stored, redoubled the energies of the fire fighters in this direction, but the fire was gaining nearer and nearer the much prized historic building. Volunteers worked faithfully in removing the most valuable articles to places of safety. Try as hard as they could the firemen could not stay the flames from the reservoir of alcohol, and after sweeping building after building from their path, they now jumped into this inflammable mass. The fire had been raging five hours and had baffled every effort to hold it in check. Now the climax had come. Instantly there was a burst of bluish flame which leaped high into the air, a magnificent scene, followed by a roaring, whistling sound. The explosion was heard many blocks distant, and for a few minutes the coloring appeared in the roaring furnace as the last vestige of the spirits was licked up in the heat. When the firemen had brought it under control after burning six hours the laboratory was practically the only building untouched by the flames. A conference of the department heads was called by Edison and preparations made that very night for restoring the plant. The loss was never published, but unofficial estimates placed it between one and two million dollars.

In an incredible space of time the immense plant was again in operation, and the thirty buildings, more or less, were soon employing thousands of operatives. Prosperity came to the inventor of the phonograph and moving pictures, both manufactured at the plant, and were with other devices bringing exceedingly large financial returns. The weekly pay roll at one time reached over $100,000. The inventions of Mr. Edison up to and including the year 1920, numbered about nineteen hundred. He is now engaged in perfecting some of his older successes, and though in his seventy-fourth year, is in good health and destined to live a long time in the enjoyment of his wonderful achievements.

CHAPTER LXXXVIII

WEST ORANGE

Organic existence was first granted the section of West Orange known as the mountain section, on March 11, 1862, when the Legislature created the town of Fairmount from parts of Orange, Caldwell and Livingston. Dissensions arising over the public schools in 1863, Simeon Harrison, James W. Fields and others petitioned the Legislature for another division from Orange, and on March 14, 1863, West Orange was set aside, the described boundaries being as follows:

Beginning at a point twelve chains westerly from the northwest corner of the bridge near the late residence of Alexander Sayre, deceased, on the dividing line between Orange and Bloomfield, thence running in a straight line to Francis Burnside's well; thence south in a straight line to the southwest corner of the gas works on White street; thence up the westerly side of said White street to the bridge; thence south in a straight line to the corner of the lands belonging to the heirs of Charles Lighthipe, deceased, and the heirs of Jacob A. Sharp, deceased, on the south side of Main street; thence south in a straight line to the easterly line of Amos Stagg's lot; thence south in a straight line to a brook in Joyce street; thence along the line of said brook south to the north side of Freemantown road; thence southwesterly along the line of said road to the county bridge near the school house; thence south down the brook to the South Orange line; thence west along the South Orange line to the southeast corner of Fairmount; thence along the line of the said township of Fairmount in its several courses to the Bloomfield line; thence along the Bloomfield line in its several courses to the place of beginning; be and the same is hereby set off from the town of Orange and annexed to and made a part of the township of Fairmount in said county, to all intents and purposes, as if said territory had originally been a part of said township; and that the act entitled, "An act to create from parts of the town of Orange and the townships of Caldwell and Livingston, in the said county of Essex, a new township to be called the township of Fairmount, approved March eleventh, Anno Domini eighteen hundred and sixty-two, shall have the same force and effect within the territory hereby annexed as they have heretofore held, and now rightfully have within the limits of said township.

And be it enacted, that the name of the said township of Fairmount be and the same is hereby changed to West Orange.

Dr. Edgar E. Marcy purchased two hundred acres of unbroken forest from Daniel C. Otis, in 1860, and proceeded to develop his tract, one of the most rugged on the mountain, and possessing a wealth of natural scenery. The tract, bounded by the ridge, Northfield road, Mount Pleasant avenue and Perry lane, was soon going through a course of pruning. Dr. Marcy, while building his home, cleared the frontage on the ridge of trees, thus providing an unobstructed view of the outlying territory extending to the great metropolis. General Randolph B. Marcy, brother of Dr. Marcy, and father-in-law of General George B. McClellan, had served as the latter's chief of staff during the time he commanded the Army of the Potomac. Seeking a place of quiet, General Marcy was soon building his home a few rods from his brother's. General McClellan occupied his home, "Maywood," in 1864, followed by John Crosby Brown and others. The Mountain Ridge road was laid out by Dr. Marcy, connecting Northfield avenue and Mount Pleasant avenue. The owners of these mountain homes enjoyed freedom from crowding, the estates, for such they really were, running back to Perry lane. This colony of famous people became very popular after the Civil War and during the summer months there was a great deal of entertaining. General McClellan was very much sought while in residence and of easy approach by the natives. Seated on his charger, "Daniel Webster," as he exercised along the mountain roads, he became a part of the very environment.

Benjamin F. Small, coming to Orange in 1860, was impressed with the pure air of the mountain, its wonderful possibilities for home making, and in 1864 purchased the Daniel S. Williams farm, which he began developing. The settlement was named St. Cloud and which is in use today. Benvenue and other avenues and thoroughfares were laid out by him and Abram Baldwin, with whom he was associated in the laying out of the land. Cottages were built and by personal influence Mr. Small induced a number of New Yorkers to make their summer homes at St. Cloud.

Efforts of the founder to popularize the venture were very successful and St. Cloud became a well settled neighborhood, but he became financially embarrassed, practically losing all his holdings. Rev. B. F. Barrett endeavored a few years before to duplicate Mr. Haskell's success at Llewellyn Park. The tract selected was south of Northfield avenue, on the mountain slope. Though plots were laid out, roads opened and inducements offered people to build their homes there, the enterprise failed of accomplishment.

West Orange was the only one of the Oranges without horse and steam railroad transportation, yet each summer an increasing number of visitors arrived in the town, giving it a lively appearance at certain hours of the day. Handsome equipages drawn by stylish looking horses passed over the mountain roads and through the parks, guided by coachmen in livery and seated in the vehicles were people of renown who had come out to the mountain country for rest and recreation. Though the town had been incorporated and privileged to conduct its affairs as the electorate directed there was no immediate desire to adopt any of the improvements in vogue in other municipalities. Not till the summer of 1868 was there a movement for the treatment of the roads with the

FAIRMONT SCHOOL, WEST ORANGE

macadam and telford system, then beginning to be used in the neighboring towns and cities. The mountainside, much of it in its virgin beauty, was now being attacked by the quarryman in the effort to secure the trap rock necessary, when ground into particles, for building the roadways.

The first meeting of the Township Committee was held in the early part of April, 1863, when Simeon Harrison was elected chairman, and on the 20th of the month Jeptha B. Lindsley, Ira Harrison and John Grannis were appointed road overseers. Mount Pleasant avenue, which had been a toll road since the early part of the century, was the only one showing any evidence of continuous care. Daniel Brennan, the pioneer in road building, according to the telford and macadam methods, was operating a quarry on the mountainside for the converting of trap rock into the specially needed sizes for the filling of his contracts in the summer of 1868, when a number of West Orange citizens secured public subscriptions to a fund for the improving of Northfield avenue. Over $3,000 was raised and applied to the much needed work on this over-mountain thoroughfare. In a few years quarries were opened at several points on the mountain-slope and the air resounded with the churning of the stone crushers as they ground the trap rock blasted from its strata into serviceable road building material. The roads in the vicinity of these plants were often the scene of processions of the stone wagons carrying their product to the outlying cities and towns. Many miles of macadamized roads were built in Essex county during the first few years of its introduction.

The town of West Orange, away from the beaten paths of travel, enjoyed a steady growth, not the fluctuating kind which often besets communities along railroad lines. Stages ran regularly from the Orange station of the Lackawanna railroad over the three principal mountain roads—Eagle Rock avenue, Mt. Pleasant avenue and Northfield avenue —for the accommodation of persons traveling beyond the valley, while the residents of Llewellyn Park, the Mountain Ridge and elsewhere enjoyed their own conveniences for transportation.

In the days before the telephone came into use the local telegraph office frequently did a rushing business sending and receiving dispatches from and for General McClellan. This was emphasized when a candidate for President in 1864. It has been said that he was bitterly disappointed in not receiving the portfolio of Secretary of War when Grover Cleveland became the first Democratic President, in 1884, in twenty-four years. Seldom has the town of West Orange had a more generous hearted man among its residents than General McClellan. He was understood by some and misunderstood by others, but the fact remains that he was of a strong Christian character and very patriotic. The Flag of Stars and Stripes was alway displayed in the entrance hall of his home. Death released him of his sufferings in the early morning of October 29, 1885.

Public affairs of West Orange were conducted in a leisurely manner and with satisfaction, ordinarily, to the taxpayer. Occasional tilts at the annual school meetings held in the St. Mark's building, now used as the Essex County Vocational School, and a contest now and then at the polls for members of the Town Committee, were the punctuation points in the quiet life of the town.

Citizens assembled in mass meeting at the Gaston Street High School on an early autumn evening in 1899, decided to petition the Legislature at its next session to incorporate West Orange as a town. A council of ten members was proposed, which would allow greater freedom of action than the limitations of the township form of government, in vogue since 1863. The times were changing. In fact there was a noticeable feeling at all the elections and other public gatherings in recent years that the days of the township were fast slipping away. The bill incorporating West Orange as a town became a law on February 28, 1900. It provided that the Township Committee should continue to function till May 1.

No provision was made in the act for a referendum, so the fact remains that the town is in possession of a form of government without the people's approving voice. An election held on the second Tuesday in April for officials to start the new government on its long journey resulted in the choice of Simeon H. Rollinson as councilman-at-large, and who was to act as the town head. Dr. William M. Brien, retiring as chairman of the old Township Committee, declined to allow the use of his name in connection therewith. Councilmen elected were W. Edward Glazier and John Otterbein, representing the First Ward, Irven A. Kenney and Thomas Cunningham, the Second Ward, Max Brodesser and Thomas Gannon the Third Ward, William E. Condit and Herman Freye the Fourth Ward. Joseph McDonough, Township Clerk, Frank A. O'Connor, Assessor, and William N. Williams, Tax Collector, were all elected.

West Orange had a population in 1900 of 6,189, and on July 1, 1901, free delivery of mail matter was begun from the office in Orange. The trolley running through the town connecting Harrison avenue with Newark and the Eagle Rock line of earlier origin were both mediums attracting residents to the sections of the town where there was a great deal of unimproved land. Watson Whittlesey's conversion of the Ira Harrison farm into the home building tract which he named Watchung Heights, now well settled, was the first noticeable real estate movement in the northern end of the town in recent years. It proved a financial success to the investor and also a help to those residents who desired to own their homes. There has been a steady demand for building lots in every part of the town.

West Orange depended upon the Police Department of Orange for

its police protection till the early summer of 1884, when the Township
Committee decided to open police headquarters in a frame building at
the corner of Valley road and Lindsley avenue, and known as Hedges
Block. A police committee, consisting of John Otterbein, Jabez H. Haz-
ard and Robert N. Drew, was appointed to arrange the rented quarters,
where two cells and a court room were placed and set the department in
motion. William H. Bamford, John Hammil and George W. Stoll were
appointed the first patrolmen and they began guarding the town peace on
June 28, 1884. Joseph K. Fields was named the first police justice, serving till 1895. Patrolman Bamford was appointed police captain on August 2, 1892, as a reward for his excellent service given the town during
the eight years he had performed regular duty, and on March 4, 1900,
was chosen chief of police by the Town Council, into which the old township committee had been merged by an act of the Legislature. Under the
guidance of Chief Bamford the peace of West Orange was conserved for
many years with a minimum of outbreaks. His familiarity with the
ways of the local evil-doers and the sharp watch maintained upon those
coming from out of town was a part of his program to prevent the commission of crimes and misdemeanors. He was most successful as the
town chief. The headquarters were changed in 1905 to the new municipal building, on Northfield road, where they have since been established.
Patrick J. McDonough, who had made several notable arrests, succeeded
Chief Bamford, when the latter retired after thirty years' service, and
the department in 1920 is in a most efficient and highly organized condition, with a total number of twenty-seven officers and patrolmen on the
roster.

Edmund Condit, whose forebears were among the first settlers of
the mountain section, succeeded Judge Fields, in 1895, and he continued
till his death in 1912 to administer the affairs of the Police Court.
Charles J. Woods, the next incumbent, lived but four months, and then
Thomas J. McLaughlin assumed the office. He, in turn, after a few
years, gave way to John B. Lander, who specialized in his dispensation of
justice to juveniles. Instead of imposing a jail sentence he placed those
he thought possible of redeeming in the custody of parents or guardians
and compelled them to report to him at certain specified dates. In one
instance two boys were compelled to forego their Christmas entertainment, but it raised such a storm of indignation all over the country that
the judge relented and relaxed the severity of the sentence. Judge Lander was a kindly hearted man and it was his constant thought to save the
infractors of the law from the atmosphere of prison life as far as possible in the hope that the error of their way would be realized and complete
restoration to society accomplished.

Three men on permanent duty and six on call comprised the first
Fire Department of West Orange, which became operative March 6,

1894, by direction of the Township Committee. Owen Kennedy was appointed foreman and John Higgins and James J. Sheehan were the drivers. The fire committee consisted of John C. Harrison, Frederick Cummings and Carl Fentzloff. Simeon H. Rollinson donated the land at the corner of Whittingham place and Valley road, where the first fire house of frame construction was erected. Here the apparatus was stored awaiting the call for service till the new building of brick was occupied a few years later, and which has remained the headquarters of the Fire Department. There is another station at Eagle Rock avenue and Washington street. The equipment in each of the houses is practically identical—chemical engine, pumper, hook and ladder truck, triple combination apparatus and an ample supply of hose. All the vehicles are motorized and with a good water supply, which was introduced in 1892. The people of West Orange have a very safe protection against fire loss. The two most destructive conflagrations which have visited the town were beyond the power of the firemen to avert. The Gaston Street High School was a mass of flames when the alarm was sounded on the night of February 27, 1913, and at the Edison fire on the night of December 9, 1914, the call was not received till it had been burning eleven minutes. There are twenty-four permanent men connected with the department in 1920, and there is also a firm alarm system attached thereto. .

West Orange is very fortunate in the possession of its parks, public and private. Eagle Rock, reserved forever as a valuable part of the system under the control of the Essex County Park Commission, is visited annually by throngs of people in their never-tiring pilgrimage to this world-renowned wonder of Nature. The northerly edge of the South Mountain reservation, also in charge of the County Commission, extends quite a distance along Northfield road, from the mountaintop westerly to the point near the reservoir owned by the city of Orange. Massive boulders and great forest trees give a rugged appearance and add much to the environment of that locality. Llewellyn Park, mentioned more fully elsewhere, has lost none of its fame of nearly seventy years as a reservation of homes on the same general plan as laid out by Llewellyn S. Haskell, the founder. The system of assessing each property for maintenance of roads and other public places continues and the natural beauty of the entire enclosure has not been marred in any way during all these years. The Essex County Country Club has preserved the Hutton Park area and its fine specimens of forest trees, ravines and other features which were so attractive to the tourists of the decade of 1820. Other acres have been attached to the tract for playing the game of golf.

Through the generosity of Mr. and Mrs. Alfred B. Jenkins, of Llewellyn Park, the town came into possession of its first playground and which is accessible to the children from every section, but more especially to those living south of Main street. The donors tendered the tract of three acres, fronting on Valley road, near Whittingham place, and extending westerly to the trolley line running to South Orange, to the Town Council in the spring of 1910, which was accepted on June 7, and arrangements were immediately made for the grading and other improvements. Dedicatory ceremonies were set for Friday, June 16, 1911, and a large crowd of townspeople wás in attendance. Superintendent Allton H. Sherman marshaled the school children into the ground in the early afternoon, and the speech of Mr. Jenkins, at the end of which he turned the keys over to Mayor Samuel A. Muta, and the latter's reply had been made when a thunder shower appeared, sending the people homeward and abruptly terminating the exercises. The Jenkins playground has for more than ten years been a most popular place in the summer and other months in which it has been opened.

A triangular plot was left in the roadway when Watchung avenue was extended from Washington street northerly, and for several years it remained unbeautified. Then Louis Peiker, a resident, quietly took the task upon himself of giving it care during the season of growth. Year after year he planted flowers and trimmed the grass till his death in 1911. Mr. and Mrs. Jenkins, for whom the faithful citizen had worked as a gardener, then planned to place a bronze memorial set in a granite block in the little park. David L. Pierson was invited to prepare the exercises of dedication, and on Saturday, September 14, 1912, they were held under favoring auspices of clear weather and a genuine outbúrst of feeling to honor a man who "went about daily doing good."

About seven acres are enclosed in the playground purchased by the late Richard Colgate, on the northern boundary of the town, the entrance being from Franklin avenue and Cherry street. The dedication occurred on a beautiful September day, in 1918, and when the ground was in thorough running order it was turned over to the Playground Commission. Mr. Colgate, who died in 1919, created an endowment fund of $25,000 in his will, the interest of which was to be used in defraying the cost of maintenance of the ground.

Over $7,000 was expended by the commission in 1920 for the upkeep of the two playgrounds under its control. The commissioners are Edgar L. Newhouse, president; Dr. J. Minor Maghee, secretary and treasurer; Mrs. Alfred B. Jenkins, Charles G. Goodrich and Frederick C. Reynolds.

Memorial Park, a triangular plot of ground, paralleling Valley road, was added in 1920 to the town reservations. It is adorned with the memorial erected as a tribute to the residents who made the supreme sacrifice while in the Federal service during the World War.

Running water was introduced into the households and other buildings during the years 1892-1893, by the West Orange Water Company, which had been permitted by the Township Committee to lay its pipes through the town. The supply was received from the upper Passaic river and was first used in the southern section on June 11, 1892. A total of thirty-two miles of mains were laid and in 1920 it had increased to forty-one, the service extending over the mountains to the Livingston line. Municipal ownership of the plant, long a public discussed question culminated in 1917 in a special election to determine if the town should acquire the plant or continue the service of the corporation. The voters decided affirmatively, but the Town Council has been unable to satisfactorily adjust the financial part of the mandate and so the town is yet supplied under the former arrangement. Consolidated with a number of other concerns into the Commonwealth Water Company, of Summit, the local service is now furnished from the plant at the Canoe Brook headwaters. There are three hundred and thirty-six hydrants ready for use in the advent of fire, and an even pressure is maintained throughout the town.

Participation in the joint outlet sewer construction by the town of West Orange along with six other municipalities was very happily advised by the authorities in the summer of 1898. Possessing excellent drainage facilities through its water courses, the town was, however, unable to provide the necessary sewerage system for carrying away the household and other waste, till the plan was set forth by Robert S. Sinclair, of South Orange, for a trunk sewer to be built by the seven municipalities, and having its outlet at tidewater. West Orange's representatives in the commission were Councilmen Thomas Cunningham, Willis E. Glazier and John J. Kenney. William Rollinson, also of West Orange, acted as the secretary. An allowance was made in the contract for the town's rights in the Summit-Millburn division of the west branch of the trunk sewer so as to provide an outlet for that portion which lies west of the First Mountain. The daily allotted capacity in gallons allowed West Orange was 3,528,000. When the entire trunk sewer was completed on June 16, 1904, the local sewers were also nearly ready for service. The line connects at South Orange with the joint outlet sewer, the pipe at the beginning being twenty-two inches in diameter. It extends along Valley road to Joyce street, then to Wheeler street, to Lindsley avenue, to Mount Pleasant avenue, to Fairmount avenue, to Valley road, through the Washington school property to the Montclair line. A branch extends through Eagle Rock avenue to Harrison avenue, to Mississippi avenue to Valley way. This was the introduction of sewerage into West Orange, one of its most useful public utilities and which has served every day since it was first used by the people on September 15, 1904. The part of the system then placed in commission was at the corner of Freeman street and Valley road. Since that day many additions have been made to it till the town is sewered in a most satisfactory manner.

The cost apportioned to West Orange for the building of the trunk sewer was $149,439.68. In addition the twenty-six miles of local construction cost approximately $200,000.

Education processes in the early days were of a limited character on account of the small number of pupils to be instructed. The first school erected in the new town was St. Mark's, on Valley road, near the entrance to Llewellyn Park, in 1865. It was built of trap rock, at a cost of $12,000, and a few years later a brick addition entailed a further outlay of $20,000. There were nine rooms in the building which accommodated about 470 pupils. Through the generosity of Richard M. Colgate, a resident of Llewellyn Park, an industrial school was opened in the St. Mark's building in 1914, and at the close of the year arrangements were made by the county educational officials to take over the school and use it for vocational purposes, open only to boys who are residents of Essex county. This removed from local control its oldest school building. The Valley school was opened in a frame building on Valley road, near Mitchell street, in 1878. In 1886 its capacity was doubled by an addition which made the value of the property about $10,000.

In 1890 the newly enacted school laws provided for the abolition of the board of school trustees and created in lieu thereof the Board of Education, to consist of eight members. The need of a High School was now most apparent and the Gaston street building was erected in 1898, at a cost of $50,000, to which the grammar grades from the fifth year through the High School were then removed. The law of 1900 changing the mode of conducting municipal affairs also affected the Board of Education. The town, now arisen to the dignity of the sub-division of four wards, each one, according to the law, was to be represented on the board by three members. Those chosen at the special election on April 10, were Orville E. Freeman, Coleman E. Kissam and Abram Overmiller, First Ward; Wendell P. Garrison, Theodore D. Faulks and John J. Kenney, Second Ward; Newell N. Smith, Frank Owen and Herbert T. Abrams, Third Ward; Alfred R. Kimball, J. Smith Pierson and Frederick E. Vogelin, Fourth Ward.

The High School was a brick structure substantially built, but its stairways were so constructed as to give a well-started fire ample room for spreading in the draft-producing area. On the evening of February 27, 1913, an exhibit of the Anti-Tuberculosis League of the State was to be given in the assembly hall of this building. A storm was prevailing and only twenty-five persons were seated, awaiting the formal opening of the evening's program, when at 8:10 o'clock the janitor rushed through the building announcing that the basement was afire. In the space of a few seconds the interior was a seething mass of flames, and the people in the auditorium were trapped in the one space not engulfed by them, though they were rapidly spreading in that direction. The telephone had been used in time to notify the West Orange Fire Department. When Chief James J. Sheehan and his firemen reached the bottom of the hill leading to the school they saw flames issuing from every window on the lower floors, and a frantic group of persons calling for help from the assembly hall. The darkness of the stormy night made the scene most spectacular and, realizing that the saving of human life was to be their one supreme effort the firemen soon had thirty-five foot ladders extending to the windows and the women and men were rescued. Several, however, jumped to the ground, but while there were serious injuries no loss of life occurred. This was the most disastrous school fire in the history of the Oranges and the loss was complete, amounting to $62,500 on the building and $4,000 on the furnishings. There was an insurance of $58,500. The records of the school were all destroyed.

Steps were taken by the Board of Education to construct another building, which was completed in time for opening at the beginning of the school year in September, 1914. Eleven recitation rooms, offices for the Board and an auditorium seating 750 persons, were provided. The cost of the building was $105,000. A total of 412 boys and girls were enrolled in 1920, part of whom were in the grammar grade.

One of the landmarks in the town is the Washington School, in its commanding location at the junction of Eagle Rock avenue, Valley road and Washington street. It has served also as a community center, its auditorium having been utilized by the people for meetings of general interest. The building was occupied in February, 1895, and its seating capacity at first was only 225, but by adding wings in 1899 and 1909 the rooms were increased till they numbered nineteen in 1920 and the attendance is 811, the largest enrolment in any of the schools.

Due to the rapid growth in the southern part of the town, the Board of Education was compelled to build a new school, the site selected being on the eastern slope of the mountain, at the top of the Hazel avenue hill. There were but few houses in the vicinity, and woods and farm lands extended in every direction. It proved an ideal location, however, as the Board was building for the future as well as for the present. Light and air were considerations weighed carefully by the commissioners, and on October 19, 1906, Superintendent Allton H. Sherman had the satisfaction of presiding at dedicatory ceremonies of the completed building, which, with an addition built in 1917, now has sixteen rooms and an attendance of 526 pupils.

Eight class rooms are provided in the Eagle Rock School, built on the north side of Eagle Rock avenue, on the eastern slope of the mountain at a cost of $65,000, and opened in September, 1917. The attendance is 316.

Occupancy of the Gregory Avenue School took place in September, 1914. Its location is near Northfield avenue, and was designed to provide for the increased population in the southern part of the town. The cost of the building and land was $20,000. Accommodation is provided for four classes, the enrolment in 1920 being 133. The Pleasantdale School, on Pleasant Valley way, near Eagle Rock avenue, was constructed in 1904, for which the contractors were paid $10,000. There are three rooms, and an enrolment of 108. Other schools in the mountain section are the St. Cloud School, having two rooms and an enrolment of sixty-five, and the Mt. Pleasant School, one room, and twenty-five enrolled. Classes for sub-normal children were started in 1914, and in the following year a house opposite the High School was rented where these classes were instructed by special methods. In September, 1920, they were moved to a house at 7 Main street. Solomon C. Strong is the supervising principal, having come to the schools five years ago. In his annual report submitted in 1920, he emphasized the need of increased accommodation, congested conditions being very much in evidence at several of the buildings. During the last ten years the number of pupils has increased fifty-four per cent. and the class room facilities only forty per cent. Twenty-nine nationalities are represented in the town enrolment at the schools of 3,012, of which 1,777 are natives of the United States.

The Board of Education now consists of five members, the commissioners in 1920 being Stephen D. Riddle, president; James T. B. Lohman, Herbert Barry, Mrs. Byron G. Harlan and Ernest T. Child.

John Crosby Brown, who became a resident of the Mountain Ridge in the town's early days, employed the most skilful talent obtainable for the beautifying of his estate. Greenhouses, in which flowers of domestic and foreign culture grew profusely were erected and in the summer months masses of them adorned the grounds. Mrs. Brown was equally fond of the beautiful blooms. In time she and Mr. Brown devised the idea of inviting a group of children living in New York to their mountain home when the warm summer sun was upon the earth. Regularly every Wednesday morning conveyances were waiting at the Orange station of the Lackawanna railroad for the happy little ones who had been promised a day's outing among the flowers and other growth on the mountains out in New Jersey. Arriving at Brighthurst, all in the party were treated to a nourishing lunch and then permitted to wander about the premises and enjoy the rare scene and health-giving atmosphere. Each week a different party was entertained and in this way several hundred children were annually given an acquaintance with the great outdoors which they otherwise would not have had but for the thoughtfulness of Mr. and Mrs. Brown. Each child upon returning from Brighthurst carried a bouquet of flowers.

Another excellent medium for life-restoring was the establishment of a cottage on the estate and to it trained nurses fatigued with their vigils were invited to come and rest. It was also the custom of Mr. Brown, on a certain Sabbath in June, when his roses were in their best bloom, to invite the congregation of St. Cloud Presbyterian Church to "worship God in Nature," by adjourning from the morning service to his place and there view the wonderful scene. This invitation was repeated in the autumn, when the chrysanthemums were in bloom. Mr. and Mrs. Brown also marked the Christian Path and with the same spirit purchased the quarry on Northfield road, which was making too much of an inroad upon the Mountain Ridge, and saved it from further encroachment.

Divided into five wards, the town is now growing toward a very uncertain future—uncertain as to its expanding possibilities. Will the fertile and lovely valley and the slopes of the First and Second Mountains be so thickly settled at a no distant day that another government for a new town will there be instituted? No one can prophecy with accuracy. But the unoccupied land west of the First Mountain will surely be opened to home-seekers before many years have passed, just as soon as transportation is provided from the eastward, connecting with its populous sections. Tunneling the mountain has been declared feasible by engineers and the memory of middle-aged men and women recalls the efforts of the Orange Mountain Cable Company to overcome the grade of the eastern slope, and the more recent undertaking of the company, financed by local capitalists and of which Frank Brewer was the moving spirit. His perseverance in overcoming the steep grade by an ingenious process of turnouts is well remembered, but the mountain residents and others failed to patronize the line in sufficient numbers and so it dropped out of existence. The Eagle Rock line still makes its trips to the foot of the reservation and may some day pass under the mountain. Then will come the new and flourishing city which it will surely be, for the fine, rolling country will lend itself most susceptibly to the building of the high type home for which West Orange of today is well known. A suggestion has been made that a viaduct, starting from Scotland street and Central avenue, wide enough for automobile traffic and also for pedestrians, be built at an easy grade to the top of the mountain. This would involve a large expenditure of money but a wonderful improvement would follow and thousands of desirable families attracted to the territory for permanent home making. The future of West Orange is promising of rich results and the desire for a home in a desirable surrounding will be the medium calling people to the valley beyond.

The population of the town, according to the Federal census, in 1920, is 15,573. St. Mark's Triangle, at the entrance from Orange on the eastward, has disappeared, and a wider driveway, with a sweeping northward curve, has been made. A Liberty Pole, from which the Flag of the Union is displayed upon the patriotic days of the national calendar, stands in the center of this vestibule, as it has been named, of the

ON THE ROAD FROM ORANGE RESERVOIR, IN SOUTH MOUNTAIN RESERVATION

MAPLE FALLS, SOUTH MOUNTAIN RESERVATION

town. In 1920 the total amount raised by taxation is $519,249.74. Of this amount, $228,207.78 is used for the local budget; $134,267.73 for maintenance of schools, and $157,258.45 for county and State requirements. There are fifty-six miles of streets in the town, nineteen of which are under county supervision and thirteen and a-half miles are unimproved.

Hampered for want of space in the transaction of town business, it was decided in 1905 to give up the quarters occupied in Hedges' Block and elsewhere and purchase the Wheeler Lindsley homestead, which had been standing on the north side of Northfield road, near Valley road, and equip it as the Municipal Building. It was occupied in September of that year and the various departments have there been housed since that time, but the increasing demand for more space indicates either the erection of an addition to the building or the placing of a new one.

John R. Rogers is mayor in 1920, and the members of the Town Council are: Alfred J. Grosso and John R. Kling, First Ward; Edwin J. Feeney and Charles Lehrer, Second Ward; Charles A. Dowd and George A. Mussler, Third Ward; Benjamin P. Laidlaw and John M. Gluchowski, Fourth Ward; James A. Reid and Louis J. Kocher, Fifth Ward.

The health of the town is looked after by a Board of Commissioners, of which Alfred N. Pierson is president, and D. D. Buckley the health officer, the others being Abram S. Overmiller, Dr. Samuel A. Muta, Otto A. Schimmel and Henry P. Mauer.

Mayor Walter D. Van Riper, looking at the future of West Orange, says that it would appear as though the town was destined to grow as a residential community rather than one of purely business or industrial interests. Continuing, he says:

True, it already has seen considerable industrial growth—claiming as its own one of the largest and most prominently known manufacturing industries in the country. However, it is a well-known fact that in order to grow industrially a town must be well equipped with transportation facilities from a railroad viewpoint. Unfortunately, this West Orange lacks! That part of it which is immediately touched by railroad line is very small, and in addition thereto it is the extreme border of the town, making transportation by railroad accessible, therefore, to a very small portion of the town.

The development which has taken place in West Orange during the last half dozen years has been largely of a residential character. The so-called "South End" of the town has witnessed an extensive development in high grade residential properties.

The Fourth Ward, including the entire mountain section, is yet to be developed. There are great possibilities for the future in the development of this vast area.

The rapidly growing population of our neighboring metropolis is assurance of the fact that people from other nearby cities will soon be seeking a home within our midst. We have plenty of room for them and can well afford to bid them WELCOME.

The Fourth Ward, of course, is lacking in many of the facilities that others sections of the town have. For the past few years it has been torn asunder by transportation agitation.

West Orange is proud of its system of roads. In proportion to population it can possibly boast of as many miles of good roads as any other municipality in the country. It has a good modern school system. Although at the present lacking somewhat in building facilities, time will, of necessity, remedy this. Its water supply and lighting system are beyond criticism. With some additional facilities placed in the Fourth Ward, it would offer every attraction to the home owner that could be asked or hoped for.

It is no reflection on our neighbors to say that from a geographical viewpoint, West Orange offers that which cannot be found anywhere about us. The height of our hills render them a vantage point for the beautiful scenery that always attracts the home owner. Undoubtedly, it will be but a few years before these hills are fairly covered with up-to-date modern homes. All that is necessary to bring this about is to keep our town modern and ever on the alert to safeguard it from untoward influences.

Let those who live here now see that we are doing something worth while and show those who are considering our town as a future home that we welcome them, and in doing so can offer them a home life that is attractive, comfortable, and what they most desire.

CHAPTER LXXXIX

THE ORANGES IN 1920

Chief among the municipal problems of Orange and East Orange is the sewerage disposal, both finding outlet in the Passaic river, the first named through the joint sewer constructed overland, and entering the water course near Belleville, and the latter entering the Newark sewers. The New Jersey Legislature has set several specified periods for the elimination of the nuisance which has polluted the once pure stream of water. The Passaic Valley sewer which is being constructed from Paterson to connect with tidewater will be completed in a few years, it having been in course of construction a long time. East Orange will find its outlet through this medium, but Orange is undecided as to the course to be pursued. The streets of the Oranges are for the most part laid with sanitary sewers, and, with the drainage system in operation, miasmatic vapors no longer rise out of the lowlands.

The Orange Memorial Hospital, at Essex avenue and Henry street, having a capacity of 150 beds in 1920, is to be further enlarged by the addition of a wing, the entire plant having proved of wonderful service to the community in its nearly fifty years of existence. The other hospitals—St. Mary's, on Center street, and the Orthopedic, on Lincoln avenue —are meeting the needs of the people suffering from ailments and accidents. The Record Ambulance, first drawn by horse and now motorized, continues its constant mission of bringing the maimed and diseased stricken human being for treatment to the Memorial Hospital. All these institutions, though located in Orange, serve the entire community of the Oranges.

Only one building, aptly named, has been erected and dedicated to the care of the aged and infirm. Its beginning was in 1881, when a "Home for Convalescents" was given a year's trial. Then the House of the Good Shepherd was started under the auspices of the clergy and women of the parishes of St. Mark's, West Orange; Grace, Orange; Holy Communion, South Orange; and Christ, East Orange. In 1891 a lot was purchased on Henry street at a cost of $4,000, and an additional $12,000 was paid for the erection of the frame building on the south side of Henry street, near Cone street, Orange. When able, the inmates pay a small charge for their accommodations.

Fraternal and benevolent organizations are doing well their share of sustaining those who have unusual burdens to carry. The Masonic Temple in Orange is the home of Corinthian and Union Lodges of that order, and in the Lyceum building of East Orange, Jersey Commandery, Knights Templar, Orange Chapter, Royal Arch Masons, Hope Lodge and

East Orange Lodge of Free and Accepted Masons are domiciled. Orange Lodge of Elks has a well established home on Main street, nearly opposite Bell street, and on the southerly side of Main street, diagonally opposite from the Elks' home, Orange Council, Knights of Columbus, has its home.

The Washington Society a few years ago purchased the building located on the east side of Prospect street, long occupied by the Orange Club. The membership of the present organization occupying the house is drawn from parishes of the Catholic churches of the Oranges, and is sustaining its place as a medium of social enjoyment for those of that religious faith enrolled in its membership.

The Orange National Bank is the oldest financial institution of the Oranges, now being in its ninety-second year, and its banking house still located at the identical site selected in 1828. It has weathered five panics and four wars. Other financial concerns are the Second National Bank, at 232 Main street, in the Metropolitan building, Orange; the Orange Valley Bank, at the corner of Scotland street and Freeman street, Orange; the First National Bank of West Orange, 313 Valley road; Orange Savings Bank, corner of Main and Cone streets, Orange; the Half-Dime Savings Bank, 228 Main street, Orange; the Essex County Trust Company, corner of Main street and Arlington avenue, East Orange, and its branch on Central avenue, near Halsted street; the East Orange Bank, corner of Hollywood avenue and Main streets, East Orange, and the Savings Investment and Trust Company, at Main street, with a branch bank on South Orange avenue, South Orange.

The Young Men's Christian Association of the Oranges is now well past its third of a century of its existence as a great moral and educational force of the community life. Clarence H. Potter is the general secretary, and the membership is over 1,500. Harry B. Watson is in charge of the community branch, installed in the Commonwealth building several years ago.

The military spirit of the Civil War days is maintained by Uzal Dodd Post No. 12, Grand Army of the Republic, and though fifty-five years have passed since the cessation of hostilities, these veterans, the survivors of a mighty army, in the twilight of their lives, retain unabated the patriotism of their youth. Memorial Day, May 30, is the rallying time of these devoted followers of Abraham Lincoln and the Flag which they helped to keep flying over the nation. Promptly at the noon hour on this day of remembrance, a group of these veterans and a few others meet at the tomb of Captain Samuel Uzal Dodd, in Rosedale Cemetery, and there conduct brief exercises in memory of the departed comrades and for the perpetuity of the Government which they defended in the long-ago period. Though the veterans have aged, the spirit injected into these brief exercises is just as fervent as it was when the elasticity of younger days was with them. Escorted by the Sons of Veterans, these

"Boys in Blue" return to their headquarters in the Reynolds building, on Main street, near Day street, where luncheon, prepared by the Ladies' Auxiliary, is served, followed by an order of exercises.

The Spanish-American War veterans are organized in Fitzhugh Lee Camp, which looks after its members and the widows and orphans of former members. Several posts of the American Legion, composed of soldiers and sailors of the World War, have been instituted in the Oranges, and are sustaining the patriotic spirit in the reconstruction days. The militia organizations were all absorbed in the army during the World War, following which the Orange Armory, on William street, corner of North Center street, became the headquarters of Company L, 113th Infantry Regiment, Captain Robert McNally being in command; Troop F, 102d Cavalry, Captain William J. Redden, commandant; and the 44th Division Signal Corps, Captain Charles Vanderpool, commandant. At the East Orange Armory, Battery A, Field Artillery, commanded by Captain Richard P. Hartdegen, is stationed, and was officially recognized by the United States Government as a part of the Federal army on November 29, 1920.

Residents of Orange and East Orange have been discussing the form of memorial to be erected in memory of the citizens who went forth to battle in the World War, but no definite conclusion has been reached.

There are five Boards of Health in the Oranges, and each had its own system of inspecting the supply of milk brought into the community, with the result of overlapping and consequent irrritation to the dealer, and more or less inconvenience to the consumer. This health-giving fluid so vitally necessary in the daily household economy, it was considered should be of the highest possible quality, since it was known to be a carrier of disease. In 1913 the Woman's Club of the Oranges, through its civic committee, offered the services of Miss Edith R. Hall, its field secretary, as an assistant for the examination of milk samples in the laboratory of the Orange Board of Health. After a year's exhaustive study of the problem, from the source of production to the consumer, Miss Hall presented a story of wasted time and duplication of money and effort in the various municipalities so intelligently and convincingly that the authorities immediately offered the funds for the creation of a joint board of supervision.

In the early summer of 1914 the Joint Milk Committee of the Oranges was formed by two representatives of each Board of Health. Dr. Frank B. Lane, of the East Orange Board, was elected president, and Frank J. Osborne, health officer of Orange, was chosen secretary. Dr. Charles A. Griffin, a graduate of the New York State Veterinary College of Ithaca, selected as the dairy inspector, began his work on July 1, 1914. An office was opened in the Orange Board of Health headquarters, where the laboratory was placed at the disposal of the committee.

One of the first problems considered was a uniform milk ordinance, in order that the requirements should be identical and that the clerical and administrative difficulties should be simplified as far as possible. With this end in view, the health officers of the several Oranges and the milk inspector drafted an ordinance grading the milk sold in the community by bacterial content and dairy scores under the three main classifications of "Certified," "Raw Tuberculin Tested" and "'Pasteurized" milk. All milk was ordered properly labeled, so the consumer would know what grade was being sold. The uniform milk ordinance went into effect July 1, 1915, and Dr. Griffin was made special inspector of each Board of Health to enforce its provisions. Of the sixty separate dealers who delivered milk in the Oranges, two of them sold in all five Oranges, four in four of them, fourteen in three, nineteen in two and only twenty-one in one. It is thus seen that the work and expense was duplicated in one or more cities in thirty-nine instances before the Joint Committee became active.

Dairy inspection was more complicated and showed still greater saving in time and money by the direct principle, since the largest dealers who distributed their product in the smaller and larger territory were situated from two hundred to three hundred miles away. At least seven hundred of these produced milk for three of the Oranges, and three hundred and fifty for all of them. Thus seven hundred of the dairies supplying milk to the Oranges were visited by three different inspectors giving presumably three different sets of instructions, while three hundred and fifty of them were thus harangued by five different men, assuming, of course, that each city was actually carrying on a complete inspection of all its dairies.

After Dr. Griffin was appointed, at a salary of $1,200 a year, all of the dairy inspections and milk examinations were turned over to him. This arrangement not only did away with the extra work and expense of each city making these inspections and examinations, to the confusion of the milkmen and dairymen, but made it possible for the various health officers, being relieved of this burden, to devote their attention to other matters not as well organized and controlled. From the central office the inspector sent out monthly and quarterly reports. The milk collections are so arranged that each municipality does its appropriate share, and the expense of the milk work is apportioned among each, on a per capita basis, which in 1914-15 was as follows:

	Population.	Appropriation.
East Orange	39,852	$1,052.00
Orange	31,968	843.88
West Orange	12,722	335.84
South Orange Village	6,612	174.54
South Orange Township	3,551	93.74
Total	94,705	$2,500.00

The plan has resulted in a financial saving of from fifty to sixty-six and two-thirds per cent.

The uniform ordinance was amended by East Orange in 1918 to permit the sale of only "Certified" and pasteurized milk, and similar action taken in 1919 by West Orange and South Orange townships. The original ordinance is still in force in Orange and South Orange.

Dr. Charles A. Griffin resigned February 1, 1916, and William B. Palmer, Assistant Health Officer of the Orange Health Department, the present executive officer of the Association, was appointed. Reorganization of the Joint Milk Committee of the Oranges was made in February, 1917, and the Milk Inspection Association of the Oranges was formed, and a constitution and by-laws, which were approved by the Boards of Health, were adopted May 17, 1920, and amendments were made and approved by them, in which they agreed to adopt resolutions to recognize the Association and abide by reports, scores and ratings used in its activities, and to appoint the executive officer of the Association as milk inspector of their respective municipalities. The object of the Association as set forth by the Constitution is: "To supervise and regulate the production, transportation and distribution of all dairy products, especially milk, sold in the Oranges, and to this end to maintain a laboratory for the examination of milk and dairy products; to employ a competent executive officer and such other employees as may be required, at salaries to be fixed from time to time by the Association, to coöperate with the Boards of Health of the Oranges, and to assist in enforcing the ordinances adopted by the several Boards or Departments of Health of the Oranges relating to the production, care and sale of dairy products, especially milk, in the Oranges."

The officers for 1920-1921 are: President, Colonel Charles A. Andrews, vice-president Board of Health, East Orange; vice-president, Dr. Samuel A. Muta, West Orange; secretary, John O'Brien; treasurer, T. Dudley Ballinger.

VOLUME XC

THE CHURCHES OF THE ORANGES

Through the two centuries and a half of the development of the Oranges, the religious spirit has predominated, and in the general character of the church organizations now maintained there is ample opportunity for the worship of God as the individual conscience desires. It is a record of which any community might well express a pride in possessing. Church life is the chief characteristic of the people, just as it was in the period when the temple in which the people worshipped the Great Jehovah was barren of comfort and of ornament. The edifices standing in every neighborhood are evidences of the strength and appreciation of a prosperous people who have kept pace with the progress of the years. The God of the Puritan forebears is with us in this later day of changing customs, the spirit of worship is sustained, and the charitable instinct finds expression in innumerable acts of helpfulness. There will surely come out of the present unrest a return to the more general recognition of the church as the rock upon which truth and all that is worth while in life securely abides.

Baptist—The First Baptist Church of the Oranges was organized in 1837, and in 1842 the corner-stone of a house of worship was laid at the corner of Maple avenue and Church place, now in East Orange. Through many discouragements the building was finished in 1858. Meanwhile, religious services had been held in the basement. The modest but substantial edifice thus acquired, the church continued to worship in it for some fifty years. During this period several other Baptist churches were organized, drawing heavily upon the feeble strength of the First church. Circumstances combined to retard its progress, and the dawn of prosperity was greatly delayed. The long pastorate of Rev. Dr. William D. Hedden, first for one year, and then, after a short interval, for twenty-four years, was a chief factor in the steady, though gradual, increase of this church in membership and influence. In April, 1892, during the pastorate of Rev. Dr. John A. Chambliss, the congregation occupied its present house of worship, corner of Main street and Hawthorne avenue, erected at a cost of fifty-six thousand dollars. The main auditorium, with the adjacent lecture and Sunday school rooms, affords sittings for about a thousand persons. Rev. Rufus Miles Traver is now the pastor.

Waverly Hall, a building standing on the north side of Main street, near North Center street, Orange, was the home of the North Orange Baptist Church till it was destroyed by fire, which occurred in December,

1860. The church was organized August 3, 1857, and on November 5 a council of Baptist churches was held for its public recognition. Rev. J. B. Morse, of Albany, was ordained and installed at this time as the pastor, but he continued less than two years. The new edifice built on South Main street was dedicated December 5, 1861. Four pastors served till May 5, 1875, when Rev. Edward Judson, a professor in Madison University, was ordained. He immediately won the esteem of his congregation by his sound preaching, fine manly presence and the intense interest manifested by him in the upbuilding of the parish. His labors were indeed greatly blessed. Evening congregations filled the pews to overflowing, and it became necessary to build a gallery on the western side of the edifice. Rev. Dr. Judson resigned on June 1, 1881, with his work in a highly prosperous condition. During his pastorate of six years an unprecedented list of 667 communicants was added to the roll. Dr. Judson then engaged in mission work in the Five Points section of New York, being impelled thereto by an overpowering conviction that he ought to labor among the destitute of the lower part of the metropolis. Another popular clergyman came to this church on March 1, 1886. Rev. James Taylor Dickinson, of Richmond, Virginia, a young man under twenty-five years of age, who accepted the pastorate, remained for seventeen years, during which he occupied a leading place in the community, being called upon to deliver addresses at public affairs and also serving on the East Orange Board of Education. A Sunday school building was added to the edifice and additions have greatly enlarged the plant located at the corner of Hickory and South Main streets. Rev. Dr. Arthur Thomas Fowler is the pastor, following Rev. Dr. William M. Lawrence, who succeeded Dr. Dickinson.

The Washington Street Baptist Church, Orange, is the outgrowth of cottage prayer meetings. At one of these meetings, held at the home of Zenas Williams, Orange, in 1873, when Rev. W. E. Howell was leading, it was voted to organize a Union Chapel. After working four years under this name, the chapel was organized into the Washington Street Baptist Church with Rev. James L. Davis as pastor. It has steadily grown under the leadership of Rev. E. D. Clough, Rev. Henry Cross, Rev. Paul Lux, Rev. Howard H. Brown, Rev. J. C. Stoddard and Rev. I. M. Thompson. During Mr. Brown's pastorate the edifice was moved from the site of the lumber yard on Washington street to its present location. Various additions have been made to the building from time to time.

The church has a membership of about 250, and is in need of a larger building in which to carry on its growing work. The problem of space is particularly acute in the Sunday school.

The Prospect Street Baptist Church, East Orange, had its origin in a mission Sunday school established by the North Orange Baptist Church in 1892, and maintained for two years in the rooms of the Woman's

BETHEL CHURCH, EAST ORANGE

Christian Temperance Union, on Prospect street, near Dodd street. In 1894 Sunday evening preaching services were instituted by Rev. E. W. Bentley. During the same year a lot was purchased at the corner of Prospect and Norman streets and an attractive building was erected at a cost of about $13,000, and dedicated February 22, 1895. On July 10 of the same year a church was formally organized with a membership of twenty-eight. Rev. M. G. Coker was called as pastor and the growth of the church became very rapid, its membership and that of its Sunday school being sufficiently large to tax the full capacity of the church building. Rev. Ernest C. Murphy is now the pastor.

Calvary (colored) Baptist Church, East Orange, was organized in 1878. One year later Rev. J. H. Travis, of New York City, was called to its pastorate, the number of communicants on the roll being forty-five. In 1891 the church purchased the building and ground on Maple avenue and the railroad, once occupied by the First Baptist Church, at a cost of six thousand dollars. The furniture was donated by the First Baptist Church. Rev. E. A. P. Cheek is now the pastor.

The Union Baptist Church, Orange, which has been located on Oakwood avenue, near Main street, for a third of a century, is the oldest colored religious organization of the Oranges, and was fostered by members of the North Orange Baptist Church in its early years. The membership has increased till today it is one of the largest evangelical societies of the Oranges. Its enrollment to date is 2,100. The frame building in which the congregation has been worshiping a number of years is inadequate to meet the demands of the growing parish, and it is hoped in the near future to supplant it with a more pretentious edifice. Rev. J. H. Hughes is the pastor. The Ebenezer Baptist Church (colored), 71 Hill street, Orange, is in charge of Rev. Walter T. Watkins, pastor. The Jerusalem Baptist Church, organized in Orange, in 1914, is the most recent of the religious organizations of the Oranges, and is located at 52 Parrow street. Rev. R. C. Pully is the pastor. A congregation of colored people is located at 17 Oak street, East Orange. It is known as the North Clinton Street Baptist Church, and the pastor is Rev. Edward D. Samuels.

The Mount Olivet (colored) Baptist Church, East Orange, was incorporated in March, 1896, with only three members. It had been worshiping in the building at William and North Clinton streets, vacated by the Calvary Methodist Episcopal congregation. Rev. George E. Reed was the first pastor, who resigned to accept the presidency of Spiller Academy, at Hampton, Virginia. A call was then extended to Rev. George W. Krygar, of White Plains, New York, who assumed charge of the parish on December 1, 1896, and is now in his twenty-fifth year as pastor. In 1897 the building, which had been rented from Richard Coyne, was vacated, and the weekly services were held in a small hall on

Main street till the present edifice on the west side of Ashland avenue, near Main street, was occupied in 1898.

Roman Catholic—Seton Hall College was removed from Madison to South Orange in 1860. Bishop Bayley and Father McQuaid were riding about the Oranges on a certain summer day when they saw an ideal site for the college, which it was thought would be more liberally patronized if it was situated somewhere in the vicinity of the community known as South Orange. The place which the two priests agreed upon as the one for the college settlement was on the southerly side of South Orange avenue, where a handsome marble house was occupied by two brothers. Negotiations for the property soon placed it in control of the college authorities, they having acquired a tract of sixty acres, besides the much admired marble villa at a cost of $35,000, the building alone having cost over $40,000 to construct. A brick structure was erected for the main college building, the corner-stone having been laid on May 15, 1860. The seminary opened in the villa on September 10 following, with fifty students enrolled. Rev. B. J. McQuaid was the first president. Near midnight of January 27, 1866, when the temperature was at freezing and sleet and snow were upon the ground, the college was aroused by the alarm of fire. It had weathered the unprofitable period of the Civil War, when other institutions had closed their doors, and now, when the immediate future seemed bright with prospects of increased attendance and interest in the college, destruction was to come to the edifice. The fire was confined to the beautiful marble building, where it originated, and though a courageous corps of volunteers worked incessantly, at the end of four hours a blackened waste was all that remained of the once stately structure. The present handsome edifice, having a facade of 134 feet and a depth of fifty feet, was erected and dedicated in 1867. Another fire occurred at noon, while the students and faculty were at lunch on March 9, 1886, in one of the dormitories of the college building. The blaze continued during a greater part of the afternoon. The loss was $35,000. Rebuilding was soon under way and the group for which Seton Hall is justly proud has remained intact since that date. Seminarians in large numbers have been graduated from the college, which is one of the leading educational institutions of the country.

The parish of St. John's, Orange, was established in the early part of 1851. During the previous years scarcely a dozen Catholic families could be found in Orange, and these little parties of devout worshipers walked to St. John's Church in Newark to attend services there. Mass was also said at times at the house of Thomas Henry, a parishioner. Captain Ward, of the United States Navy, then a resident of Orange, became interested in the growing need of a house of worship, and at his suggestion and with his help a fund of about $3,000 was raised by subscription. A plain frame building originally less than one hundred feet in length

ST. JOHN'S CATHOLIC CHURCH, RIDGE AND WHITE STREETS, ORANGE

INTERIOR OF ST. JOHN'S CATHOLIC CHURCH, ORANGE

and fifty in width, its interior quite simple in arrangement, was erected
at the corner of Chapel and White street. An altar with little decoration,
a few pictures, a loft for the choir and a melodeon, comprised the church
furniture. The dedication was on the first Sunday of October, 1851, the
land having been purchased by Captain Ward, and the deed made over
by him to the congregation. Rev. Louis Senez, famed as a missionary,
became temporary pastor, and ably seconded Captain Ward's efforts
toward finishing and occupying the little church. Father Senez remained
but a short time on account of his duties as a traveling missionary, and
was succeeded by Father McLaghlan, a Scotchman by birth and a Span-
iard by education. Proficient in Gaelic and Spanish, but unfamiliar with
English, he failed to interest through his inability to make himself understood. Hearing of a congregation of Highlanders in Canada who were
desirous of a pastor, he was relieved at his own request and went there.

In 1852 Rev. Terence Kiernan was appointed priest in charge of St.
John's parish, and he remained till March, 1854, when he was succeeded
by Father Hubbersty, who is remembered by the surviving pioneers of
the parish as a hale and hearty Englishman who made many friends.
He was of noble descent, and often related the bitter experiences of his
ancestors under Henry and Elizabeth. Rev. John Murray, who came in
1856, worked with great energy in his new field. Tall, well-built, of a
vigorous habit, iron constitution, affable and pleasing in his manners, he
steadily and firmly attached himself not only to his own people but to
many non-Catholics. His first work was to enlarge the church, after which
he projected his main work—the building of the first parochial school in
the Oranges. Father McKay became pastor of St. John's during the Civil
War. He was a man of deep learning, and his eloquence won the hearts
not only of his own people but even of non-Catholics. He resigned the
rectorship in 1865, and returned to Ireland, where he died about fifteen
years ago.

The year 1865 was eventful in the history of St. John's. The spread
of the hatting and other industries in Orange notably increased the number of Catholics. With insufficient accommodations for adults and children both in church and school, it was apparent that building operations
could not long be delayed. It was at this critical time that Rev. E. M.
Hickey came to Orange. The necessities of the hour demanded of the
new pastor qualities of head and heart and hand capable of untiring and
continuous work. Father Hickey plunged into his difficult tasks with his
accustomed energy. The spiritual needs of his flock were his first
thought. No night was too dark, no road too stormy, when his ministra-
tions of comfort and help to his people necessitated his loving care and
solicitude. The property at the corner of Ridge and White streets was
bought for $10,000—a very large sum in that day for a congregation
having no wealthy members. But the opportunity was seized, and the

highest spot in Orange east of the Mountain, easily reached and in a delightful neighborhood, was secured. Ground was broken for the new church in June, 1866. Llewellyn S. Haskell, philanthropist and founder of Llewellyn Park, offered his quarry to the builders, which was accepted with gratitude. Not content with contributing their humble portion of money, the laboring force was every evening reinforced by a crowd of devoted workmen who offered their toil after having worked at their various trades from ten to twelve hours during the day. The survivors of this devoted band, depleted in number, met at St. John's five years ago, the fiftieth anniversary of their achievement, and were the honored guests of a grateful congregation.

Thus the building arose, stone by stone, until three years after the excavation of the foundation, one of the most beautiful church buildings in the State was dedicated to the service of God under the patronage of St. John the Evangelist, on October 10, 1869. Before the dedication, Father Hickey, broken in health, was sent to Europe by the congregation to recuperate. After three months of rest, he returned to the parish and again took up his burden, but the task proved beyond his strength, and to the great sorrow of his people he was forced to take up lighter duties in the South. In May, 1873, Right Rev. M. A. Corrigan, Bishop of Newark, appointed Rev. Winand M. Wigger as pastor. He afterwards succeeded Dr. Corrigan as Bishop of the diocese. The disastrous panic of 1873 struck St. John's with crushing force, and finding the burden too great Dr. Wigger resigned after a few months. Rev. Hugh P. Fleming next came on March 12, 1874. He was a young priest, just ordained, but possessed of executive ability and well adapted for the important work awaiting him. In addition to enlarging the cemetery, which was one of the most pressing needs of the time, he erected the tower and spire which now surmount the beautiful church.

Ground for the present Columbus Hall was broken in 1892 and the commanding edifice erected. As a school building there is none more complete in the State of New Jersey, and as a home for works of art, the life gathering of Father Fleming, it is unique and very valuable. The unveiling of the main altar of the church, a splendid work of art executed in Belgium, the gift of the late Francis C. O'Reilly, occurred at this time. A special feature of the altar is the large number of statues of exquisite carving in enduring oak. Father Fleming, after a pastorate of thirty-four years, retired from active service in the ministry in the spring of 1908.

Rev. Matthias McDonald succeeded Father Fleming in September, 1908. To the task of continuing the institutions founded by his predecessors, Father McDonald devoted himself with unremitting zeal. He will be remembered for his successsful efforts in founding two greatly needed new parishes—the one in First Ward of East Orange, known as the

REV. HUGH P. FLEMING

Church of the Holy Name, and the other in the Watchung Heights section, the Church of Our Lady of Lourdes. Rev. Father McDonald passed away suddenly on September 6, 1914, while engaged in the school registering the names of the pupils on the opening day.

Father McDonald was succeeded on October 14, 1914, by the present pastor, Rev. Paul T. Carew, Ph. D., LL. D., formerly rector of St. Mary's Church, Dover. Father Carew is ably assisted in the work of the parish by Rev. Edward F. Hillock and Rev. Thomas J. Herron. The parish has since made gratifying progress spiritually and temporally. Columbus School has an attendance of one thousand pupils, about fifty of whom are graduated from the commercial grade each year. St. John's has been a powerful influence in all matters relating to the civic and social betterment of Orange, and has been found in the forefront of every movement of progress initiated by the citizens of our community. During the anxious years of the World War, when the people of every community were called upon frequently and urgently for Red Cross and Liberty Loan contributions, the parish did its duty nobly, sending nearly five hundred of her sons into the ranks, and absorbing hundreds of thousands of dollars worth of Liberty Bonds. It is on record at the national headquarters of the Liberty Loan that $342,200 of Liberty Bonds were bought by the parishioners of St. John's, at the personal solicitation of committees organized from the parish.

As a specimen of Gothic architecture, the church is one of the most notable examples in this section. It is surmounted by a tower of great beauty, with a clock having an electric connection and church chimes for ringing the Cambridge quarters. The instrument was the gift of former Mayor George Huntington Hartford, and cost over $4,000. It was a tribute to the church he loved so well and in which he was baptized into the Roman Catholic communion, the ceremony being the first administration of baptism performed in the church, on the day of its opening in October, 1869. This gift, with other benefactions, was an earnest of his desire and purpose to aid the parish in every way possible, which he faithfully carried out to the day of his death.

The passing away of Mayor Hartford in 1917, at the age of eighty-four years, was a serious loss to the city of Orange and especially to St. John's parish. His gentle dignity, his unfailing kindly courtesy, his magnificent nobility of character, stamped him as a model and exemplar that recalls the glory of the Chevalier Bayard of the days of chivalry, "the knight without fear and without reproach."

In the same month of that year occurred the death of Mrs. Francis C. O'Reilly. Mr. and Mrs. Francis C. O'Reilly were of great assistance to St. John's in its crucial days of Father Hickey's pastorate. The beautiful altars are their monument and the bronze Columbus statue at the entrance and the Sacred Heart atop Columbus School will ever recall in grateful memory the many benefactions of another generous soul, the late Colonel Minahan. The St. Anthony altar and confessional also enshrine the memory of the late Laurence T. Fell.

During the seven years of Father Carew's pastorate, the church debt has been reduced from $155,000 to $59,000, and improvements have been effected costing $38,000.

St. John's Church was the only Catholic organization, excepting Seton Hall College, in the Oranges till 1873, when the population of the southern part of the town known as Freemantown and later as Orange Valley, demanded another parish of that faith. The Orange Valley Congregational Church having vacated its stone edifice at Valley and Nassau streets, the Catholics living in that neighborhood purchased it as their place of worship. On September 8, 1873, the Church of Our Lady of the Valley was instituted, Rev. G. A. Vassallo was chosen the first rector, and Patrick Hayes and Edward B. Maroney the first trustees. Rev. William M. R. Callan, who become rector on July 28, 1879, continued till January 25, 1898, and was popular with all the people of Orange Valley during this long term of nearly twenty years. Rev. Thomas A. Wallace, who succeeded Father Callon, raised the subscriptions which were used in defraying the building operations of the Lyceum, one of the most notable adjuncts of the parish. Father Wallace resigned February 1, 1903, and then became Chancellor of the Newark diocese. Rev. John F. Boylan, who had successfully built a handsome church at Franklin Furnace, was next assigned to the charge, which he has ever since administered with zeal and success. Through his efforts the funds for the erection of the building, now so prominently situated on Valley street, were raised among the parishioners. The corner-stone was laid on August 29, 1909, and the dedication services of the completed edifice were held on February 26, 1911. The property of the parish occupies an entire block, bounded by Valley, Nassau, Church and McChesney streets.

Standing at the corner of North Clinton and Main streets, East Orange, the Catholic Church of Our Lady Help of Christians is one of the handsomest in the community. The parish was founded in the spring of 1882, by Right Rev. Bishop Wigger, and its first rector was Rev. Maurice P. O'Connor, a young priest whose zealous and successful work in organizing it soon proved the wisdom of the Bishop in his selection. Father O'Connor soon after his settlement purchased the finely located lot and began the erection of a temporary house of worship on the northerly end fronting North Clinton street. The priest was soon afterwards transferred to East Newark to rehabilitate a declining parish and was succeeded first by Rev. Pierce McCarthy, and later by Rev. Michael J. Kirwan, who, stricken with paralysis in September, 1893, died on May 10 following. Rev. John P. Callaghan, who had been acting as administrator of the parish during Father Kirwan's last illness, was appointed rector after his death, and the result of his labors was apparent. The marble church in which the congregation now worships is a monument to his untiring labor and ability. In addition to this beautiful church the parish owns a fine brick parochial residence immediately adjoining the old church building and parochial school on North Clinton street, and a brick residence used as a sisters' home, on Main street, two doors west of the parochial residence. Rev. J. A. O'Brien is the present rector.

Catholics of South Orange had their choice of attending services at Orange, Newark, or Seton Hall College, till 1887, when the parish of Our Lady of Sorrows was erected, and Rev. J. F. Solaum was installed as the first rector. Property was secured on Fourth street, and the church construction was begun by Rev. Dr. Charles Mull, who succeeded to the rectorate in 1888, and which was completed by Rev. L. C. M. Carroll, appointed September 12, 1889. The dedicatory services were held on the third Sunday in September of this year. The property has a frontage of a whole block along Fourth street, from Academy street to Prospect. street. Rev. W. F. Grady is the rector now in charge.

The Church of St. Venantius was established as a place of worship for Catholics of German tongue, at the corner of Henry street and Cone street, in August, 1887. Father Seeber was appointed first rector, and the frame edifice and school adjoining were soon built and in use. The rectory was added in 1892. Under the able management of those called to the head of this parish it has had a prosperous career. Rev. Peter Kurz is the rector.

Rev. Nicholas Marnell, an associate priest of St. John's Church, saw the need of a parish in the northern part of West Orange on his missionary trips about the community, and through his efforts, in 1914 the Church of Our Lady of Lourdes was organized in the Watchung Heights section of that town. There are 2,000 communicants enrolled on the parish register. Rev. Mr. Marnell has been the only rector.

Our Lady of Mount Carmel is the name of the church built on the easterly side of Center street, nearly opposite Reock street, for the accommodation of the Italians possessed of the Catholic faith. Its priests have all been popular, and to Father Romanelli, the first rector, is the honor ascribed for starting the St. Mary's Hospital, now one of the leading retreats for the care of the sick and injured in New Jersey. The rector in 1920 is Rev. James Zuccarrelli.

The parish of the Blessed Sacrament was begun as a mission of the Church of Our Lady Help of Christians about 1914, for those families living in Elmwood who desired a nearer place of worship. On May 21, 1916, the parish was instituted and Rev. William V. Dunn was assigned as the first rector. A brick church was soon built on Elmwood avenue, near Shepard avenue, and a rectory erected on Rhode Island avenue. The membership is 400 in 1920.

Rev. Thomas O'Shea is rector of the Church of Our Lady of All Souls, located on Rutledge avenue, East Orange.

St. Michael's Church, situated on Tremont avenue, East Orange, for the worship of Italians living in that vicinity, is in charge of Rev. Sylvester Neri.

Early in the Twentieth Century a mission attached to St. John's Church was started in the First Ward of East Orange, being served by the curates of the mother parish of Catholicism of the Oranges. The corner-stone of the frame edifice was laid in 1903, and the dedicatory services held in the following year. Rev. Matthew J. Farley, who was assigned to the church, which was designated the Holy Name, as its first rector, came from St. Joseph's Church, Jersey City, and took charge on May 8, 1910. He has remained there ever since.

Congregational—The Highland Avenue Congregational Church, Orange, was exceptionally fortunate in its first settled pastor, Rev. Dr. George Blagdon Bacon, who was of a family which boasted of three generations of widely known preachers and teachers. He came directly from his studies to Orange, was installed on March 27, 1861, and served till his death in 1876. His able preaching and administrative ability gave the church its high standing throughout the community. He was one of the most eloquent and popular speakers of the region during the Civil War. In 1869 he delivered the first Memorial Day address given in the Oranges. He is also recognized as the organizer of the New England Society. Rev. Joseph A. Ely, who succeeded Dr. Bacon, possessed also a taste for literary pursuit, writing verse with a clearness, rhythm and solidity. The third pastor, Rev. Dr. Jeremiah E. Rankin, too, wrote freely, his hymns being printed in large number. He was author of the Christian Endeavor favorite, "God be with you till we meet again." After leaving the church, Dr. Rankin became president of the Howard University at Washington, D. C., an institution which has done a great deal in educating the colored race. The first edifice was sold to the Church of Our Lady of the Valley, and the one on Highland avenue, and still in use, was built in 1868, the chapel added in 1880, and the parsonage in 1886. A feature of the church is the chime of bells stationed in the tower, and in securing which the Mason family was very active. Dr. Lowell Mason's name is inscribed on the large bell. Rev. Charles A. Savage, who followed Dr. Rankin, died in 1899. Rev. Frank W. Hodgdon then became pastor, and after a few years, in 1904, Rev. George P. Eastman assumed charge of the parish and remains there today. He has been connected with a number of the local enterprises for the public uplift, and is especially interested in the patriotic work of the community. The name of the Orange

Valley Congregational Church was discarded in 1916, and that of the Highland Avenue Congregational Church adopted.

Independence Day, July 4, 1866, was chosen as the time to discuss the creation of a new church by residents in the vicinity of Main and Grove streets, East Orange. The Congregational form was adopted, and about August 1 the formal organization took place. Two plots of land at the corner of the two streets were donated by Aaron P. Mitchell and George P. Mitchell, and a small strip of land by Jotham Hedden, to give symmetry to the property. On December 18, 1867, a brown stone building was completed and dedicated. Rev. Allan McLane was then the pastor. An addition was made to the church in 1871 at a cost of $5,000. On August 13, 1888, the cornerstone of the edifice now standing at the corner of Grove street and Main street was laid with imposing ceremonies. Dr. Harriet C. Hinds, organist of the church, composed this hymn, sung to the tune "America," for the first time:

> Thou great and holy King!
> Thy loyal children bring
>   An earnest prayer.
> Lift up our hearts to Thee
> On waves of harmony.
> While praising only Thee,
>   Thy mercies share.
>
> Before thy throne we bow,
> Seeking a blessing now,
>   Dear Lord, from Thee.
> 'Tis only in Thy name—
> We make no other claim—
> This house of God to frame,
>   For worship free.
>
> Where now this stone we lay,
> Let in the coming day
>   These walls ascend!
> That we may labor here,
> In love and godly fear—
> May all sad hearts and drear
>   Here find a friend.
>
> And may it ever be
> A blessed ministry.
>   This church to come!
> And open portals wide,
> For all in Christ to bide
> Until earth purified,
>   We're gathered home.

The completed edifice was occupied in 1890. The pastor is Rev. Thomas B. Powell.

Trinity Congregational Church became a reality in January, 1870, when a meeting of members of different Protestant churches residing in the Brick Church neighborhood of East Orange was held at the house of Rev. Dr. Frederick A. Adams, on Prospect street, for the purpose of considering the formation of a Congregational church in that vicinity. The first public services of the new congregation were held in Lyric Hall, corner of Main and North Harrison streets, on the first Sunday of the following March, and were conducted by Rev. Dr. George E. Adams, of Brunswick, Me. On March 17 articles of association were adopted, and five days later the formal organization was completed and the corporate title of "Trinity Church" was accepted. The church was recognized by the Council of Congregational Churches May 4, and a unanimous call was extended to Rev. Dr. George E. Adams, who accepted and began his pastoral duties at once. The services were held in Lyric Hall until May, 1872, when an unpretentious frame church on Harrison street near the railroad was completed and dedicated. This building was enlarged and improved several times, and twenty years afterward the present modern and attractive brick structure was erected and dedicated October 5, 1893, the cost, with its furnishings, being about $26,000. The edifice occupies the identical site of the first structure. Rev. Dr. Adams, who resigned his pastorate in May, 1875, died at his home in East Orange in December following. Rev. Richard T. Green succeeded Dr. Adams shortly before the death of the latter, and he resigned his pastorate July 1, 1889. Rev. Dr. Fritz W. Baldwin was settled December 8, 1889, and was succeeded by Rev. David Brewer Eddy, and he by Rev. Howard J. Chidley. Rev. Joseph H. Robinson is now the pastor.

The Swedish Free Congregational Church of East Orange had its origin in a Swedish Sunday school started in 1886 by Miss Carlina Darrow, which met in Trinity Congregational Church, on Harrison street. In 1892 preaching services in Swedish were begun in the same place by Rev. C. F. Blonquist, who stayed here for six months. Early in 1893 Rev. A. P. Nelson was called, and in April of that year the Swedish Free Congregational Society was organized. Six months later the Swedish Free Congregational Church was formally instituted, with thirty-four members and the Rev. A. P. Nelson as pastor. In 1895 a lot was purchased on Ashland avenue, near William street, and a building was completed and occupied October 13, 1895. Rev. Joel Fridfelt is the pastor now in charge of the parish.

Rev. John Kjobsness is pastor of the Norwegian Congregational Church, located at 253 Cleveland street, Orange.

Reformed Dutch—The first parish of the Reformed Dutch denomination in the Oranges is the one worshiping at the corner of Main and Halsted streets, East Orange, and known as the First Reformed Dutch Church. The movement which resulted in its organization had its origin in a difference of opinion in regard to the administration of the temporal affairs of Brick Presbyterian Church, between Rev. Dr. Bishop, then pastor of that church, and other officers and members. Dr. Bishop resigned his pastorate in the spring of 1875, and accompanied by about one hundred and thirty members of the church, began holding divine services in Lyric Hall, at the corner of Main and North Harrison streets. The First Reformed Church was formally organized by the Classis of Newark, May 12, 1875, and the erection of a building at the corner of Main and Halsted streets was begun almost immediately, being completed before the close of the year. The edifice is of attractive brown stone, with a seating capacity, after two enlargements, of about eight hundred. A further addition for the accommodation of the Sunday school was built on the south side of the building. No debt has ever rested upon the property. Rev. William Warren Giles was installed pastor in November, 1907. Dr. Bishop was then retired from the active ministry and became pastor emeritus. He died March 12, 1914, and in the following January a tablet in his memory was placed on the church, having engraved thereon this inscription :

To the Glory of God
and
in loving Memory of
Rev. George Sayles Bishop, D. D.,
Who founded this church on May 12, 1875.
Was pastor till February 1, 1907,
And pastor emeritus until his death,
on March 12, 1914.
Faithful to his people,
Devoted to the Church,
Consecrated to his God.

Whosoever liveth and believeth in Me shall never die.—John xi., 26.

In 1903 a Union Sunday school was established in the Hyde Park section of East Orange, which merged into the Hyde Park Reformed Church, under the direction of the Newark Classis. The clubhouse was purchased April 16, 1904, for $5,000 and converted into an edifice. Rev. Frederick B. Pullan was pastor for several years and the weekly meetings were well attended. Rev. Charles A. Hallenbeck is the pastor.

Episcopal—St. Mark's Episcopal Church was incorporated in 1827. Just before the death of Rev. Benjamin Holmes, which occurred August 4, 1836, James A. Williams, a young layman of the parish and a graduate of the General Theological Seminary in New York, was ordained deacon by Rt. Rev. Dr. George W. Doane, Bishop of New Jersey, on July 10, 1836, ordained priest on August 13, 1837, and on September 9 formally instituted rector. Thus began a successful and eventful ministry lasting for forty-seven years, in which his fidelity to the duties of his office, his solid worth as a man, and his wise administration of such financial interests as were committed to him, made him highly esteemed by the parish and the community.

In 1845 the present rectory was built, and the nave was extended in 1851 and two transepts and a chancel were added at the north end of the original building, thus furnishing about 180 additional sittings. Stained glass windows took the place of the ones of plain glass and a new organ was installed at the southern or front end of the church. These changes were completed and the church reoccupied September 7, 1851. In the following year the basement of the new part of the church was finished and furnished for the use of the Sunday school.

In 1861, very material changes were made in the general appearance of the church building; the nave was extended about fifteen feet toward the south, the old tower which stood in the middle of the front was removed and a new front built with a tower and spire at the southwest corner, a slate roof was placed on the entire building, and a new ceiling built in the interior. In 1877, the parish building on the east side of the church was built, thus affording ample room for the Sunday school and for meetings of the various guilds.

The long and faithful service of Rev. Dr. Williams was brought to a close by his death, on September 2, 1883.

Rev. Dr. Frank B. Reazor, still in office, became the rector October 15, 1891. A beautiful side chapel was constructed in the parish building, and other important changes made during his pastorate of nearly thirty years.

Grace Episcopal Church, Orange, had its origin as an offshoot of St. Mark's Church, on March 5, 1854. Services were first held in Bodwell's Hall, corner of William and Park streets. The lot on which the edifice now stands was purchased from the trustees of the First Presbyterian Church, and the building operations were completed and consecration services held on July 16, 1857. Rev. James Bush, first rector, served through the stormy Civil War period, and acted well the part of the patriot-clergyman. He was very popular in the community. Rev. Anthony Schuyler, the second rector, came in 1867, being then of middle age, but he entered heartily into the parish work. A rectory was added the following year, in the rear of the church, fronting on William street, and in 1877 the Sunday school building was erected. There were then 250 members on the communion roll. In 1872 a brown sandstone transept and chancel were added to the edifice. Rev. Alexander Mann, called as assistant to Dr. Schuyler, became rector on the latter's death. Then Dr. Mann was called to Trinity parish of Boston in 1905, and Rev. Charles Thomas Walkley assumed charge of the parish in the following year. The Alice Broome Memorial parish house, the gift of Mr. and Mrs. Jonathan J. Broome, dedicated early in the new century, has since been the workshop of this very busy parish. Rev. Mr. Walkley continues as the rector. The installation of a handsome new pipe organ, one of the largest in the country, is soon expected.

The Church of the Holy Communion (Episcopal) was organized in South Orange on October 8, 1859, and a freestone edifice built at the corner of South Orange avenue and Ridgewood road, upon a lot donated by Thomas Loundes. Rev. David Magot, the first rector, remained only a year, resigning in 1861. During the next four years Rev. Elisha Mulford had charge of the parish, and in 1865 he was succeeded by Rev. William J. Frost. The latter was the first to occupy the new rectory, built at a cost of $6,000 on a lot diagonally opposite the church. Rev. Louis Cameron, who was chosen rector about 1895, is remembered by a host of people in the Oranges for his very kindly ways and his remarkable sunshine nature. He died in office in the early autumn of 1909. The present rector is Rev. George A. Hanna.

The organization of an Episcopal church in the Watsessing neighborhood of East Orange was begun in 1869, and it was under the charge of Christ Church of Bloomfield. A small chapel was erected on Myrtle street and opened for service January 30, 1870. The accommodations were soon outgrown, and five years later it was removed to a more advantageous location on the corner of Dodd and Meadow streets, and substantially enlarged. The church continued to be a mission of Christ Church, Bloomfield, until the spring of 1876, when it was established as an independent mission. The parochial organization was perfected November 22, 1876, when it was admitted to the Diocesan Convention as St. Paul's Church of East Orange. In 1893 a lot was purchased at the corner of Prospect street and Renshaw avenue, and in January, 1896, the new edifice of Pompton granite and of an attractive gothic style of architecture, was dedicated. The first rector of St. Paul's was Rev. William White Wilson, who served from May, 1876, to June, 1880.

Rev. John W. Williams, who assumed charge of the parish November 27, 1892, was one of its most popular rectors, serving for nearly ten years. A convenient and well-appointed parish house adjoins the church on Renshaw avenue. Rev. William P. Taylor, of Morristown, the present rector, was installed on St. Paul's Day, January 25, 1902. He composed a hymn, "Onward," which was distributed in large numbers to the soldiers in France during the World War, and has written other verses.

Christ Episcopal Church, East Orange, is the outgrowth of a meeting held October 10, 1867, for the purpose of considering the expediency of establishing an Episcopal Church in East Orange. The formal organization of the new parish, known as St. John's parish, was not effected until nearly a year later, at a meeting held in the old Arlington avenue railroad station, September 15, 1868. Ten days afterward the name was changed to Christ Church parish. The first service was held August 1, 1869, in the school rooms of Rev. John G. Mulholland, on Main street, at the Junction, and until September, 1870, Mr. Mulholland conducted the services and provided a place of worship without cost to the congregation. Rev. Horace S. Bishop began his work as rector September 11, 1870, and continued till April, 1894, when he resigned on account of ill health, and was succeeded by Rev. William Whiting Davis. Rev. Dr. Bishop remained as the honored and beloved rector emeritus until his death, April 1, 1898. Shortly before Mr. Bishop's settlement a lot was purchased on Main street, and a frame building erected thereon. It was completed at a cost of nearly $10,000, and the first service was held one week before Christmas of that year. This building received several additions, and on Sunday morning, December 23, 1888, it was destroyed by fire. For two years the congregation worshiped in Commonwealth Hall, until the completion of the present beautiful building at the corner of Main and North Burnet streets, occupying the site of the old church and the adjoining lot, formerly occupied by the rectory. The new building was opened for services and dedicated March 27, 1891. Rev. Charles E. Hutchison, present rector, was called to the parish in 1906.

The Church of the Holy Innocents was erected in St. Cloud, West Orange, in 1877, as a memorial to Mrs. Douglas Robinson. The first rector was Rev. T. Jefferson Danner, followed by Rev. Dr. C. H. W. Stocking, who was prominently connected with the community life for several years. Rev. Alfred W. Arundel is now the pastor.

A mission of St. Mark's Church was begun in the school house, corner of Valley road and Forest street, Orange, in 1876. Eighty-five communicants were present when the chapel was opened at the corner of Forest and Tompkins streets, on September 14, 1879. It was named St. Mark's, and Rev. William Richmond, curate, was in charge. Various clergymen took up the work there till April, 1885, when the parish was divided, and that part south of Glebe street and extending to the South Orange line was set off and named All Saints on April 13, 1885. The chapel was continued as the house of worship, but the problem of securing a more commodious building was soon pressing itself upon the people. Land was secured at the corner of Forest and Valley streets, and there the stone church was erected and used for the first time on the second Sunday after Easter, April 24, 1887, the old church serving as the chapel. Rev. Mr. Richmond continued for a number of years as the rector. Rev. Clarence M. Dunham is the rector in 1920.

St. Andrew's Church, at the corner of Center street and Stirling avenue, South Orange, was the offspring of Grace Church, and was organized December 24, 1892, under the direction of Rev. Alexander Mann, assistant to Dr. Schuyler. The new edifice was opened for service in July, 1893. Rev. Samuel H. Bishop was the first rector. The office is now held by Rev. F. Creswick Todd.

The Holy Trinity Episcopal Church, West Orange, had its origin in a series of cottage services held early in the decade of 1880 in the home of Mrs. Lyons, an invalid, who lived in the Burnside residence at Mead and Washington streets. The services were continued for a few years till a Sunday school was started. Rev. Frank C. Cantine, under the direction of Rev. Bishop Falkner, then rector of St. Mark's Church, took charge of the work as lay reader and superintendent of the school. Two rooms in the house, owned by Elias M. Condit, were rented, where services were held for several years, and in 1890 subscriptions to the amount of $2,100 were secured by Rev. Mr. Falkner and Mr. Cantine, with which they built a chapel on Columbia street. It was used for seventeen years as St. Mark's Mission Chapel. In December, 1905, Rev. O. F. Humphreys began holding regular morning services on Sunday, and on April 2, 1907, the organization of Trinity Episcopal Church was accomplished, with Mr. Humphreys as the rector. The Ryder homestead, having a frontage of 410 feet on Eagle Rock avenue and 226 feet on Franklin avenue, and another strip of land were purchased as the site of the new edifice. The corner-stone was laid by Bishop Edwin S. Lines on Sunday, September 15, 1909, and the first service of holy communion in the edifice was held at midnight on Christmas eve. In June, 1919, Rev. Mr. Humphreys resigned as rector to take a special course at Oxford University, England. Through his efforts the mortgage was cancelled and burned at a service arranged for that purpose, and he left the parish free of debt. Rev. Paul Roberts is the rector.

St. Agnes Episcopal Church, East Orange, began as a mission of Christ Church, and was the first one installed by Bishop Edwin S. Lines, who succeeded Bishop Thomas A. Starkey, deceased. The first meeting was held in the club house at Hyde Park, on St. Agnes Day, January 21, 1904. A lot was secured on the lane leading northward from Central avenue, just west of Munn avenue, in 1906, and the building thereon was remodeled for church purposes. Rev. Dwight W. Graham, then the rector, continued the administration of the charge committed to his care for a number of years. In 1910 the mission became an independent parish. Rev. William W. S. Hohenschild is the rector.

The Church of the Epiphany was instituted as a mission of Grace Episcopal Church, of Orange, for the colored people embracing that faith. A church was built at the corner of Pierson and Center streets, in 1911, three years after the rector, Rev. George M. Plasket, came to the parish. There are about three hundred communicants on the parish register.

The Church of the Incarnation, which owns property at 513 North Grove street, East Orange, near Rutledge avenue, and extending westerly to North Maple avenue, was instituted in 1911 as a mission of the Episcopal Diocese of Newark. Rev. Dwight W. Graham, the officiating minister at St. Agnes Church, gave part of his time to the new movement, till Rev. Carolus R. Webb, who had been assistant to Rev. Charles T. Walkley, of Grace Church, Orange, was called as rector, which office he yet holds. A parish house was first erected, in which the congregation is now worshiping. The rectory was built afterwards, and the parish, now grown to the number of two hundred and twenty-three communicants, is considering plans for the erection of a new edifice.

St. George's Episcopal Church, of Maplewood, is in charge of Rev. Frederick A. Richey.

Disciples—The Church of the Disciples of Christ, at Nineteenth street and Park avenue, East Orange, had its beginning in May, 1901, when a number of residents of the Fifth Ward who had been holding services in a business office had advanced far enough in numerical and financial growth to permit of arrangements being made for the erection of a house of worship. A chapel was first erected on the lot, and in 1908 the present stone edifice was dedicated. The congregation has steadily grown in interest and influence. Rev. Walter Haushalter has been pastor for several years.

Methodist Episcopal—The congregation of the Orange Methodist Episcopal Church, which had been settled on the plot adjoining the Masonic Temple, on Main street, for over three score and ten years, decided in 1903 to rebuild on another location at the corner of Park avenue and Day street. Jacob Roth purchased the edifice and land in the summer, and on September 20 a historical sermon was preached by Rev. Dr. Frank A. MacDaniel, pastor, at the last service held there. Pending the erection of a new meeting house, arrangements were made for holding the regular services in Library Hall, on Main street, next west of the First Presbyterian Church. Wilbur S. Knowles, architect, prepared the plans for the new edifice and, in July, 1904, special exercises were held in Music Hall, when Rev. George P. Eckman, former pastor, addressed the congregation, after which adjournment was made to the site and ground broken for the foundation walls. The corner-stone was laid on October 1, 1904, the exercises being directed by Rev. Dr. MacDaniel. Rev. Dr. W. L. Hoagland, district superintendent, read the address to the people, prayer was offered by Rev. Dr. Fred Clare Baldwin, of Calvary Methodist Episcopal Church, East Orange, and other clergymen were assigned parts in the program. Among the many articles of interest placed in the box deposited in the corner-stone were an autographed photograph of Thomas A. Edison, one of the first records of the phonograph, and a plate of one of the original electric storage batteries invented by him. In the spring of 1905 the Miller Memorial Chapel, erected in honor of Louis P. Miller, father of Mrs. Thomas A. Edison, and founder of Chautauqua, of Akron, Ohio, was occupied and dedicated. The main edifice was dedicated on November 12, 1905, by Bishop Henry Spellmeyer, who preached at both services. The meeting was featured by the contribution of $30,000 (the amount asked for), toward paying for the new church. It was under the splendid leadership of Rev. Dr. MacDaniel that the enterprise was brought to a successful close. The parsonage was built on a lot east of the church in 1909. Rev. Dr. Harry W. Murkland is now the pastor.

Over seventy years ago, in 1848, the foundation of the Methodist Episcopal Church of South Orange was laid when the congregation first worshiped on the village green, with only the blue canopy of heaven above them, and the trees and shrubbery surrounding this early company of Methodists. Then the Ladies' Aid Society made a tent which was the first enclosure of the congregation. Five years later, in 1853, a lot was purchased during the pastorate of Rev. J. M. Freeman and a chapel located thereon, at a cost of $1,000. The location was on Prospect street, near South Orange avenue. The parish from 1853 to 1860 was a part of the circuit covered by Middleville, Irvington and Maplewood, but in the latter year the South Orange Methodists withdrew and became an independent parish. During the Civil War, all but three of the men of the congregation served their country in the Federal ranks. Rev. James Montgomery, who became pastor in 1871, erected the first edifice, and the dedication services, presided over by Bishop Matthew Simpson, took place in 1874. The enterprise cost $12,000. In 1895 the property at the corner of Prospect street and South Orange avenue was purchased, and the house standing upon it was used as the parsonage till the one now in use was built in 1901. Bishop E. G. Andrews, assisted by Bishop Thomas Bowman, officiated at the exercises of the laying of the corner-stone of the present handsome stone edifice on October 12, 1901, and the church was dedicated by Bishop Charles C. McCabe, on October 26, 1902. Rev. Thomas M. Pender is the pastor of the church today.

From 1858, the date of organization, till 1870, the name of the Methodist Episcopal Church of Jefferson Village remained in the minutes of the Annual Conference, in distinction of the Methodist Church of South Orange, both being in the township of South Orange. Jefferson Village dropped its name in favor of Maplewood, and the change was accordingly made in designating the church located there. In 1890, during the pastorate of Rev. John I. Morrow, the edifice was removed from its site on Ridgewood road and Claremont avenue to Lennox place, near Ridgewood road. The last service was held in the church at its old location May 4, and the remainder of the year was devoted to rebuilding and enlarging the edifice. Dedicatory services were held on Sunday, December 14, 1890. Mr. Morrow was the beloved pastor, and during his ministry of three years made enduring friendships with his congregation. In 1911 the present handsome church of stone was erected. The name of the Morrow Memorial Methodist Episcopal Church was applied to it in his memory. The enrollment is nine hundred. Rev. Dr. John E. Charlton is the pastor.

Up to the time of the organization of Calvary Church, East Orange, the Methodists of Orange, East Orange and West Orange worshiped in the First Methodist Church of Orange, for more than half a century the only church of that denomination in all this region. The agitation for the establishment of a Methodist church in East Orange began in 1868. In 1870 a lot was purchased at the corner of Mulberry (now North Clinton) and William streets, and the building was completed and dedicated July 12, 1870, soon after the formal organization of the church. The first pastor was Rev. Charles S. Ryman, who began his labors April 1, 1870, and he remained in charge for two years. Owing to the demands for enlarged accommodations, it was decided in 1885 to build a new edifice, and on August 5 of that year ground was broken for the imposing brownstone structure which now stands at the corner of Main and Walnut streets. The cost was nearly $80,000, nearly all of which was raised by subscription, so that it was dedicated free of debt. Owing to the failure of the contractors, the work was not completed till early in 1887. Additions and improvements have been made to the plant since then, including a chapel and a foyer for the main edifice. Rev. Dr. Fred Clare Baldwin, who was called to the pastorate in the spring of 1901, served continuously for nineteen years, it being the longest in the history of the Newark Conference. He retired to accept the office of superintendent of the Newark District. During his long service in the local parish, Dr. Baldwin won the good will of his congregation and a host of people unidentified with it. His preaching and public speaking made him popular far beyond his church limits.

After several months of discussion in Calvary and Roseville Methodist Episcopal churches concerning a new religious enterprise in the territory lying between these two churches, resolutions were adopted February 19, 1893, favoring the establishing of a mission in the neighborhood of Park avenue and Grove street, East Orange, under the patronage of the Church Extension Society. Delay occurred in securing the building, so that the work did not progress until the following autumn. A temporary chapel was opened on Sunday afternoon, September 10, 1893, when the Sunday school of forty members was enrolled, with George R. Howe as superintendent. The first preaching service was held immediately at its close and was conducted by Rev. Dr. L. C. Muller, superintendent of the Newark City Church Extension Society. The new chapel and furniture cost about $1,700. The Sunday school grew so rapidly that it was found necessary to enlarge the building in the following spring. A room for the primary department was added on the north side of the building at a cost of over $500. This growth led to the purchase of the lot for $3,300. Rev: W. W. C. Walker was appointed as the first pastor. The portable building was abandoned in a few years and the edifice now in use erected, a parish house provided and a highly organized parish in full operation. Rev. Henry J. Johnston, who is now the pastor, acquitted himself with great bravery as a Y. M. C. A. secretary in France during the World War.

The religious work which resulted in the establishment of the Sandford Street Methodist Episcopal Church, East Orange, had its beginning in a Sunday school established in the summer of 1893. Frederick E. Daum, who was the first superintendent, served four years, being succeeded by Henry Roberts. In 1895 Dr. M. H. C. Vail donated a lot on Sandford street, near Tremont avenue, to the mission, and soon afterward a chapel was erected thereon at a cost of $2,600. Early in 1896 the site of the edifice was changed to a lot on the west side of Sandford street, about one hundred yards south of Central avenue. The first service was held there on February 23 of that year, and was conducted by Rev. John Scarlet, who was, however, not settled as the pastor, but who ministered to the congregation about seven years. The first pastor was Rev. George P. Eckman, a student of Drew Seminary. During the pastorate of Rev. Thomas G. Spencer, the present church was dedicated on October 14, 1907. Rev. Frederick George Wiley is now the pastor.

Beginning with cottage prayer meetings and developing into a Sunday school and then the holding of preaching services in the Franklin School house, the Ferry Methodist Episcopal Church, Dodd street, East Orange, took positive form in 1879. Rev. Edward S. Ferry, who was given charge of the mission, induced the people to build a frame chapel, which was dedicated in the autumn of 1880. The name was bestowed in honor of former Mayor George J. Ferry, of Orange, who contributed liberally toward the building enterprise, father of the pastor, and a prominent member of the Orange Methodist Episcopal Church. Rev. George Anderson Hill is now the pastor.

The First Methodist Episcopal Church of West Orange, at the corner of High and Ridge streets, was organized April 2, 1899, but is now without a settled pastor. Rev. R. G. Waters is pastor of the St. John's Methodist Episcopal Church (colored), on Hickory street, Orange. The Hilton Methodist Episcopal Church is in charge of Rev. J. Fred Bindenberger.

New Church—The first New Church services in Orange were held at the home of Rev. B. F. Barrett, about 1855. He lived at the point now known as Main street and North Essex avenue. Rev. Charles H. Mann was called as pastor of the society in 1866. Regular services were held for several years in a room rented in Library building. The founders of the church were Rev. Charles H. Mann, Mr. and Mrs. David N. Ropes, Mr. and Mrs. William Lewis, Mr. G. Woolworth Colton, Mrs. G. E. Hooker, and Mr. and Mrs. James Root and two sons, Horace and Thomas, and their daughter, Miss Anna H. Root.

Rev. Mr. Mann remained pastor for twenty-nine years, and then resigned on account of ill health. During his many years of residence in Orange he took an active part in municipal affairs and was a member of the Orange Board of Education for nine years. He died in New York City in 1918, aged seventy-eight years.

The present pastor, Rev. Adolph Roeder, was called from Vineland, N. J., to Orange in February, 1896, and has been here for over twenty-five years, serving the community most faithfully through the Civic Association and being called upon frequently to deliver addresses upon various subjects.

Presbyterian—Oldest of all the churches of the Oranges is the First Presbyterian, the story of which is narrated in various chapters of this history. The landmark, at the corner of Main and Day streets, Orange, where the town clock is situated, is familiar to thousands of persons who have passed through the community. Its colonial style of architecture appeals to the artistically inclined, and has proved well the ability of Moses Dodd, the architect of 1812, as a designer of edifices. Special services beginning on November 9 and ending on November 12, 1919, featured the attainment of the two hundredth anniversary of the "Old First." The pastor, Rev. Harmon H. McQuilkin, preached an historical sermon in the morning of the first day, on "The Propulsive Power of the Past," and in the afternoon a tablet in memory of Rev. Dr. Eldridge Mix, pastor, 1867-1881, was dedicated with an address by Rev. David O. Irving, pastor of Bethel Presbyterian Church, and prayer by Rev. Dr. Herman C. Gruhnert, pastor of the German Presbyterian Church. Tablets had been erected in recent years to the memory of Rev. Dr. Henry M. Storrs, pastor, 1882-1894, and Rev. Dr. Charles Townsend, pastor, 1895-1914. Thus all the nine deceased ministers of the parish have been remembered with memorials. At the evening service, Rev. Dr. Robert Brewster Beattie, pastor of the Munn Avenue Presbyterian Church, East Orange, preached a sermon, taking as his subject, "The Church and the Nation." The historical service was held on the following night, November 10, when a number of addresses were delivered and on Wednesday evening the celebration was closed with a reunion of present and former members.

Brick Presbyterian Church, corner of Prospect and Main streets, East Orange, had its beginning at a meeting held on March 30, 1830, which is fully told in its proper place in the history. The original title was "The Second Presbyterian Church of Orange," but in 1890 it was changed for the one now in use. In 1878 the edifice was remodeled and enlarged at an expense of $18,000. The bell first hung in the belfry was sold to a church at Roseland, and the one now heard on the Sabbath and other occasions was installed. Rev. Dr. Henry F. Hickok, who retired as the pastor, in 1895, was made pastor emeritus, and Rev. Dr. Alexander N. Carson was chosen as his successor. After two years he was succeeded by Rev. Dr. James F. Riggs. A new chapel was added in 1907, the corner-stone being laid on Sunday, September 30, 1906. The build-

FIRST PRESBYTERIAN CHURCH, ORANGE

ing used also by the Sunday school was named the Hickok Memorial Chapel, in memory of Rev. Dr. Hickok. Rev. George M. Gordon succeeded Rev. Dr. Riggs, who died in the pastorate on January 21, 1918.

Instituted in 1831, the First Presbyterian Church of South Orange depended upon stated supplies for its preaching services till January 21, 1840, when Rev. Joseph Vance was installed pastor and the first edifice of frame construction was placed upon a lot donated by Samuel Brown. The cost of building amounted to $3,250. The congregation continued to worship in the old frame building, and in 1880 the present brownstone edifice was contracted for and occupied five years later. Among the pastors called to the parish none made a deeper impression upon the people through his ministerial activities than did Rev. Dr. George Lawrence Spinning, who began his labors on December 1, 1893, but was not installed till May 2, 1895. He was a soldier in the Civil War, and strongly associated with the Grand Army of the Republi· As a pulpit orator he ranked among the leaders of the State, and he was frequently called upon to deliver addresses outside of his parish. Advancing years brought on the resultant waning strength, and the pastor reluctantly offered his resignation on October 30, 1906, after a service of thirteen years. Dr. Spinning was then placed upon the church records as pastor emeritus. Rev. George A. Edmison is the pastor.

Officially, the name of the Munn Avenue Presbyterian Church, East Orange, is the First Presbyterian Church of East Orange. It was organized in June, 1863, when the Brick Church, first parish erected in the city, was known as the Second Church of Orange. To Rev. Dr. James M. Ludlow, the clergyman-author, is credited the longest pastorate in the more than fifty years of the life of the parish. He was installed on March 12, 1886, and his scholarly attainments and ripe judgment brought to the church a new spirit and interest. In a comparatively brief time the attendance at services and the work of the parish had increased perceptibly. An addition was made to each side of the church and a new lecture room was built in 1876, at a cost of $9,537.24. In 1888, after Dr. Ludlow had been pastor two years, another enlargement of the main auditorium was made which cost $39,537.24, and a new organ installed. Literary productions of the pastor include several volumes, among them being "Incentives for Right Living," dedicated to Theodore Roosevelt, President of the United States, and who was parishioner of Dr. Ludlow in New York City in his younger years. The Munn Avenue Church prospered and became the leading one of the Oranges in that denomination for membership and parish activities. On September 28, 1902, the commodious and handsome "Andrew Reasoner Memorial Chapel'" was dedicated as the gift of Mrs. Reasoner, wife of the one memorialized. A few years afterward, Dr. Ludlow resigned his pastorate so that he might devote his time to literary pursuits, and Rev. Dr. John Douglas Adam, a forceful pulpit orator, took his place. He resigned two years later, and Rev. Robert Brewster Beattie, who became the pastor, has successfully carried on the work of the large and influential parish for the past ten years.

Churchgoing was popular in the days following the close of the Civil War, and on January 20, 1867, the Central Presbyterian Church of Orange was organized by the Presbytery of Passaic, with thirty-three members. Rev. Edward D. Youmans, the first pastor, began his work on the first Sunday in May, 1867, and died suddenly on August 26, 1868. His brother, Rev. Alfred Youmans, of Bellefonte, Pennsylvania, who took his place, served from January, 1869, to March, 1889, when he also died suddenly. The chapel and main edifice were erected at a cost of over $90,000. Rev. Dr. Rufus S. Green was next installed as pastor, and his resignation having been accepted, Rev. Dr. John Fulton Patterson, of Pittsburg, Pennsylvania, was called and duly installed in February, 1894. He has served ever since as the pastor of one of the most highly organized parishes in the Oranges. All departments are working in accord with each other, and there is a fine degree of church spirit existing between pastor and people. This is shown in a remarkable manner in the attendance and interest manifested in the Men's Bible Class on Sunday mornings. The church and parsonage occupy the entire frontage on Main street, between Oakwood avenue and Prince street.

Under the ministration of Rev. Richard Rosenthal, the First German Presbyterian Church grew from a struggling organization in 1867 to full possession of its edifice, on William street, which was dedicated on December 28, 1869. He was followed by Rev. Herman Carl Gruhnert, a student at the Bloomfield Theological Seminary. After his graduation from the seminary he was ordained and installed by the Presbytery in July, 1874. The church was burdened with a heavy, altogether disproportionate indebtedness, amounting to over $8,000. But again the churches of the Oranges and the Presbytery of Morris and Orange, and also numerous outside friends, manifested a most generous interest in the feeble organization, so that by their liberal help, as well as by the earnest efforts of the people themselves, the debt was lifted in comparatively few years, while the church grew in numbers and efficiency. In 1886 a new and commodious parsonage was completed, on the site of the old one. In 1889 a fine pipe organ was installed, and in 1899 the Sunday school annex was erected in the rear of the edifice. The activities of the church are attested by faithful attendance at worship, and by a number of auxiliary societies, two Ladies' Societies, a Men's Club and two Young People's Societies, as also by an efficient force of teachers in the Sunday school. Rev. Mr. Gruhnert is the oldest settled pastor of the Oranges, having served forty-six years.

Bethel Presbyterian Church, at the corner of Midland avenue and

Dodd street, was evolved out of the Franklin Union Sunday school and organized by a committee of the Presbytery on November 13, 1870. A frame building erected four years before on the south side of Dodd street, near Brighton avenue of today, was occupied by the congregation till 1891, when a new stone church was built at the corner of Midland avenue and Dodd street. Rev. James H. Marr, first settled pastor, remained till January 1, 1882, when he resigned, and his place taken by Rev. David O. Irving, who was ordained and installed pastor on May 4, 1882. In 1906 an extension was added to the edifice. Mr. Irving has remained the pastor since his ordination, and has served as a member of the Board of Education of East Orange.

Preaching services were held in the completed edifice atop of the Mountain in the St. Cloud section of West Orange, on Sunday, June 10, 1877, and the occasion also marked the institution of the St. Cloud Presbyterian Church by a committee of the Presbytery of Morris and Orange. The edifice was built of free stone and dedicated on September 13 following. Rev. William Force Whitaker, of Southold, Long Island, installed as pastor on November 22, continued till the late autumn of 1894, when he accepted a call to the First Presbyterian Church at Albany, New York. In 1880 a chapel was added to the church, the gift of Mrs. John Crosby Brown, and in memory of Rev. Dr. William Adams, her father, who assisted in the institution of the parish. General George B. McClellan, who was an original elder, died on October 29, 1885, and a polished brass tablet was placed on the wall of the church, containing the following inscription:

George Brenton McClellan, Major-General U. S. A.
Governor of New Jersey. Elder of this Church.
October 29, 1885
"I have fought a good fight; I have finished my
course. I have kept the faith."

Missionary work inaugurated by Richard Purdue, in the Elmwood district of East Orange, marked the beginning of the Elmwood Presbyterian Church, at the corner of West street and Elmwood avenue. Mrs. Anna M. Trippe donated the lot on which a small frame building was built and first used by the Sunday school, on March 1, 1874. The work was carried on under the auspices of the pastor and members of the Munn Avenue Church. Rev. George S. Webster, who was called to the pastorate in 1882, had the pleasure of seeing the new frame building completed in December, 1889. The chapel, having become self-sustaining, was given recognition as the Elmwood Presbyterian Church, in 1898, by the Presbytery of Morris and Orange, and in 1910 the present edifice was erected during the administration of Rev. Charles B. Bullard, who was installed February 5, 1900. He increased the work and interest of the parish till he resigned in February, 1914. Frederick M. Shepard, who

had been superintendent of the Sunday school since 1881, died on June
30, 1913, and on November 30 a bronze tablet in his memory was unveiled upon the church walls. The inscription reads:

In loving memory of
Frederick M. Shepard,
The Friend of Elmwood.
Superintendent of the Sunday School
1881-1913
President of the Trustees
1898-1913.

Rev. A. Frederick Dunnels is the present pastor of the church.

In January, 1907, Rev. Mr. Bullard began the publication of "The
Elm Leaf" each month, which he continued till the end of December,
1913, a valuable historical contribution to the life of the parish.

The Hillside Presbyterian Church, Orange, held its first meetings in
Westcott's private gymnasium on Highland avenue, beginning on July
31, 1887, and on November 21 following the Presbytery of Morris and
Orange formally organized the parish. In 1888 the first unit of the present church plant was built in the form of a chapel on Hillside avenue,
near Scotland street. The present church proper was built in 1891.
Since then a parish house, a memorial chapel and study for the minister
have been added. The first pastor was Rev. Dr. Stanley White, who accepted the call of the congregation upon his graduation from Union
Theological Seminary, and remained for twenty years, resigning to accept a secretaryship of the Presbyterian Board of Foreign Missions. He
was a graduate of Princeton College. His successor was Rev. Robert Service Steen, a graduate of Princeton University and Union Theological
Seminary. Mr. Steen had served three years on the faculty of the Syrian
Protestant College at Beyrout, Syria. His pastorate was notable for brilliant preaching and exceptional personal leadership, but death brought it
to an end after a period of eight months.

The present minister is Rev. Franklin Boyd Edwards, a graduate
of Williams College and Union Seminary, whose pastorate began in 1910.
The staff consists of the pastor, also a director of religious education, Dr.
Miles B. Fisher, and a trained leader of girls' work, Miss Elizabeth Ste-
phens. The church also supports a missionary in China, a missionary in
Utah, and assists in the maintenance of a kindergarten in China.

Rapid growth of the Fifth Ward of East Orange soon made most
apparent, after the advent of the last decade of the Nineteenth Century,
the need of a new church because of the increasing attendance at the
neighborhood prayer meetings. These resulted, first, in the opening of a
Sunday school on June 19, 1891, then in an evening preaching service
begun in February, 1892, in a carriage house at 20 Hamilton street, and
conducted by Rev. John Martin Thomas, a student of Union Theological

Seminary of the class of 1893. A permanent society was formed on November 10, 1892, and the name Arlington Avenue Presbyterian Church applied to it. Rev. Mr. Thomas was ordained and installed on Friday, June 9, 1893, and upon a lot selected at the corner of Arlington and Springdale avenues, the complete house of worship was dedicated the day previous. Rev. Mr. Thomas left the parish in 1907, to assume the office of president of Middlebury College, in which he became very successful. Rev. Walter S. Davison is now the pastor.

Trinity Presbyterian Church, South Orange, was organized on January 27, 1892, when the name was officially given and sixty-eight members were enrolled. Dedicatory services of the new edifice were held on November 27, 1892, it being built at the corner of South Orange avenue and Grove road, and the entire cost of lot and construction was $11,000. Rev. Asa Wynkoop, of Union Theological Seminary, was ordained and installed the first pastor June 28, 1893. Rev. Edwin E. White is the pastor in 1920.

The Pleasant Valley German Presbyterian Church, erected on the western slope of the First Mountain, was organized May 26, 1878. Rev. Franz Hartig, a student at the Bloomfield Theological Seminary, was installed as the first pastor.

Rev. John F. Kern, another student at the Bloomfield Seminary, was ordained and installed pastor of the Orange Valley German Presbyterian Church, July 24, 1891, and in 1893 the edifice at the corner of Scotland street and Fairview avenue was occupied. Mr. Kern has continued as pastor to the present day.

The latest parish organized by the Presbyterians was the Prospect Street Presbyterian Church, of Maplewood, in 1917. Rev. Charles A. Anderson, a native of Orange, was installed the first pastor.

The West Orange Presbyterian Chapel had its beginning in a Sunday school opened in Bennett Hall, at 39 Washington street, on January 11, 1903. Though the day was very stormy, thirty-two children and twenty adults from the Central Presbyterian Church, Orange, attended. The movement was started by the session of this parish. Prayer meeting was first held on Friday, January 16, being conducted by Rev. Dr. John Fulton Patterson, pastor. A lot having a frontage of one hundred feet on Washington street was selected as the site for the edifice, which was first occupied on the afternoon of Christmas, 1904. Spencer S. Marsh, superintendent of the Sunday school, reviewed the progress made during the nearly two years of the existence of the parish, and Dr. Patterson delivered an address. Rev. Wellington P. Francisco was the first pastor, beginning his work on July 1, 1905. The enrollment is now 500 in the church, and 450 in the Sunday school. Rev. Henry A. Pearce, the present pastor, took charge November 1, 1920.

The Ridgeview Presbyterian Church, West Orange, was instituted by the Presbytery of Morris and Orange, in 1911. The pastor is Rev. H. A. Stemme.

Scientist—The First Church of Christ, Scientist, in Orange, informally organized in December, 1895, began services and a Sunday school in Berkeley Hall, East Orange, the membership being confined to those who had experienced the healing efficacy of Christian Science. The church was incorporated in 1898, and the building site on Cleveland street, near Main street, was purchased the following year. Indiana limestone was the material worked into the edifice, which was completed in 1911, providing a seating capacity for about 1,000 persons. Services were first held in the new church on Thanksgiving Day, 1911, but the dedication was deferred to December 31, 1916, when the announcement was made that the debt was entirely removed. The cost of building operations was $65,000. A free reading room is maintained by the church at 191 Main street, Orange.

Another First Church of Christ, Scientist, meets at 317 Main street, East Orange.

Unitarian—The first service of worship under Unitarian auspices was held in Masonic Temple, Orange, on Sunday, January 12, 1890. Rev. John White Chadwick, of Brooklyn, poet and successor of Rev. Samuel Longfellow, brother of Henry Wadsworth Longfellow, also a Unitarian, preached the sermon. The service was soon followed by incorporation, the first trustees being Henry Foster Hitch, president; W.C. Swift, treasurer, and Warren Delano, Jr., Nathan L. Handy, Mrs. Margaret L. Aborn, Clemens Herschel, Isabel Furman. Rev. Edward Hale, the first minister, was installed April 2, 1891. Among the noted preachers who served the new church, before the installation of Mr. Hale, were Rev. Edward Everett Hale, Francis G. Peabody, Price Collier, Robert Collyer. The cornerstone was laid December 22, 1892, and the new church dedicated in May, 1893.

The church has held a steady and prosperous group from the first. Rev. Edward Hale resigned in July, 1897, to accept a professorship in Harvard University. For a year and a half the church was without a settled minister. In November, 1898, the present pastor, Rev. Walter Reid Hunt, was called, and is continuing the work to this day. The church has had but two ministers.

Early in the present pastorate the church debt was paid and the mortgage burned. Shortly after this a pipe organ was installed. This was soon followed by the erection of the parish house, the gift of a devoted member of the church in memory of her husband. The church and parish house now occupy the church lots on Cleveland street, bordered by beautiful shrubbery.

Its working departments are the Sunday school, the Unity Club, the Woman's Alliance and the Laymen's League, all active in furthering the cause of pure religion in every way. The church is without a debt, completely equipped, growing each year in membership and interest.

In 1920 the Unitarian denomination conducted a campaign to raise $300,000. The quota assigned the Orange church was $5,000. It at once raised $7,500, exceeding its quota fifty per cent.

Lutheran—The Evangelical Lutheran Church, at 15 Ridge street, Orange, is in charge of Rudolph S. Ressmeyer.

Hebrew—In the fall of 1873 a few of the Hebrew residents of the Oranges met in the old Library Hall, adjoining the First Presbyterian Church, and began worshiping as a Reformed Jewish Congregation of Sharey Tefilo ("The Gates of Prayer"). Having outgrown its meeting room, a synagogue was built on Essex avenue which was dedicated in January 27, 1889, and has been in constant use since then, services being held on Friday night of each week. The congregation numbers eighty, drawn from the Oranges and surrounding towns. Rev. Nathan S. Barsch is the rabbi.

The Congregation A. A. A., Jewish, meets at 36 Park street, Orange. Rev. Schlaeme Swartz is the rabbi.

CHAPTER XCI

THE INDUSTRIES OF THE ORANGES

Products of our local industries have been known in the world for a century and a half. When the settlers pushed their way from Newark over the mountains they found the hemlock tree growing in profusion, the acid extracted from the bark of which was used in tanning leather. This developed the tanning industry, crude indeed, but answering the needs of the people of a primitive era. Naturally boot and shoe making followed, first carried on by the itinerant who went from house to house in quest of orders. Then came the miniature factory in which the laborious processes of hand-making the footwear of the people ten or twelve hours each day, excepting on the Sabbath, was the feature of the industrial life. In time the product not needed locally was shipped to the metropolitan market. Thought was given in the manufacture more to serviceableness than to comfort or appearance and thus the industry thrived. Cider-making and the distillation of apple whiskey produced thousands of gallons of the beverages every season, the orchards, as we have learned from the early history of the community, flourishing in large numbers. Cooperage, the making of barrels, firkins and hogheads for the storing of the product, was also a popular industry, and large quantities of staves and headings were taken out of the forests every year. Shipments of them were also made to other markets, the income derived therefrom being not inconsiderable. The sawmills and gristmills also added their share to the annual output of the local industries of the latter part of the Eighteenth Century. These have all, these many years, been extinct in the life of the Oranges.

The manufacture of hats, alone of the industries inaugurated in this awakening century, survives after a century and a third. But the manufacture of boots and shoes continued till a few years after the Civil War, when machine-equipped factories in other places produced a cheaper article and consequently the local concerns, unable to compete with the manufacturers elsewhere, were compelled to go out of business. Labor has and always will be the principal element in the product of merchandise, but it is difficult to visualize in these latter days, with the growing indifference among the men and women working at the various industrial pursuits, the vital interest employees manifested in the plants where they performed their daily task. As a rule they toiled five hours in the morning and five in the afternoon, with an interim of an hour at noon. The prevailing custom during a larger part of the Nineteenth Century was the enjoyment of dinner at exactly 12 o'clock noon every day in the year. Employee and employer were practically living on the same social plane, and all adjourned to their respective homes for refreshments and rest when the sun reached the meridian. Keen interest was shown by the journeymen in their output, and there was a value placed upon articles of commodity not computed by the dollar sign. Individuality was a characteristic of the labor of the early days, and the welfare of the employer was considered, and not alone the few dollars received at the end of each week. Skilled labor, such as it was in the first half of the Nineteenth Century, usually commanded from one dollar to one dollar and a half for a day's toil of ten hours. This wage provided well for the homes, together with the produce raised on the premises. There was, it can be stated, with reasonable certainty, a larger proportion of contentment than in these latter days when the toil is not so onerous and the wages allowed the journeymen are in many instances excessive.

Introduction of steam revolutionized not only the industrial life of the community, but the economic and social conditions as well. Of course, the change did not come overnight nor in a few years, but the invention of machinery for the production of goods made by hand not alone increased the output but also brought lighter work to the employee. Fear was expressed that there would not be enough remunerative employment for all the operatives when the machines made an appearance, but this was overcome in the course of time and increasing wages dissipated all thoughts of an untoward character. The transition from hand-made to machine-made industrial activities was, in so far as it related to the Oranges, attended with no unpleasant incidents. Machinery first introduced here was placed in the hat factories, which was thriving by leaps and bounds in the decade of 1850. The water courses, chiefly the east branch of the Rahway river running through the Orange Valley and the Second river, in the Doddtown section, were utilized by the manufacturers, their factories being erected on the bank and sometimes over the stream. The water furnished was ideal for washing the headgear, a necessary part of the manufacture.

Though the industry has been intimately related to our local prosperity for a century and a third, there is little or no familiarity on the part of the people with the processes necessary to develop the hats made in the Orange district from the raw material to the finished product. Fur of rabbits, muskrats, coney and other animals, gathered in various parts of the world, carefully mixed and shrunken into a composite mass, pliable and durable, make up the body of the felt hat. The shrinking of the fur is an interesting process. First it is formed into a long cone by means of suction, in an atmosphere of "live steam," then dipped alternately into hot and cold water, pounded and rolled by hand and machinery to the required size. They are then dyed, starched, blocked and shaped into the shape of crown and brim desired. Rubbing, ironing, shaping, with much hand work follow, and then trimming, entirely performed by women, completes the finished product. Thirty distinct and separate processes are necesssary to bring the hat up to its final stage for inspection and delivery to the jobber.

Hat forming was entirely hand-made till about 1850, when the introduction of the Wells hat forming machine invented a number of years previously, brought the first change in the industry. Firms employing a small number of operatives were compelled to retire from business, as the machine could do the work of thirty or forty men. Felt hats were very much in demand during the decade of 1850, being popularized by the Hungarian exile, Louis Kossuth, who wore this style of headgear on his visit to the United States, and who was entertained in Newark in April of 1852.

The Gill hat forming machine, invented by Ira Gill, of Walpole, Massachusetts, father of John Gill, mayor of Orange, in 1894, was an improvement upon the Wells machine, and quickly found favor in the Orange district. The Gill machine was patented in 1857, and it radically differed from the one first introduced, in construction, method of operation, and of results accomplished, yet Mr. Gill was compelled to defend a long and costly litigation in the courts, the owners of the Wells machine claiming that Mr. Gill had infringed upon their patent. Expenditure of large sums of money in legal fees was required of him before being allowed uninterruptedly to proceed with the manufacture of his machine. A monopoly was also sought by the owners of the Wells machine in restricting the number in use by the hat makers to seventy-two for the districts of Orange, Danbury, New York, Philadelphia and Boston.

John Gill settled in Orange, his home being at the corner of Cleveland and White streets. In 1872 he and his brother, George H. Gill, established the hat-forming factory on the east side of Lumber street, afterward renamed Essex avenue, the style of the firm being J. & G. H. Gill. Prosperity came to the firm, and it was continued till 1892, when the junior member retired. John Gill continued the business for a few years longer. A feature of the plant was its peculiar-toned whistle, which was a strong rival of the town clock in popular favor. It blew with a regularity and accuracy at 7 in the morning, 12 and 1 at noon, and 6 at night, excepting on Saturday, when the week's work ceased one hour earlier. The whistle was used also in sounding an alarm of fire. The instrument became practically the timepiece of the housewife and business man as well as the factory employer and employee. Once it was destroyed by fire, but was replaced with little or no impairment to its volume and tone. Another fire visited the factory in 1905, which stilled forever the sound of the whistle.

Fires and floods caused considerable loss in the Orange hat manufacturing district at various times, and in 1892, the year marking the centenary of the industry, there were twenty-one firms engaged in the trade. The value of the plants at the end of the one hundred years, was estimated at $1,091,575, the number of employees being 3,722, and approximately 397,850 dozen hats or a total of 4,774,800 hats were the year's product. The valuation was estimated at $4,849,940. The production in 1852, the fiftieth anniversary of the industry, was about 195,000 dozen hats per annum.

A few of the manufacturers of the decades of 1870 and 1880, when the industry grew toward its greatest height, were the firms of McChesney & Fischer, Austin, Drew & Co., F. Berg & Co., Cummings, Matthews & Co., Puff & Youmans, McGall Brothers (Quinton and William), William Clorer, the No Name Company, Porter, Crofut & Hodkinson (the latter Thomas Hodgkinson, being one of the most popular salesmen in the entire industry), John J. Perine, Augustus Dykeman, C. B. Rutan & Co., James Young & Son, Laurence T. Fell, Damon Stocker, James Young & Son, Edwin B. Whiting, Harrop, Gist & Co., Henry Smith & Son, Thomas Walker, Crowe, Quinlan & Moore, Augustus Brandies, Brennan & Carr, John Otterbein, John R. Long & Son, George H. Gill, Connett, Read & Co.

There are now (1921) only five hat factories in the Orange district, with a total capacity for turning out 250,000 dozen hats per annum. These are the factories of the No Name Company, F. Berg & Co., E. V. Connett & Co., the Trimble Company, the C. B. Rutan Company—the survivors of the long list of factories which formerly comprised the Orange district.

Oldest of the hat manufacturing plants in the Orange district is the No Name Company, situated on Mitchell street, at South Jefferson street, in the section known as Orange Valley. The founder was Stephen Stetson, who over one hundred years ago was in business on Main street, in the Brick Church section of East Orange. It is believed that he later moved to the site now occupied. Henry T. Stetson, his oldest son, born May 4, 1817, mastered the trade and became a manufacturer with his brother, Napoleon. They were operating the plant at its present location. In 1850 the output of the factory conducted by the brothers exceeded that of any one other establishment in the district, of which there was a large number. Henry Stetson was killed on August 8, 1853, while riding on a train from New York to Orange. The business was then carried on by Napoleon Stetson, who became very active in local public life, was elected a member of the first Common Council in 1860, and was looked upon as the leading manufacturer of his day.

Henry Stetson, his son, born on January 12, 1857, entered the factory after receiving his education, and after familiarizing himself with the trade became a member of the firm. Unable to decide upon a name for the plant, when it was agreed in 1882 that it should be incorporated, the strange designation "No Name" was decided upon by the men

NO NAME HAT MANUFACTORY, ORANGE

F. BERG & CO. ORANGE

directly interested. John B. Stetson, brother of Napoleon Stetson, and who afterward became famous as the head of the Philadelphia house. of hatters of that name, was chosen first president of the No Name Company. In 1893, when the company was reorganized, Henry Stetson, who a few years later was elected mayor of Orange, became president, and, inheriting many of the executive traits of his grandfather, brought the No Name factory to a high state of prosperity. His son, Stephen L. Stetson, great-grandson of the founder, is in 1921 identified with the company. The product is sent to all parts of the country, and is known far and wide for serviceableness and style. The members of the firm are all wide-awake and keenly interested in the industry, now approaching its centenary of identification with the life of the Oranges.

The name of Berg is familiar in every home in the Oranges. For fifty-seven years it has been associated with the factory, located at the corner of South Jefferson and Nassau streets, Orange Valley, where hundreds of operatives (500 men and 200 women) are engaged in turning out thousands of dozens of hats annually, and which go out.to all parts of the country.

Frederick Berg, the founder, was engaged in the industry in the summer of 1862 when he heard the call of Abraham Lincoln for nine months' troops to augment the ranks of the Union army. On his return to Orange in June, 1863, he set about to engage in business as a manufacturer of fine grade felt hats. It was begun in 1864, in a factory of frame construction, and with only a few articles of furnishing, but soon became a place of intense activity. Thirty-two men were at first employed, and it was the one idea of Mr. Berg that the best possible product should be turned out of his factory. Gradually the business increased, and as his sons, Fred., Jr., Henry, Charles and Christopher, completed their education, they were admitted to the firm, which was styled F. Berg & Company. The firm prospered till June 19, 1902, when a night fire completely destroyed the plant, leaving practically no salvage worthy the name.

With characteristic energy, the firm immediately engaged an unused factory in Newark, and after adjustment had been made with the underwriters, in which, it is believed, about $300,000 was allowed for the loss, a new factory of steel and concrete construction, six stories in height, was erected, with every modern facility for carrying on the industry, and which gave a capacity of 2,500 dozen hats per week. In the early days the water for sizing the hats was heated in kettles, under which fires were built, but today steam coils have made the old-time practice seem primitive. Ironing shells were heated by means of iron slugs; now the heating is done by electricity. And so the story could be told of the wonderful advances made in the manufacture of hats. Sanitary appliances of the latest approved pattern have been added to the equipment as they have been suggested. From the moment the stock is taken out of the large storeroom, every care is exercised in its handling, especially in the dyeing, the colors of the Berg factory being famous for their variety and durability. Four two-hundred horse-power boilers supply the steam so necessary in the manufacture of the hats, and the entire plant is lighted by electricity.

Eugene V. Connett, who settled in South Orange in 1865, was the founder of the hat manufacturing plant known as the E. V. Connett Company in 1920. For half a century and more this well known firm has manufactured the fine line of felt hats so prominently associated with the name of Connett. The factory is located on the west side of South Jefferson street, in the Orange Valley district, and operatives can always depend upon full time employment if there is any movement worth while in the trade. The building is familiar to all who have any association, permanent or temporary, with this section of Orange. Mr. Connett introduced at the very beginning, sterling principles for the conduct of the plant, and there has been no deviation from them in the long and excellent career of the organization. At the time of the factory's beginning there were a large number of factories in the locality, all situated along the course known as the east branch of the Rahway river, the water of which was especially adapted for the washing of the hats during the process of making into a perfect article for the market. The founder was possessed of a strong personality and enjoyed the confidence of those with whom he was associated and also the operatives in his plant. During the years when differences over the bill of prices with them required skill and tact in settlement, Mr. Connett succeeded in several instances in avoiding lockouts and strikes. The labor situation was very keen at times, but the workmen in the Connett factory took a pardonable pride in the goods turned out by them. Today the high standing of the E. V. Connett Company is due in very large measure to the splendid ability of the founder in steering the concern clear of friction, as far as it was possible to attain, with his employees. While the factory is one of the five survivors of those of the latter part of the Nineteenth Century, it is third oldest in the district, being led by the No Name and the Berg factories.

The Orange Hat Box Company, at 9 Mitchell street, Orange, incorporated in 1906, manufactures the paper board boxes in which the hats are placed for shipment and also the wooden cases which contain them. The average value of the material manufactured is $85,000. There are forty-six employees operating the plant.

Forty years ago, in 1880, George J. Seabury, a resident of Llewellyn Park, West Orange, and the founder of the Seabury & Johnson Pharmaceutical Works, in 1867, built the brick building on Glenwood avenue, between Franklin street and the Watchung railroad, East Orange, and installed his plant, which has been enlarged several times and is now one of the largest industrial establishments of the Oranges. Plasters, surgical dressings, absorbent cotton, antiseptic specialties and other necessities in the medical and surgical profession are manufactured in large consignments and sent to every part of the world. Extreme care is constantly exercised lest deleterious matter may enter into the product, which must be absolutely sterile to be of service in amelioration of the ills of humankind. The value of the product manufactured in this plant in 1920 is three million dollars. There are 600 employees, 150 men and 450 women engaged in operating the concern, whose product has for half a century and more been known in the world.

Thomas A. Edison, the foremost inventor of his time, transformed the quiet of the vicinity of Lakeside avenue and Valley road, West Orange, into one of bustling activity soon after installing his laboratory there in the decade of 1880, first by erecting the building in which phonographs were manufactured for the entertainment of the people of the world. Thousands upon thousands of the instruments have been sent broadcast into the markets, and in seasons of mild weather the sounds of music can be plainly heard by passersby, as new records are being made by musicians famous in the operas and other fields of the persuasive art. These internationally popular products of the inventor's brain brought large financial returns, and increasing employment to several thousand employees. The Edison dictating machine is also manufactured in the plant, which has grown into the largest establishment in the Oranges devoted to industrial pursuits. It occupies land on both sides of Lakeside avenue and extends northward to Alden street and eastward to the tracks of the Erie railroad. The Bates hand numbering machines, widely used for the consecutive numbering of tickets, et cetera, have been manufactured many years in the Edison plant. Storage batteries, being the heaviest duty battery used in the country, are turned out in increasing numbers annually. These are applied as the motive power for electric automobiles, auto trucks, baggage trucks, transportation of passengers and to store light for the miner and light for the farmer. Primary batteries are manufactured at the Silver Lake plant, in Bloomfield. The Thomas A. Edison Company was incorporated in 1896, with a capital today of three million dollars. The average value of the product per annum is fifteen million dollars and the number of employees is seven thousand, of which two thousand are engaged in making the storage batteries.

Another large manufacturing plant is operated by the Crocker-Wheeler Company, in the Ampere section of East Orange, which has one thousand two hundred operatives on its payrolls. Dr. Schuyler Skaats Wheeler, the noted inventor, is the president of the corporation which manages the heavy production, amounting to four million dollars annually in value. Electric motors and other electrical devices are there made, but the industry was temporarily halted during the period of the World War, and munitions were there made for use by the Federal army and navy.

The Sprague works, partly in East Orange and partly in Bloomfield, at Lawrence street and the Erie railroad, is an auxiliary of the General Electric Company. One of the most important products is the unit motor and controller, adapted for installation as motive power for individual machines in factories. Motors, generators, electric hoists, electric fans. ozonators, controllers, rheostats and compensators are also manufactured in the Sprague plant.

Magnetos, automotive starting and lighting systems and portable house lighting and power plants are manufactured by the Simms Magneto Company, at 275 North Arlington avenue, East Orange, incorporated in 1910. It has recently begun to manufacture "home lite" outfits, an ingenious equipment which makes electric light possible in places isolated from the centers. It consists of a set of storage batteries and a compact generating plant. An air-cooled portable engine, with tank and starting motor, complete with fan and a Sims magneto for charging batteries, comprises the outfit contained in a small box. Placed in the basement of a house, it forms an independent light unit. Its noise and vibration are so slight that little disturbance is caused. Adjoining this factory, the A. P. Smith Manufacturing Company, at Norman and Lawrence streets, East Orange, is carrying on a large and remunerative business in producing valves, hydrants, water main tapping machines and water supplies. They are standards in the water departments of New York, Boston, Buffalo, Cleveland, Detroit, and other large cities. During the World War the plant was converted into a shell-producing factory for the Government of the United States. There are 185 employees.

The Edison Lamp Works, a branch of the General Electric Company, is located at Nineteenth street and Springdale avenue, East Orange. Incandescent lamps are turned out in large numbers every year by the 466 employees making up the working force of the plant.

Tons of ore are refined at the factory, corner of Alden and High streets, Orange, by the United States Radium Corporation, seeking to obtain only a tiny grain of radium. The minutest part of it is used to make luminous a paint used for dials and hands for watches and other indicators. On Standish avenue, not far away from the radium plant, the Cromlow Film laboratories make positive prints for leading producers of moving pictures. The Hart Roller Bearing Company, at 559 Main street, Orange, opposite the Erie station, manufactures the Hart roller bearings in which it has been engaged since 1916. Foodstuffs are prepared and shipped to many centers at the factory of the Purity Cross, on the north side of Central avenue, west of the Lackawanna

MONROE FACTORY IN 1913

MONROE PLANT, SHOWING NEW UNIT

railroad. Across the thoroughfare the Standard Music Roll Company makes player piano music rolls; the Arto Company manufacturers phonograph records, and the Standard Paper Box Company includes among its other products the boxes which contain the music rolls.

Nearly a third of a century the Orange Machine and Manufacturing Company has been engaged in machine building and repairing and oxy-acetylene welding and cutting, at 354 South Jefferson street, Orange. R. W. Gardner & Co., pharmaceutical chemists at 376 Henry street, near the Memorial Hospital, and the French Pearl and Jewelry Works, at 345 Henry street, Orange, are both kept busy the year round turning out their products. The Vosburgh Miniature Lamp Company, at 263 Main street, Orange, which began in 1912 turning out miniature incandescent lights, employs seventy-five operatives. Riley & Downer, manufacturers of wood cases and paper boxes, have been doing business at 226 William street, Orange, since 1887. They employ eighty-five operatives. The Chronicle Publishing Company, at 15 Essex avenue, employs thirty-eight men and women.

The Mystic Mit Company, at 521 Main street, East Orange, is engaged in making a pot cloth which is woven of cord and flattened wire, used in scouring cooking vessels. Die castings in large numbers are made at the plant of the C. M. Gray, Manufacturing Company, at 358 Central avenue. At 24 Sterling street, East Orange, the Jephson-Scott Body Company makes automobile bodies, and the New York Cornice and Sky-light Works, which name suggests its output, is located at 6 Sterling. street, East Orange. The Nitram Company, makers of knitted shopping and school bags, tapestry fabrics and polished twines, is located on Long street, a short distance from the corner of North Park and Dodd streets, in the First Ward of East Orange.

There are two factories in South Orange, one, the Orange Screen Company, at 515 Valley street, Maplewood, makes screens for windows, etc., sash and metal weather strips, employing sixty-five hands. The Sill-cock-Miller Company, at Parker avenue, in business since 1910, is the maker of celluloid specialties and finds employment for fifty-five men and twenty women.

"The Romance of the Monroe" is the story of the machine that has made all figuring as easy as turning the crank—another exemplification of the fact that America is the mother of invention. Her offsprings are found in every clime and in every variety of service. Not the least among them is the machine which users have termed "A mechanical brain that thinks for you."

Along the line of the Lackawanna railroad, in the environs of Orange, is a plant as modern and scientifically perfect as may be constructed. This is the home of this mechanical thinker, which is small enough to be carried from office to office, and large enough in "brain capacity" to record a saving in the Tax Department of the State of New York in one year of $85,000. In this plant is housed the machinery which is turning out Monroe Calculating Machines by the thousands.

While this introductory statement may seem to some dull and uninteresting in these days of mechanical perfection, it has an important bearing upon the efficiency of the present day. Without this machine and other mechanical improvements of the day, business could not now be conducted on the enormous scale with which we are all so familiar. We would be back in the days of not very long ago when the head bookkeeper carried the figure-load of the firm in his head on a salary of thirty dollars a month. Often he had to carry the books home and dig out the results at night with pencil and pad-upon-pad of discarded figures. He continually existed in a state of fear and trembling because he did not know when some error might creep through that would cause him to lose his salary and his livelihood.

Mr. Frank Stephen Baldwin, the inventor of the Monroe Calculating Machine, is alive and still a force in the business, and had reached the age of eighty-four years when this article was written. He it was who invented and patented the Recording Lumber Measure. This was a machine which automatically measured and recorded four different kinds of lumber at the same time. It was this device which set Mr. Baldwin thinking about computing machines. This point really marks the birth of the Monroe.

In the office of a life insurance company at St. Louis, Mr. Baldwin had seen the Thomas type of calculating machine, devised by C. X. Thomas, of Kolmar, France, about 1820. He contrived the plan of substituting one cylinder for the nine cylinders in that machine, making a working model which is now in the Patent Office at Washington, D. C. It was on this model that Mr. Baldwin had William S. Burroughs, of adding machine fame, do some work for him. Mr. Burroughs' father had a small general machine shop in St. Louis. About 1880, Mr. Burroughs started work on his own adding machine with the keyboard setup. The meteoric success of the Burroughs business is now history.

In 1872 Mr. Baldwin moved to Philadelphia and rented a small shop and started to manufacture ten of his calculating machines. While thus engaged, he designed an adding machine which he named the Arithmometer. This patent, dated July 28, 1874, was the first one of the kind granted to Mr. Baldwin by the Patent Office at Washington. It was one of the first adding machines ever sold in the United States. It was at this time that the Franklin Institute of Philadelphia awarded the John Scott Medal to Mr. Baldwin for his calculating machine as a meritorious invention of the year. The only other man to receive a similar honor that year was George Westinghouse, for his air-brake.

The vicissitudes of the inventor of the Monroe Calculating Machine were many. It was not until 1911 that his fortunes changed. It was during that year that he first met Mr. Jay Randolph Monroe. Mr. Monroe was then associated with the Western Electric Company in New York City. He had always been of a mechanical turn of mind, and fortunately his work following his graduation from law at Michigan had been along clerical and commercial lines, rather than following the law. This brought him in close touch with calculating machines and the various uses to which they were being applied. He began to study them for their weaknesses, endeavoring to devise ways in which they could be improved.

When Mr. Monroe first saw Mr. Baldwin's machine, he at once recognized its possibilities. He was convinced that it measured up to the specifications which he knew business would eventually demand, namely, a machine which anyone could operate after a brief explanation; a machine which could accomplish the work with a minimum of effort; a machine which was portable; one that was simple in construction; one that furnished a visible check; a machine with a keyboard set-up; a machine that would not only add, but multiply, divide and subtract as easily as it could add.

Having met on a common ground, these two men joined hands and set about to design a machine and make it as nearly perfect as possible in its adaptation to the needs of modern business. Mr. Monroe immediately set about to organize the company which now bears his name. Work was started at the present location with three drill presses and a single lathe, the total value of the machinery at that time being about five hundred dollars. The manufacturing space required a part of one floor of the original site. Since that time the company has witnessed as much growth in seven years as many concerns have seen in thirty. Additions have been made to the old site from time to time, and in the fall of 1920 a four-story fire-proof structure of brick and concrete was completed to make room for the rapidly expanding business. The actual floor space has quadrupled since the Monroe first found its way on the market. About five hundred employees are now engaged in the manufacturing of this machine. Over one hundred and fifty offices rendering Monroe service are found in the principal cities of the United States and Canada, and in many of the larger cities throughout the world.

Many so-called calculating machines require weeks, often months, of training before the operator is equipped to apply same and obtain accurate results. Not so with the Monroe. The simple two-way mechanism enables anyone to handle successfully the most complicated figurework, from simple addition to complicated figuring involving cube and square root, after very little practice. The range of application is as wide as accounting itself. There is no figure-work known to pencil and pad which the Monroe cannot reduce to an easy machine process.

To give the reader an idea of the versatility of this machine, it was selected by the Government during the World War to compute the points necessary to range-finding at the various artillery fields. The reason that it was chosen for this important work was because of its speed in arriving at the results, as well as its absolute reliability. An artillery-man has to know his range in order to hit a certain spot, before he "lets go," and it was on this important job that the Monroe was used at many of the Government's proving grounds. One of the greatest drawbacks to the old style method of figuring by pencil and pad, not taking into consideration the errors that were likely to result, was the brain fatigue and the drudgery of it. Since the advent of the Monroe Calculating Machine, the employee is able to conserve his valuable brain energy for the essential policies of the business. Under the old-style method, the employee went home so brain-weary after poring over masses of figure detail that often he could not sleep; in fact, his time was so taken up during the day with figure detail that there was no possible way by which he could develop himself or improve the business. The Monroe Machine, by relieving this condition, not only leaves the employee time to improve himself physically, but to devote more and more of his time to constructive business policies.

The big idea back of the Monroe Calculating Machine Company is not so much that the company is selling machines, but that it is defining a service, of which the machine is but the instrument. To give the reader some idea of how the Monroe is defining its service to users—in seven years of active operation it has never known of a single dissatisfied user among the thousands that now dot the globe. Every year, service letters are sent out to all Monroe users seeking criticisms and suggestions, and it is inspiring to read the testimony of those who are fortunate enough to have Monroe Machines in their offices.

In a plant where mathematics and exactitude dominate, one would not be surprised if the human side of life were missing. In the Home of the Monroe, however, the human element is uppermost, and this feature is directly traceable to the pull-together spirit that makes for coöpera-tion in its highest form. It is a true example of what the American manufacturing organization can become—a school, social center, a place where work is a question of love and loyalty rather than enforced obli-gation. It is this spirit within the Monroe ranks which is the spirit of a great many American institutions and which has been responsible for the country's phenomenal progress within the past decade.

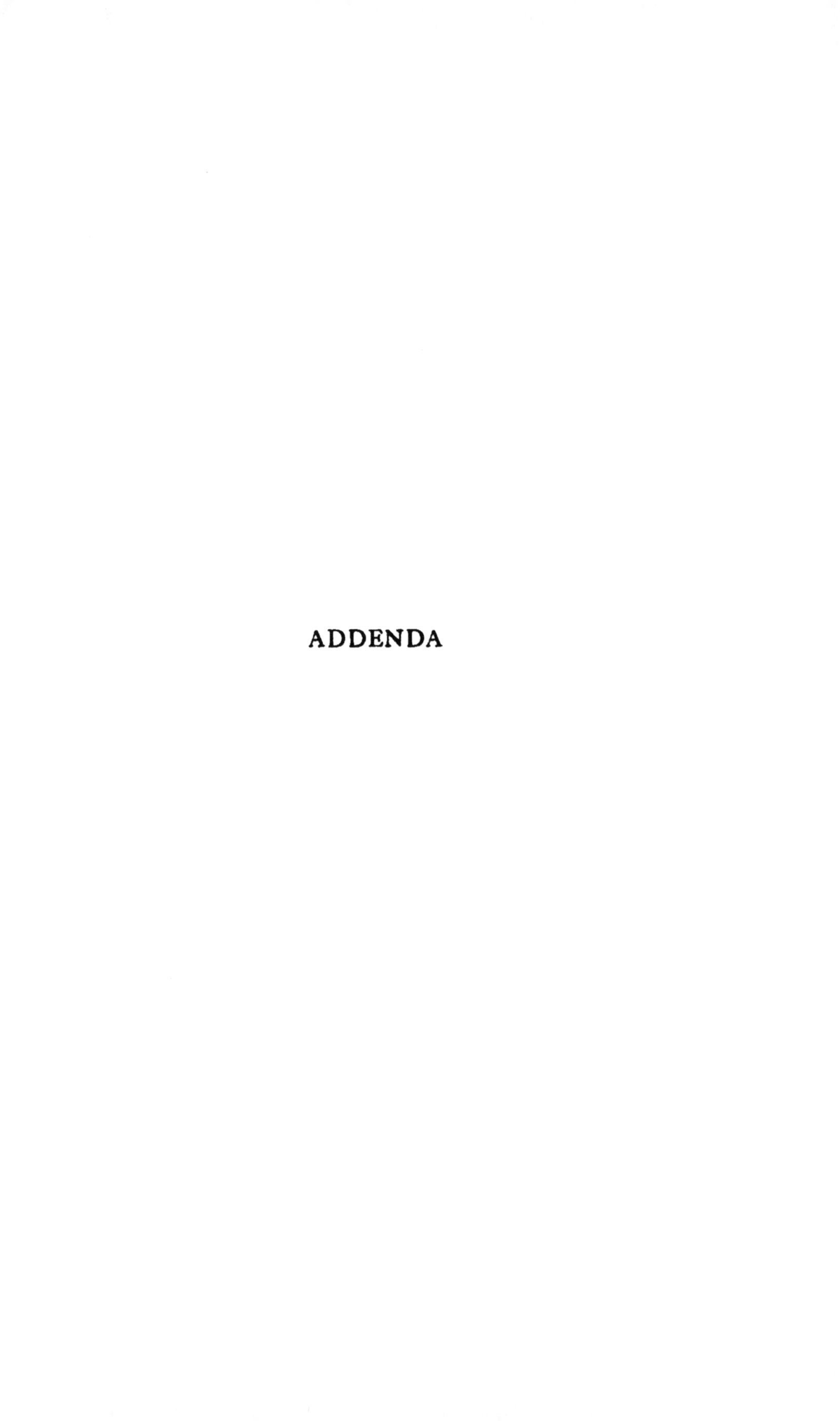

ADDENDA

RAILROAD JUNCTION, EAST ORANGE

ADDENDA

Advantage is being taken of the long interim following the preparation of the "History of the Oranges" and its presentation to the public, for the continuance of the narrative through the year 1921, principally for the purpose of having placed in this record an account of the extensive improvements being made along the Lackawanna railroad in East Orange. This is the final track change in the great system extending westward from Hoboken, and is the result of nearly twenty years of negotiations between the city and the railroad officials. The undertaking is one of the costliest in the entire chain of improvements along the line, and has not only changed topographical features of the city and destroyed landmarks, but has also disturbed innumerable business concerns. Operations began in the spring of 1921, the office of the directing engineer being in a building formerly occupied as a dwelling at the corner of Burnet street and the Lackawanna railroad.

In the vicinity of the Brick Church station the transformation was very noticeable. Shifting of the tracks southward to McKinley avenue left but a narrow sidewalk along the former thoroughfare for pedestrians. Evergreen place became a "dead-end" street, a high wire fence being constructed between the tracks and the sidewalk, which made it impossible for persons to reach the lane from the north side except at Harrison, Halsted and Clinton streets. Then came the destruction of the Brick Church depot, and with its disappearance business dropped low in Washington place and Railroad place, which had for years been a beehive of industrious tradesmen. Both East Orange and Brick Church depots were consolidated at a point on the south side of the tracks near Clinton street. The vicinity of the former Brick Church depot was forlorn looking, indeed. Next followed the ousting of the owners and tenants of the brick and wooden buildings extending along Railroad place from the westerly point of the old station to Harrison street, among the buildings removed being Berkeley Hall, a brick structure associated with many of the society events of a third of a century ago, and fronting on Harrison street. The removal of this building alone involved $45,000, the amount paid by the city of East Orange for the property.

Even greater changes were made around the East Orange station, where the row of brick buildings extending from Arlington avenue westerly and known at one time as the Doan block, were razed and a new street opened on the site. Other buildings were removed on Main street, some were partly destroyed, and one large brick structure owned by Richard Coyne was moved several feet southerly from the south side of Main street. The familiar old time "Junction," so named because of the street railroad tracks crossing there, has completely vanished. Notwithstanding the disrupted condition of the main thoroughfare at this section, the trolley and steam railroad service was but little deranged.

Corps of workmen under skilful guidance continued the operations every day in the week and late in the evening along the entire distance of about one mile and also on the Montclair branch, taking in the section known as Ampere which is incorporated in East Orange. The actual cost of the improvement will amount, it is believed, to about four million dollars, and East Orange will pay about five hundred thousand dollars. The tracks are to be elevated on an embankment, while the approaches to the East Orange, Brick Church, Grove street and Ampere stations are to be treated as ornately as the latest engineering devices can secure. Attractively arranged pillars made of concrete will support the roadbed, and the stations and shelter houses will be of the most approved and latest fashioned designs of architecture. They will surely be of great convenience to travelers on the road. It is expected to run trains over the new roadbed in August, 1922.

One of the direct results of these changes in the landscape was a blessing in disguise for the New Jersey Society, Sons of the American Revolution, which had occupied an office in the Berkeley Hall building since May 1, 1920. The Society was organized in 1889 for the purpose of maintaining the patriotic spirit created by the founders of the Republic, and to preserve traditions of the formative days, spread the gospel of Americanization, preserve the flag from the commercialist and the vandal, mark historical sites and scenes connected with the War for Independence, and to create a lively interest in the history of the American people. Ordered to vacate the premises, the board of managers saw no alternative but to secure permanent headquarters where the activities could be carried on undisturbed. On the anniversary of former President Theodore Roosevelt's birthday, October 27, 1921, the headquarters were removed from East Orange to 33 Lombardy street, Newark, where a handsome brownstone building was purchased and the Society ensconced most comfortably for the first time in nearly thirty-three years.

An acquisition to the general intellectual interests of East Orange is the institution of the Baptist International Seminary in the home formerly occupied by David S. Walton, at 34 Munn avenue. Another property was purchased at No. 32, which gives a complete plant for carrying on this feature of the educational work of the Baptists, which is to equip young men of foreign peoples for the ministry. The institution was dedicated on Columbus Day, October 12, 1921. Rev. Dr. Frank L. Anderson is president of the faculty, and Rev. Dr. Frank Austin Smith, of Elizabeth, is president of the board of trustees.

The Rotary Club of Orange, which meets once each week for lunch or dinner, is formed on the unique plan of one active and representative man from each line of business and profession in the community. The objects are to foster high ethical standards in business and professions, the ideal of service as the basis of all worthy enterprise, the active interest in civic, commercial, social and moral welfare of the community, the development of a broad acquaintanceship as an opportunity for service as well as to aid to success, the interchange of ideas and of business methods as a means of increasing the efficiency and usefulness of the members, and the recognition of the worthiness of all legitimate occupations as affording an opportunity to serve society. The Club has been well officered and has fulfilled the obligations of its members. Merrick R. Baldwin is the president at the end of the year 1921.

A long hoped for installation came in the latter part of the year, when the new electric lighting of Main street, from Brick Church to Arlington avenue, in East Orange, shed a glow over the thoroughfare, which fairly dazzled those who saw it for the first time. This long sought benefit was a Christmas gift, being introduced on December 3. Housing conditions, which were very embarrassing on account of the stoppage of building operations during the World War, show some signs of improvement during this year of 1921. It was said that in the year 1919 there were twenty thousand homeless families in Essex county. There was not an empty dwelling in the entire area, and in many instances homes were used by two or more families. The builders are at work, however, and the lack of dwellings will soon be overcome. As a quickening incentive, the Legislature of New Jersey offered through an act to exempt all dwellings from taxation for five years if built within a certain prescribed time, from October 1, 1920, to October 1, 1922.

The health of the community continues most excellent, under the constant watchfulness of the various Boards of Health, and there is grave doubt if an epidemic of any character will ever visit our community in the future.

An intensive American spirit having seized a number of Orange citizens of Italian birth, they have under the leadership of Raymond Bocca purchased the house and ground at the corner of Main and South Jefferson streets, Orange, where it is proposed to Americanize newly arrived countrymen. Formal dedication of the building, named the Dante House, in remembrance of the great Italian poet, occurred on the anniversary of the adoption of the Constitution of the United States, September 17, 1921. A central feature of the celebration was the dedication of a Liberty Pole from which the flag of Stars and Stripes has since been displayed. On the day of dedication the first emblem to be drawn to the top of the staff was the offering of Orange Chapter, New Jersey Society, Sons of the American Revolution. Its president, John Lenord Merrill, being absent, the presentation address was made by David L. Pierson, a former president of the chapter. During the program which followed, Mayor William A. Lord, Judge Ovido Bianchi,

Mr. Pierson, Miss Addie Crommelin, Ogden H. Bowers, and others, delivered addresses. Mr. Bocca presided, and music was furnished by a brass band. This was the only formal observance of Constitution Day in the Oranges, though the church bells were rung at the noon hour for three minutes.

Through the Community Chorus, organized several years ago by several hundred residents of the Oranges, a great deal of pleasure has been given the public. Rehearsals are given on stated evenings, and on June 9, 1921, an outdoor concert with dramatic effects was arranged in the Orange Park. Though a rainstorm interfered with the plans, the numbers were given with artistic skill and finish. Mrs. F. Westervelt Tooker is the leader in this enterprise.

Rev. Dr. Arthur Thomas Fowler, who has been pastor of the North Orange Baptist Church several years, resigned his charge in November, and is about to embark in a missionary survey in the Latin-American Republics. A fine spirit of service was displayed by about forty men and boys on Saturday afternoon, October 1, when, responding to the call of the president of the Old Burying Ground Association, they assisted in clearing the sacred tract at the corner of Main and Scotland streets, Orange. The party vigorously attacked the weeds, underbrush and other growth, while moving pictures were taken. On account of the high cost and scarcity of labor, the oldest cemetery in Essex county had been uncared for during the past three years, a condition brought about by the war. A plan is now being formulated to incorporate the association, secure a large endowment, and divert the interest toward the maintenance of the cemetery. Scotland street from Main street to Central avenue is paved with enduring material, making it a most attractive bouvlevard.

Dr. Edwin C. Broome, who administered the office of Superintendent of Public Schools of East Orange so thoroughly for the past seven years, resigned his position in April, 1921, and Dr. Clifford J. Scott was chosen as his successor.

A branch of the Kiwannis Club has been organized in East Orange, having Dr. George P. Olcott, Jr., as its president. The Club meets on Tuesday of each week, enjoys lunch, indulges in jocularity, and then projects some serious work for the community welfare.

Red Cross seals are sold each holiday season in the Oranges, as they are elsewhere, for the relief of the people from the white plague, or tuberculosis. The funds thus provided have assisted greatly in stamping out this disease which has slain thousands in the past years.

A number of the streets of Orange have had their names changed by order of the City Commission. Cone street has been eliminated and South Day street substituted therefor. Several other names have been changed.

Chief of Police John Drabell, who had faithfully served the Department of Public Safety of Orange for many years and who had attained the age of three score and ten, was retired on December 31, 1920, and on February 15, 1921, Joseph T. McGonnell was advanced from the ranks to the office vacated.

The maternity wing which had been in course of construction at the Orange Memorial Hospital during 1921, is now in use, the capacity of the hospital being about two hundred beds. Among its many useful agencies is the Graves Laboratory, contributed by Dr. William B. Graves.

Judge Worrall F. Mountain, who served acceptably as mayor of East Orange, is now a judge of the circuit, and sits in the Essex County Court House.

APPENDIX

APPENDIX

EARLY RECORDS

The following comprises the contents of the Record Book of the Annual Town Meetings of the Township of Orange from 1807 to 1845, the same being reproduced as nearly verbatim as modern types will allow. To these are added interesting extracts from the old Township Committee Book for the same series of years. The old Record Books were discovered by accident in the Orange National Bank building, and in 1897 were republished in "The Orange Chronicle."

1807.

April 13th, 1807. The first annual town meeting of the inhabitants of the Township of Orange was held at Orange Meeting house when the following Town officers were appointed and the following resolves were passed.

Moderator, Amos Harrison Esq.; Town Clerk, & c., Henry Stryker; Assessor, Doctr. Isaac Pierson; Collector, Nathan Squire; Township Committee, Daniel Williams, John Dean, Abijah Harrison, Stephen D. Day, Thomas Baldwin; Surveyors of the Highway, Stephen Tichenor, Jonas Smith; Judge of Election, Jabez B. Baldwin; Chosen Freeholders, John Lindsley, Esqr. Samuel Condit; Overseers of the Poor, Caleb Tichenor, John N. Baldwin; Committee of Appeal, David Meen, Jabez D. Kilburn, Abram Winans; Constables, John Quinby, Noah Matthews; Pound Master, Thomas Baldwin; Overseers of the Roads, Asa Perry, Joel Condit, Capt. Zenas Pierson, James Williams, Caleb Williams, Danl. Kilburn, Cyrenus Baldwin, Joseph Condit, Matthias Pierson, Jr., David Meen, Peter Dean, Daniel Dod, John Hedden, Jabez D. Kilburn, Stephen Jaggers, John Earl, Abraham Harrison, Thomas Baldwin, Joseph B. Ball, Timothy Ball, Daniel Edwards.

Resolves passed. That the Dog tax be appropriated to support the poor. That the business of the poor be left in the hands of the Overseers. That the sum of three hundred & 50 dollars be raised for the support of the poor the present year. That the pound master shall advertise three weeks in a public paper before sale. That the next town meeting be held at Thomas Bucbee's. That the election for the present year open at John Ming's and close at Samuel Meen's.

Henry Stryker, Clk.

1808.

April the 11th, 1808. The second annual Town Meeting of the Inhabitants of the Township of Orange was held at Orange Meeting house when the following Town officers were appointed and the following resolves were passed.

Moderator, Amos Harrison, Esqr.,; Town Clerk, Caleb Quinby; Assessor, Nathan Squire; Collector, John Quinby; Town Committee, Stephen D. Day, Thomas Baldwin, Daniel Williams, Jabez Pierson, Samuel Condit; Surveyors of the Highways, John Harrison, Josiah Baldwin; Overseers of the Poor, Caleb Tichenor, John N. Baldwin; Chosen Freeholders, Amos Harrison, Esqr., John Lindsley, Esqr.,; Commissioners of Appeals, Abraham Winans, Samuel Brown, Jonas Smith; Constables, Noah Matthews, Samuel Munn; Road Masters, Isaac Looker, John Corby, Samuel Williams, Jr., Zenas Pierson, Abijah Harrison, David Ogden, Jotham Condit, Jonathan Baldwin, Joseph Taylor, Moses Condit, Jr., Wm. Williams, Amos Freeman, Jeptha Baldwin, John Rewk, Henry Osborn, Moses Hand, Cyrus Freeman, Jotham Quinby, Moses O. Baker, Ethan Baldwin, Abner Crowel.

Resolves Passed. that the poor be farmed out to the lowest bider: that the sum of Six hundred and fifty Dollars be Raised for the Support of the poor the present year: that all the fines and astrays goes to the farmers of the poor the poor farmed out to Samuel Purey for the sum of three hundred and ninety-six dollars and twenty-five cents: that dog tax be appropriated to the support of the poor: that if any of the poor that is in dispute fall on this township that they Remain in the hands of the said overseers of the poor: that the overseers of the poor attend to the tuition of poor children: that if any of the poor that is farmed out that do not belong to this township the farmer to receive the same proportion of pay as in the first sale thereof. that the Election for the present year open at John Woodruff at Camptown and Close at Moses Condit jr's Orange: that the next annual town meeting open at Samuel Munn at Orange.

Caleb Quinby, Clk.

1809.

April 10, 1809 The third annual Town meeting of the Inhabitants of the Township of Orange was held at Orange Meeting house when the following Town officers were appointed, and the following resolves were passed.

Moderator, Major Jabez Pierson; Town Clerk, Nathl. Bruen; Assessor, Dr. Isaac Pierson; Collector, John Quimby; Town Committee, Daniel Williams, Abm. Winans, Saml. Condit, Capt. Thomas Baldwin, Josiah Baldwin; Surveyors of the Highway, Stephen Tichenor, Jonas Smith; Judge of Election, Samuel Munn; Overseers of the Poor, Capt. Caleb Tichenor, John N. Baldwin; Freeholders, Samuel Condit, Samuel Lyndsley; Commissioners of Appeal, Abijah Harrison Daniel Dod, Abm. Harrison; Constables, Noah Matthews, Peter Dean, Nathan Tichenor; Overseers of the Highway, Jonathan Condit, junr. John Corby, Erastus Pierson, Henery Townley, John Williams, Daniel Ward, Ichd. Harrison, Ezra Baldwin, Joseph Condit, Abm. Winans, John Peck Jun. Amos Freeman, William Stockman, Abner L. Kilburn, Elias Osburn, Deacon Saml. Pierson, Enos Tompkins, Aron Quimby, Joseph Durand, Capt. Thomas Baldwin, Thomas Tichenor.

Resolves Passed. That the Township unite with the county in building a poor house. That the poor Shall be farmed out this year in the same manner that they were the last year & that the education of the poor Children shall be under the direction of the Overseers at the expense of the Township. That the emoluments arising from the Dog-tax be appropriated for the support of the poor. That the money arising from the sale of strays be paid to those who farm the poor, & that the farmer indemnify the Town against any additional expense for the present year on account of the poor. The poor farmed out to John N. Baldwin for Three hundred & eighty nine Dollars. That six hundred Dollars be raised for the support of the poor the present year. That any person suffering their Swine after the age of three months to run in the public highway without a ring in the nose from the 1st of May to the 1st of November shall pay to the Overseers of the poor Seventy-five Cents each for the use of the Township & that it shall be the duty of the Overseers of the poor on complaint to prosecute for the same. That the bal. on hand due to the Township held by Stephen Day be disposed of by the Town committee to the best advantage at interest. That the next election for Members of Assembly & other officers be opened at Henery Squire's & closed at Saml. Munn's.

Nathl. Bruen, Clk.

At the third annual Town Meeting the place for opening the fourth Annual T. Meeting was neglected, on account of which neglect a Special meeting of the Electors of the Township were called as the law directs which met at Samuel Munn's. Capt. Isaac Matthews was chosen Moderator.· Resolved that the fourth Annual Town Meeting be opened at Samuel Munn's Hotel.

Nathl. Bruen, Clk.

1810.

April 9, 1810. The fourth annual Town Meeting of the Inhabitants of the Township of Orange was held at Orange Meeting House when the following Town officers were appointed and the following resolves passed.

Moderator, Amos Harrison, Esq.; Town Clerk, Nathl. Bruen; Assessor, Daniel Condit; Collector, John Quimby; Town Committee, Thomas Baldwin, Daniel Williams, Stephen D. Day, Josias Baldwin, Saml. Condit.: Surveyors Highways, Jonas Smith, Daniel Dod; Judge of Election, Samuel Munn; Overseers Poor, Caleb Tichenor, John N. Baldwin; Freeholders, Samuel Condit, Amos Harrison, Esq., Commissioners of Appeal, Isaac Matthews, Abijah Harrison, Samuel Brown; Constables, Noah Matthews, Peter Dean, John Hedden. Overseers of Highways, Enos Pierson, Joel Condit, Samuel Williams, junr. Zenas Pierson, Aron Harrison, Ebenezer Matthews, Linas Dod, Jonathan Baldwin, John Harrison, Peter Dean, Lewis Munn, Amos Freeman, Josias Baldwin, Ebenezer Havens, John Earl, Moses Hand, Cyrus Freeman, Jotham Quimby, Ezekiel Ball, Ethan Baldwin, Linas Ball.

Resolves passed. That the Poor be farmed out this year in the same manner they were the last excepting..........& four children, the children to be bound out and a place provided with suitable accommodations for..........under the direction of the overseer. That Five hundred dollars be raised for the support of the poor the present year. That the monies arising from the sale of strays be appropriated to the use of the Township. That the money on hand due the Township be disposed of by the Town Committee the whole or in part as may be necessary in putting out the poor children, if any overplus to be loaned out at interest. That a pound be erected at Capt. Thomas Baldwin & that Capt. T. Baldwin be the pound master. The swine tax to be continued in force from the present to the next annual Town Meeting. The Poor farmed out this year to Samuel Perry for Three hundred and sixty eight Dollars, & to indemnify the Town against any additional expense, to provide cloathing & Provisions for them.

8. That the Election for the present year open at Henery Squire's & close at Moses Condit Junr's.

9. That the next Town Meeting open at Moses Condit, Jun. at Orange.

Nathl. Bruen Clk.

1811.

April 8, 1811. The fifth Annual Town meeting of the Inhabitants of the Township of Orange was held at Orange Meeting House when the following Town officers were appointed & the following resolves passed.

Moderator, Amos Harrison, Esq.; Town Clerk, Nathaniel Bruen; Assessor, Daniel Condit, Junr.; Collector, John Quimby; Town Committee, Daniel Williams, Josias Baldwin, Capt. Thos. Baldwin, Stephen D. Day, Esqr., Aron Harrison; Surveyors of Highway, Stephen Tichenor Junr. John Ball; Judge of Election, Major Jabez Pierson; Overseers of the Poor, Samuel Condit, John N. Baldwin; Freeholders, Amos Harrison, Esq. Samuel Lindsley; Commissioners of Appeal, John Harrison, Samuel Brown, Daniel Dod; Constables, Noah Matthews, John Hedden; Overseers of Highway, John Perry, Israel Brundridge, Zephia Condit, Henery Townley, Benjamin Williams, Junr. Matthew Williams, Timothy Ward, John N. Campbell, Caleb Hedden, Capt. Moses Condit, Isaac Munn, Jabez Pierson, Davis Kilburn, Moses Stockman, Doctr. W. Bonnel, Stephen Bruen, Joseph B. Telue, John Quinby, Capt. Abeel Hays, Ethan Baldwin, John Ball.

Resolves Passed. 1. That the poor be farmed out this year to the lowest bidder. That..........be included among the number of the poor farmed out the present year. That four children belonging to the family of the Poor be bound out this year. (Then follow the names which are suppressed for obvious reasons.) That five hundred Dollars be raised for the support of the Poor the present year. That the Town committee shall pay the funeral expenses of Stephen Osburn. That no pound shall be erected in the Township. That the Township unite with the county in building a Poor house. The Poor farmed out this year to Aron Quinby for Three hundred and eighty six Dollars. That the election for the present year open at William Stockman's Camptown, & close at Samuel Munn's Orange. That the next Town meeting open on the green below the meeting house.

Amos Harrison, Moderator, Nathl. Bruen, Clk.

1812.

April 12, 1812. The Sixth Annual Town Meeting of the Inhabitants of the Township of Orange was held at the meeting house when the following Town officers were appointed and the following resolves passed.

Moderator, Amos Harrison, Esq., Town Clerk Nathaniel Bruen; Assessor, Daniel Condit,; Collector, John Quinby; Town Committee

Daniel Dod, Enos Pierson, Abner Crowel, Josiah Baldwin, Abijah Harrison.; Surveyors of Highway Major Jabez Pierson, Daniel Kilburn; Judge of Election, Jeptha Baldwin; Overseers of the Poor, John Harrison, Abm. Baldwin; Freeholders, Amos Harrison Esqr. Samuel Condit; Commissioners of Appeal, Capt. Jonas Smith, Simon Condit, Cyrus Jones.; Constables, Noah Matthews, John Hedden; Overseers of Highway, Nathan Williams, Asa Perry, Amos Williams, Zenas Pierson, Zenas Williams, Joel Williams,. Ichabod Harrison, Lewis Dod, William Williams, Joseph Condit Junr., David Munn, Major Jabez Pierson, Benjamin Lindsley, Aron Hedden, Elias Osburn, Nathaniel B. Gardner Jacob Walker, Hiram Quinby, Abm. Harrison, Ethan Baldwin, Job Crowel, James Reynolds.

Resolves Passed. That the poor be farmed out this year to the lowest bidder; That Three Hundred Dollars be raised for the support of the Poor the present year; That the Town Committee be instructed to procure a Book in which they are to designate and make out to each Overseer of the Highway his particular district in such a manner as shall be distinctly understood; A motion was made (and carried by vote to be laid over for the consideration of the next Town Meeting) for the destroying of destructive birds. The poor farmed out this year to Asa Perry for Three hundred and fifty-eight dollars.; That the election for the present year open at the House of Henery Squire, (if the sign of public admittance continue) otherwise at the house of William Stockman, Camp Town, & close at Moses Condit's; That the next Town meeting open on the green below the meeting House.

Amos Harrison Moderator, Nathaniel Bruen Clk.

1813.

April 12, 1813. The Seventh Annual Town Meeting of the Inhabitants of the Township of Orange was held at the Meeting House when the following Town officers were appointed and the following resolves passed.

Moderator, Amos Harrison, Esqr.; Town Clerk, Nathaniel Bruen; Assessor, Daniel Condit, Junr.; Collector, John Quinby; Town Committee, Abijah Harrison, Abner Crowel, Enos Pierson, Josiah Baldwin, Abraham Winans; Surveyors of Highways, Jonas Smith, Samuel Brown; Judge of Election, Noah Matthews; Overseers of the Poor, Abraham Baldwin, William Williams; Freeholders, Samuel Condit, Amos Harrison, Esqr.; Commissioners of Appeal, Stephen Tichenor, Samuel Brown, Joel Harrison; Constables, Josiah Leonard, John Reuck; Overseers of Highways, Reuben Ward, William Perry, Henery Townley, Stephen Tichenor, Uzal Dod, Caleb Hedden, Timothy Williams, Caleb Harrison, John Peck, Freeman, Benjamin Lindsley, Moses Osburn, Elihu Crowel, Timothy Ball, Cyrus Freeman, Ezra Gildersleeve, Joseph Durand, Stephen Hedley, Junr. Aron Crowel, Daniel Dod, Abijah Harrison, Erastus Pierson, Jacob Harrison.

Resolves passed. That four hundred Dollars be raised for the support of the Poor for the present year; That the Poor be farmed out the present year in the same manner they were the last with the exception of Mrs. ———. That the Overseers of the Highway for the present year be enjoined to render in to the Town Committee on the Second monday of May, next ensuing, the bounds of their several districts, with the number of persons and names employed in each; The Poor farmed out this year to Stephen Tichenor for Four hundred Dollars with whom it is understood the following persons are in connection. (Here follow the names.) Mrs. ———— is to be provided for in a separate manner under the direction of the Overseers. That the election for the present year open at Frederick Gruet's Camp Town & close at Ire Munn, Orange. That the next annual Town Meeting open on the green below the Meeting House.

Amos Harrison Moderator, Nathl. Bruen, Clk.

1814.

April 11 1814. The Eighth Annual Town Meeting of the Inhabitants of the Township of Orange was held at the house of Moses Condit, Junr. when the following Town Officers were appointed.

Moderator, Noah Matthews; Town Clerk, Daniel Kilburn; Assessor, Daniel Condit, Junr.; Collector, John Quinby; Town Committee, Daniel Dod, Abijah Harrison, Abraham Winans, Josiah Baldwin, Abner Crowel.; Surveyors Highway, Moses Condit, Junr., Joel Harrison; Judge of Election, Noah Matthews; Overseers of Poor, William Williams, Jeptha Baldwin; Free Holders, Samuel Condit, Nathan Squier; Commissioners of Appeal, Timothy Williams, Samuel Brown, Moses Condit; Constables, Josiah Leonard, John Reock; Overseers of the Highway, Ira Pierson, John Corby Junr., Henry Townly, Samuel Condit, Zebina Dod, Lewis Dod, Isaac Pierson, Daniel Lindsley, Cyrus Jones, John Hedden, John Lindsley, Esqr., Abraham Baldwin, John Taylor, Nathaniel Brown, Abrm. P. Meeker, Amos Harrison, Junr., Abial Hayes, Ethan Baldwin, Joseph B. Ball, Daniel Porter, Moses R. Gardner, Jashia Condit, Jacob Walker.

Resolves passed. 1st. That Six Hundred Dollars be raised for the support of the poor the present year. 2d. That the poor be farmed out the present year in the same manner they were the last year. 3d. The poor farmed out this year to John Perry, Junr., for five hundred & seventy nine Dollars fifty Cents. 4th. That the Election for the present year open at the house of Frederick Gruet in Camp town and Close at the house of Moses Condit, Junr. in Orange. 5th. That the next Annual Town meeting open at the house of Ira Munn.

Noah Matthews, Moderator, Daniel Kilburn, Clk.

In Consequence of the Refusal of Isaac Pierson to serve as Overseer of the Highway a special Town Meeting was Called agreeable to law—

Major Abraham Winans was appointed Moderator.

The meeting made choice of Daniel P. Stryker as overseer of the highway in the place of Isaac Pierson, declined.

Orange May 5, 1814.

Abraham Winans, Moderator, Daniel Kilburn, Clk.

1815.

April 10, 1815. The ninth Annual town meeting of the inhabitants of the township of Orange was held at the house of Ira Munn when the following town officers were appointed.

Moderator, Amos Harrison; Town Clerk, Daniel Kilburn; Assessor, Daniel Condit, Junr; Collector, John Quinby; Judge of Election, Jabez Pierson; Town Committee, Abraham Winans, Abijah Harrison, Abner Crowel, Josiah Baldwin, Nathan Williams; Surveyors of the Highway, Joel Harrison, Aaron Brown; Overseers of the Poor, William Williams, Jeptha Baldwin; Freeholders, Amos Harrison, Nathan Squier; Commissioners of Appeal, Moses Condit, Samuel Brown; Constables, David Ball, John Reuck; Overseers of Highway, Moses S. Williams, Asa Perry, Henry Townley, Moses Williams Junr. Timothy Weirel, Jun'r. Noah Baldwin, Nathaniel Harrison, Noah Matthews, Isaac Munn, Job Brown, Uzal Baldwin, Abraham Baldwin, Nathan Tichenor, William Young, Samuel Freeman Junr. Jonas Smith, Obadiah Crane, Isaac M. Tichenor, Aaron Ball, Moses Dodd, Benjamin Williams Junr. Daniel Williams Junr., Peter Peck.

Resolves passed. 1st. Resolved that One Thousand Dollars be raised for the support of the Poor. 2d. Resolved that the poor of the Township be left in the hands of the Overseers of the poor to be provided for in such manner as they shall think proper. 3d. Resolved that the next Annual Election open at the house of Frederick Gruet's in Camp Town and close at the house of Ira Munn's. 4th. Resolved that the next Annual Town Meeting open at the house of Moses Condit, Junr.

Orange April 10th 1815.

Amos Harrison, Moderator, Daniel Kilburn, Clerk.

1816.

April 8th 1816. The tenth annual Town Meeting of the Inhabitants of the Township of Orange was holden on the Common opposite the House of Moses Condit Junr. when the following Town Officers were elected.

Moderator, Amos Harrison; Town Clerk Daniel Babbit; Assessor, Daniel Condit Junr Collector, John Quinby; Judge of Election, Noah Matthews; Town Committee, Abraham Winans, Josiah Baldwin, Daniel Dod, Abijah Harrison, Abner Crowel, Surveyors of the Highway; Daniel Smith, Joel Harrison; Overseers of the Poor, Noah Matthews, Jeptha Baldwin; Chosen Freeholders, Amos Harrison, Samuel Condit. Commissioners of Appeal, Moses Condit Junr. Jonas Smith, Samuel Brown; Constables, John Reock, Cyrus Baldwin; Overseers of the Road, Lewis Pierson, John Corby, Joseph Pierson Junr. Abraham Day, Abiel Dod, Lewis Dod, Isaac Matthews, Daniel Smith, Ichabod Jones, Amos Freeman, Jeptha Baldwin, Sayers Roberts, John S. Taylor, Timothy Ball, Abrm. P. Meeker, John Quinby, Aron Allen, Ethan Baldwin, David J. Beach, Daniel Dod, Charles Harrison, Caleb Pierson, John Ensley.

The poor of the township were set up at public sale & knocked off to Aron Quinby, for Seven Hundred & fifty Eight Dollars, & the town to be indemnified.

Resolutions of the Town Meeting. 1st. That the Poor of the Township be farmed out the present year. 2d. That one thousand Dollars be assessed on the Township, for the Support of the Poor the present year. 3d. That the Elections for the present year, open at Gruet's Tavern in Camptown & close at Moses Condit Junr's Tavern in Orange. 4th. That the next annual Town Meeting be opened at the House where Ira Munn now lives. 5th. That this meeting instruct their Chosen Freeholders to use their influence with the Board of the Chosen Freeholders of the County at their next annual meeting in establishing a County Poor House—but, should they fail in this, that they request the Town Committee to call a Special Town meeting to consult on the Expediency of procuring a poor house for the use of the Township of Orange.

Danl. Babbit, Clk.   Amos Harrison, Moderator.

Sept. 26th, 1816. A Special Town meeting convened at the house of Moses Condit Junr. agreeably to previous notice given when Col. Abrm. Winans was chosen Moderator.

The Subject of providing a Poor House for the use of the Poor of the Township—the Object for which the Meeting was called—was taken up, discussed, & the following Resolutions were unanimously adopted.

1st. That the Town Committee be instructed to make application to the Legislature of this State at their next Sitting, for a Law to exempt the Township of Orange from their liability to pay their proportion of the Expenses of a County Poor House, on Condition that the Township of Orange should provide a House for the use of their own Poor.

2d. That the Town Committee be instructed to make diligent Enquiries, on what terms a suitable plan for the accommodation of the Poor may be obtained—& should the above mentioned Law be passed & other circumstances in their opinion render it necessary, that they be authorized and required to call a special Town Meeting to take the matter into consideration.

3rd. That Notice of the application about to be made to the Legislature be given in the public prints. Adjourned.

D. Babbit, Clk.   Abrm. Winans, Moderator.

1817.

The eleventh annual Town Meeting of the Inhabitants of the Township of Orange was held at the house of Daniel Kilburn, when the following Town officers were duly elected.

Moderator, Amos Harrison; Town Clerk, Daniel Kilburn; Assessor, Daniel Condit, Junr.; Collector, John Quinby; Judge of Election, Jabez Pierson; Town Committee, Jonas Smith, William Williams, Josiah Baldwin, Daniel Dod, Abijah Harrison; Surveyors of Highway, Joel Harrison, Moses Condit, Junr.; Overseers of Poor, Noah Matthews, Jeptha Baldwin; Chosen Freeholders, Samuel Condit, Amos Harrison; Commissioners of Appeal, John Harrison, Samuel Brown, Timothy Williams; Constables, John Reuck, Cyrus Baldwin; Overseer of Roads, Ira Mun, Henry Meyers, Bethuel Harrison, Benjamin Mun, Junr., Jonathan Lindsley, Frederick Gruet, Isaac T. Tichenor, Stephen Bruen, Joseph B. Tillou, Caleb Smith, Obadiah Crane, Phineas Baldwin, Linas Ball, Daniel D. Condit, Benjamin Williams, Junr., Bethuel Williams, Moses Harrison, John Perry, Junr., Ambrose Condit, Benjamin Townley, David D. Baldwin, Ichabod Harrison, Noah Baldwin.

RESOLUTIONS OF THE TOWN MEETING.

1st. That all the Children belonging to the Town that are eight years old and upwards are to be bound out, the boys till they are fifteen years old, and the girls until they are eighteen, with The exception of Nathaniel Condit.

2d. That the poor of the Township be farmed out for the present year.

3d. That One Thousand Dollars be raised for the support of the poor the present year.

4th. That the Election for the present year open at the house of Isaac Combs in South Orange and Close at the house of Daniel Kilburn.

5th. That the next annual Town Meeting open at the house of Moses Condit, Junr., at two o'clock P. M.

6th. That this meeting instruct their Chosen Freeholders to apply to the Board of Freeholders of the County to build a County Poor House.

The poor farmed out the present year to Moses Jones for Nine Hundred forty nine Dollars and the Town to be indemnifyed.

Daniel Kilburn, Clk.   Amos Harrison, Moderator.

1818.

April 13th, 1818. The twelfth Annual Town Meeting of the Inhabitants of the township of Orange was held at the house of Moses Condit, Junr. when the following town officers were duly Elected.

Moderator, Noah Matthews; Town Clerk, Daniel Kilburn; Assessor, Daniel Condit, Junr.; Collector, John Quinby; Judge of Election, Noah Matthews; Town Committee, Abijah Harrison, Abraham Winans, Abner Crowel, Nathan Williams, Jonas Smith; Surveyors of Highway, Moses Condit, Junr. Daniel Smith; Overseers of the Poor, Noah Matthews, Jeptha Baldwin; Freeholders, Amos Harrison, Josiah Baldwin; Commissioners of Appeal, John Harrison, Saml. Brown, Jabez D. Kilburn; Constables, John Hedden, John Reock; Overseers of Highway, Ezra Gildersleeve, Abial Hays, Ethan Baldwin, Joseph B. Ball, Daniel Dodd, Abiathar Harrison, Japhia Condit, Jotham Freeman, Benjamin Ward, Moses S. Brundage, Samuel Pierson, Josiah Frost, Silas Munn, Lewis Dodd, Isaac Pierson, Wheeler Lindsley, Jabez Pierson, John T. Munn, Jabez D. Kilburn, Aaron Hedden, Daniel Baldwin, Timothy Baldwin, William Smith.

The Poor farmed out to Abraham P. Meeker for six Hundred and seventy-three Dollars and He to indemnify the Town.

RESOLUTIONS OF THE TOWN MEETING.

1st. The Poor to be farmed out the present year. 2d. That Eight Hundred dollars be raised for the support of the Poor the present year. 3d. That the town Committee consider the turnpike road through Orange beginning at the Great Meadow Brook as respects the number of hands to be set off to work the same as a district road and the South Orange turnpike road to be worked on the same principle. 4th. That the next Annual Election open at the house of Nathaniel Seabury in Camp Town and close at the house of Moses Condit, Junr. in Orange. 5th. That the next Annual Town Meeting open at the house of Daniel Kilburn at 2 o'clock P. M.

Noah Matthews, Moderator, Daniel Kilburn, Town Clerk.

1819.

April 14th 1819. The thirteenth annual Town meeting was held at the house of Daniel Kilburn, when the following Town-officers were duly elected, viz:

Moderator, Amos Harrison; Town Clerk, Danl. Kilburn; Assessor, Danl. Condit; Junr—; Collector, John Quinby; Judge of Election, Jeptha Baldwin; Town Committee, Abraham Winans, Abner Crowel, Timothy Williams, Noah Matthews, Jonas Smith; Surveyors of Highway, Moses Condit Junr., Ichabod Condit; Overseers of the Poor, William Williams, John Ball; Commissioners of Appeal, Cyrus Jones, Saml. Brown, Abraham Winans; Freeholders, Amos Harrison, Josiah Baldwin; Constables, John Reock, John Hedden; Road Masters, Jotham Quinby, Abial Hays, Stephen Headley, Aaron Brown, Saml. B. Williams, Jotham Pierson, Stephen Harrison, Danl. Pierson, Asa Perry, Zenas Pierson, Ichabod Locey, Caleb Hedden, Stephen D. Day, Zebulon Myses, Saml. Brown, Wm. Peck, Jeptha Baldwin, Abraham Baldwin, John S. Taylor, Saml. Pierson, Saml. Freeman Junr.

The Poor farmed out for the present year, to Saml. Freeman, Junr. for

RESOLUTIONS OF THE TOWN MEETING.

1st. That Mrs. C—— be put out to David S. Roff, at six shillings per week. 2d. That J—— W—— be put out to Moses Quinby at twelve shillings per week. 3d. That the Poor be farmed out for the present year. 4th. That one thousand dollars be raised for the support of the poor the present year. 5th. That the Town Committee put the law in force against all delinquent Road Masters. 6th. That the Town Committee deliver certificates to each Road Master of their appointment. 7th. That the next annual election open at Isaac Combs's & close at Daniel Kilburn's. 8th. That the next annual Town meeting open at Isaac Comb's at o'clock P. M.

Amos Harrison, Moderator, Danl. Kilburn, Clerk.

1820.

April 10th, 1820. The fourteenth annual Town Meeting of the Inhabitants of the Township of Orange was held at the house of Isaac Combs, when the following Town Officers were duly elected.

Moderator, Noah Matthews; Town Clerk, Daniel Kilburn; Assessor, Daniel Condit, Junr.; Collector, John Quinby; Judge of Election, Abraham Winans; Town Committee, Noah Matthews, Cyrus Jones, Jonas Smith, Joel Harrison, Daniel Dodd; Surveyors of Highway, Ichabod Condit, Moses Condit, Junr.; Overseers of Poor, Edwin Gray, William Williams; Commissioners of Appeal, Daniel Dodd, Abraham Winans, Henry B. Campbell; Freeholders, Amos Harrison, Josiah Baldwin; Constables, John Reuck, John Hedden; Overseers of Highway, Isaac Baldwin, Abraham Harrison, Enos Baldwin, Joseph B. Ball, Ira Harrison, Silas D. Condit, Hiram Quinby, Ira Pierson, Asa Perry, Henry Townley, William P. Soveril, John S. Baldwin, Moses Condit, Junr., Stephen Condit, Edwin Gray, Viner Van Zandt Jones, Benjamin Lindsley, Joel Harrison, Jabez B. Baldwin, Stephen Ball, Ziba Tompkins, Ichabod Harrison.

RESOLUTIONS OF THE TOWN MEETING.

1st. That eight hundred (800) Dollars be raised for the support of the Poor. 2d. That the next Annual Town Meeting open at the house of Moses Condit Junr. at 2 o'clock (P. M.) 3rd. That the Annual Election open at the house of Isaac Combs in South Orange and close at the house of Moses Condit Junr. in Orange. 4th. That N—— W—— and

Mrs. W—— be farmed out for the present year and the farmer to indemnify the Town and the remaining poor now on the Town be left in the hands of the Overseers.

The Poor farmed out to Isaac T. Tichenor for two hundred and twenty (220) Dollars and he to indemnify the Town against all the Poor that may come in the Town for one year.

Noah Matthews, Moderator, Daniel Kilburn, Clk.

July 17th, 1820. A Special Town Meeting convened at the house of Daniel Kilburn for the purpose of appointing an Assessor, in the room of Daniel Condit Junr. decd. agreeable to previous notice given when Noah Matthews was chosen Moderator.

Assessor, Jonas Smith.

In consequence of appointing Jonas Smith Assessor there was a vacancy in the Town Committee and John Harrison was chosen to fill the same.

Noah Matthews, Moderator, Daniel Kilburn, Town Clerk.

1821.

April 9th, 1821. The fifteenth annual Town Meeting of the Inhabitants of the Township of Orange was held this day at the house of Lydia Condit, when the following Town Officers were duly elected.

Moderator, Noah Matthews; Town Clerk, Daniel Kilburn; Assessor, Jonas Smith; Collector, John Quinby; Judge of Election, Noah Matthews; Town Committee, Ambrose Condit, Abraham Winans, Ichabod Condit, Daniel Dodd, Stephen Bruen; Surveyors of Highway, Daniel Kilburn, Stephen Condit; Overseers of the Poor, William Williams, Edwin Gray; Commissioners of Appeal, Abraham Winans, Joel Harrison, Daniel Smith; Chosen Freeholders, Amos Harrison, Josiah Baldwin; Constables, John Reuck, John Hedden; Overseers of Highway, Jonas Smith, Obediah Crane, Jotham M. Baldwin, John Dreever, Benjamin Williams, Junr. Amos Williams, David Walker, Ira Pierson, Asa Perry, John P. Crowel, Samuel Condit, Junr. Caleb Hedden, Joseph Lyon, John Doane, Caleb Harrison, John Peck, Jeptha Baldwin, Stephen Jaggers, Stephen Tichenor, Nathaniel Brown, Abiathar Freeman, Samuel M. Dodd.

RESOLUTIONS PASSED.

Resolved, 1st. That four hundred Dollars be raised for the support of the Poor. 2d. That the next annual Town Meeting open at the House of Daniel Kilburn at two O'Clock (P. M.) 3d. That the Annual Election open at the house of Nathaniel Seabury in Camptown and close at the house of Daniel Kilburn in Orange.

The Poor Farmed out to Isaac Taylor for two hundred Dollars and he to indemnify the Town against all the poor that may come on the Town for the space of one year.

Noah Matthews, Moderator,
Daniel Kilburn, Clerk.

1822.

April 10th, 1822. The Sixteenth Annual Townmeeting of the Inhabitants of the Township of Orange was held this day at the house of Daniel Kilburn when the following Town Officers were duly Elected.

Moderator, Joel Harrison; Town Clerk, Daniel Kilburn; Assessor, Jonas Smith; Collector, John Quinby; Judge of Election, Noah Matthews; Town Committee, Jeptha Baldwin, Joel Harrison, Abraham Winans, Ichabod Condit, Ambrose Condit; Surveyors of Highway, Stephen Condit, Henry B. Campbell; Overseers of Poor, William Williams, Edwin Gray; Commissioners of Appeal, Samuel Brown, Daniel Dodd, Daniel Smith; Chosen Freeholders, Amos Harrison, Josiah Baldwin; Constables, John Reuck, Bethuel Pierson; Overseers of Highway, Daniel Quinby, Abraham Harrison, Stephen Hedley, Joseph B. Ball, Nathaniel Williams, Linas Williams, Joseph Matthews, Ira Condit, Benjamin Townley, Ira Harrison, David Brown, Samuel Camp, Charles Lighthipe, Aaron Peck, Thomas D. Kilburn, Ebenezer Havens, Zebulon Jennings, David Hand, Abraham Pellacker, Stephen Dodd, Lewis Dodd.

RESOLUTIONS OF THE TOWN MEETING.

Resolved that the next Annual Election open at the house of Nathaniel Seabury in Camptown and close at the house of Lydia Condit in Orange.

Also that the next Annual Town Meeting be opened at the House of Lydia Condit at two O'Clock (P. M.) That eight hundred Dollars be raised for the support of the Poor the ensuing year. The Poor farmed out to John Hedden for five hundred sixty eight dollars for one year and he to indemnify the town against all the Poor that may come in the Town in one year.

Joel Harrison, Moderator,
Daniel Kilburn, Clerk.

1823.

April 14th 1823. The Seventeenth Annual Town Meeting of the Inhabitants of the Township of Orange was held at the house of Lydia Condit when the following Town officers were duly elected.

Moderator, Amos Harrison; Town Clerk, Daniel Kilburn; Assessor, Amos A. Harrison; Collector, John Quinby; Judge of Elections, Abraham Winans; Town Committee, Ambrose Condit, Joel Harrison, Ichabod Condit, Daniel Dodd, Jonas Smith; Surveyors of Highway, Jabez D. Kilburn, Ichabod Harrison; Overseers of Poor, William Williams, Caleb Harrison; Commissioners of Appeal, John Dean, Benjamin Williams, Junr., Moses Lindsley; Freeholders, Amos Harrison, Josiah Baldwin; Constables, John Reock, Bethuel Pierson; Overseers of Highway, James Smith, Phineas Baldwin, John S. Orsborn, David J. Beach, Ichabod Williams, Daniel S. Williams, Joseph Harrison, John Perry, Jotham Condit, Ambrose Condit, Benjamin Townley, Daniel Ward, Daniel Dodd, John Lindsley, Wm. Peck, Jeptha Baldwin, Moses Stockman, Alvin Tichenor, Daniel Reeves, Amos Freeman, Junr., Abial Dodd, Noah Baldwin, Moses Lindsley.

The Poor farmed out to Abraham P. Meeker for

A Motion was made to change the mode of working the Highway and on taking the vote it was carried that the roads should be worked as usual instead of raising money by Tax.

RESOLUTIONS PASSED.

First, That twelve hundred Dollars be raised for the Support of the Poor. 2d. That the following list of Paupers, be left in the hands of the overseers of the Poor viz, Mrs. Phebe C——, John T——, Mary T——, Joannah T——, John T——, Berton W——, Amzi W——, Joseph T——, & Nancy C——. 3d. That the overseers of the Pay Samuel Dodd twenty-five dollars provided he will take Mrs. G——'s child and keep it till of full age. 4th. That the Poor be farmed out and the farmer to indemnify the Town. 5th. That forty Dollars be appropriated to Phebe C——, and her friends to indemnify the Town for one year. 6th. That the Overseers of the Highway make returns to the Town Committee of those that do road duty or be fined for neglect of duty. 7th. That the next election open at the house of Isaac Combs, and close at the house of Daniel Kilburn. 8th. That the next Annual Town Meeting open at the house of Daniel Kilburn at 2 O'Clock P. M.

Amos Harrison, Moderator, Daniel Kilburn, Clk.

At a Special Town Meeting held this seventh day of May, 1823, at the house of Daniel Kilburn to fill the vacancy caused by the declension of Daniel Dodd as an overseer of the highway and to fill the vacancy of Commissioner of Appeal occasioned by the neglect of Moses Lindsley in not returning his qualification, Daniel Dodd was chosen Moderator When Daniel D. Condit was elected to supply the place of Daniel Dodd as overseer of the highway and Moses Lindsley was reelected commissioner of appeal.

Daniel Dodd, Moderator, Daniel Kilburn, Clk.

1824.

April 12th 1824. The Eighteenth Annual Town Meeting of the Inhabitants of the Township of Orange was held this day at the house of Daniel Kilburn, when the following Town Officers were elected and Resolves Passed.

Moderator, Joel Harrison; Town Clerk, Samuel D. Kilburn; Assessor, Jonas Smith; Collector, John Quinby; Judge of Election, Henry B. Campbell; Town Committee, Daniel Dodd, Joel Harrison, Ichabod Condit, Ambrose Condit, Aaron Peck; Surveyors of the Highway, Ichabod Harrison, Stephen Dodd; Overseers of the Poor, William Williams, Daniel D. Condit; Commissioners of Appeal, Benjamin Williams, Junr., Jotham Condit, Stephen Bruen; Chosen Freeholders, Jeptha Baldwin, Amos Harrison; Constables, John Reock, Bethuel Pierson; Overseers of Highways, Isaac Baldwin, Crowel Wilkinson, Stephen Hedley, Junr., Benjamin Meeker, Benjamin Williams, Junr., Silas D. Condit, John Endsley, Ira Pierson, Matthias Wilkinson, Ambrose Condit, Benjamin Townley, Bethuel Williams, Daniel Dodd, Chester Robinson, Stephen Peck, Benjamin Lindsley, Lyman S. Averil, Matthias I. Snyder, Stephen Bruen, Allen Dodd, Rufus Freeman, Ichabod Harrison, Henry W. Culverson, John Hedden.

RESOLVES PASSED.

1st. That twelve hundred Dollars be raised for the support of the Poor the present year. 2d. That all the children that are now on the Town of six years and upwards be left in the hands of the Overseers of the Poor to be bound out on the best terms possible. 3d. That Jabez P—— and Phoebe C—— be left in the hands of the Overseers of the Poor. 4th. That the remainder of Poor be farmed out and the farmer to indemnify the Town against all the Poor that may come on the Town for one year.

5th. That the Town give thirty dollars for the support of Daniel E——
and his friends to indemnify the Town for one year. The Poor was
farmed out to Abraham Pellecker for five hundred and ninety seven Dollars. 6th. That the next Annual Town Meeting open at the house of
Lydia Condit at 2 O'Clock (P. M.) 7th. That the next Annual Election
open at the house of Matthias Ross and close at the house of Lydia Condit, And that the next Congressional and Electoral Election open at the
house of Isaac Combs and close at the house of Daniel Kilburn.

Joel Harrison, Moderator,
S. D. Kilburn, Clk.

1825.

April 11th 1825. The Nineteenth annual Town Meeting of the Inhabitants of the Township of Orange was held this day at the house of
Lydia Condit, when the following Town Officers were elected and Resolves passed.

Moderator, Joel Harrison; Town Clerk, Jabez Pierson; Assessor,
John Quinby; Collector, Adonijah Osmun; Judge of Election, Henry B.
Campbell; Town Committee, Abram Winans, Aaron Peck, Ambrose
Condit, Joel Harrison, Ichabod Condit; Surveyors of the Highway, Ste-
phen Condit, Ichabod Harrison; Overseers of the Poor, William Wil-
liams, Daniel D. Condit; Commissioners of Appeal, William Pierson,
Jotham Condit, Benjamin Williams, Junr.; Chosen Freeholders, Jeptha
Baldwin, Amos Harrison; Constables, John Reuck, Bethuel Pierson;
Overseers of the Highway, Jotham Quinby, Oliver Hays, John S. Taylor,
Abner Crowel, Nathanel Williams, Hiram Quinby, Lewis Williams,
Moses Condit, Jr., John Corby, Benjamin Townley, Matthew Williams,
Elijah C. Pierson, Bethuel Williams, Chester Robinson, Abraham R.
Marsh, Elias Tomkins, Ezekiel Ball, Thomas P. Gale, Isaac A. Baldwin,
Daniel Kilburn, Abraham P. Meeker, Ichabod Harrison, Kelita Brown,
Daniel Squier, Amos Baldwin.

RESOLVES PASSED.

Resd. 1st. That one Thousand Dollars be raised for the support of
the Poor the present year. 2. That the following list of paupers be left
in the hands of the Overseers of the poor viz. Phoebe C——, Simon
M——, John T——, Nathaniel L——, Joseph T——, Amzi A. W——,
Hannah T——, Morgan Y——, Amos S——, Jonas H——, Zelpha J——.
3d. That Forty dollars be paid Phoebe C——, & Julia C——, their
friends previously indemnifying the Town from further charges for one
year. 4th. That Daniel E——, be paid Thirty dollars, the Town being
indemnified. 5th. That the remaining poor be farmed out and the
farmer indemnify the Town. 6th. That Lewis Dodd be paid ten dollars,
for services rendered, Joseph White, decd. 7th. That the next annual
Election open at the house of Bethuel Pierson & close at the house of
Daniel Kilburn. 8th. That the next annual Town Meeting be opened at
the house of Daniel Kilburn at two o'clock P. M. 9th. Ambrose Condit,
Amos Harrison & Jonas Smith were appointed a special Committee to
obtain information as to the advantages & disadvantages of a poor house
establishment from Townships where the same are in operation & if
in their opinion they are advantageous they ascertain the probable cost
& where a suitable farm can be procured for the purpose & Report the

same at the next annual Town Meeting. The poor was farmed out to Daniel Reeve for three hundred twenty two dollars & fifty cents.

Joel Harrison, Moderator,
Jabez Pierson, Clk.

1826.

April 10th, 1826. The Twentieth annual Town Meeting of the Inhabitants of the Township of Orange was held this day at the house of Danl. Kilburn when the following Town Officers were duly Elected and the following Resolutions passed—viz.

Moderator, Henry B. Campbell; Town Clerk, Amos A. Harrison; Assessor, John Quinby; Collector, Adonijah Osmun; Judge of Election, Ichabod Harrison; Town Committee, Abram Winans, Aaron Peck, Joel Harrison, Ichabod Condit, Benjm. Williams, Junr.; Surveyors of the Highway, Stephen Condit, Jotham Condit; Overseers of the Poor, William Williams, Danl. D. Condit; Commissioners of Appeal, Jonas Smith, Moses Lindsley, Wm. Pierson; Chosen Freeholders, Jeptha Baldwin, Stephen Dodd; Constables, Ichabod Harrison, John S. Orsborn, Richard Ward; Overseers of Highway, Ezra Gildersleeve, Oliver Hays, Stephen Hedley, David I. Beach, Benjm. Williams, Junr., Joseph Matthews, John Perry, Jonathan S. Williams, John Corby, Clark Townley, Saml. Condit, Danl. Dodd, Caleb Pierson, Chester Robinson, Lewis Munn, Jeptha Baldwin, Matths. W. Ross, Jno. Orsborn, Danl. S. Reeves, Peter Groshong, William I. Smith, Albert Harrison, Henry D. Reeve, Moses N. Combs, Adonijah Osmun.

RESOLUTIONS PASSED.

The Committee appointed at the last annual Town Meeting to make enquiry as to the advantages of a Town Farm on which to keep the poor of the township, Reported favorable to the plan—Whereupon it was Resolved, 1st. That a farm for the purpose above set forth be purchased as soon as is expedient. 2d. That the Town Committee conjointly with the Overseers of the poor be Instructed to purchase a Suitable Farm. 3d. That the sum of Three Thousand Dollars be assessed upon the Inhabitants of the township the present Year for the support of the poor, and paying toward the contemplated farm. 4th. That the poor of the Township be left in the hands of the Overseers, by them to be provided for. A motion was made and Seconded to work the public highways by Tax Which motion was decided in the negative. 5th. That the next annual Election open at the House of Bethuel Harrison, at South Orange, and close at Lydia Condit's. 6th. That the next Annual Town Meeting open at the Widow L. Condit's at two O'clock P. M.

Henry B. Campbell, Moderator,
Attest, Amos A. Harrison, Clk.

A Special Town Meeting of the Inhabitants of the Township of Orange held this 8th day of May 1826 at the house of Lydia Condit, by order of the Town Committee to appoint one Constable, one Chosen Freeholder, two Commissioners of Appeals, and two Overseers of Highways. Henry B. Campbell was chosen Moderator, and the meeting then elected Stephen Harrison Junr. Constable; Amos Harrison, Chosen Freeholder; Ira Pierson and Jotham Condit, Commissioners of Appeals; Matthias B. Corby and Abijah Harrison Junr., Overseers of the Highways.

Henry B. Campbell, Moderator,
A. A. Harrison, Clk.

1827.

April 9th, 1827. The twenty-first annual town meeting of the Inhabitants of the township of Orange was held this day in the Church at Orange, when the following Town Officers were duty Elected and the following Resolutions passed, viz—

Moderator, Daniel Kilburn; Town Clerk, Moses S. Harrison; Assessor, John Quinby; Collector, Adonijah Osmun; Judge of Election, Henry B. Campbell; Town Committee, Abraham Winans, Ichabod Condit, Ambrose Condit, Daniel Dodd, Aaron Peck; Surveyors of the Highway, Elias Tompkins, Jonas Smith; Overseers of the Poor, William Williams, Daniel D. Condit; Commissioners of Appeal, Jotham Condit, Amos A. Harrison, Joel Harrison; Chosen Freeholders, Amos Harrison, Jeptha Baldwin; Constables, Stephen Harrison, Jur., John Reuck, Bethuel Harrison; Overseers of the Highway, Jonas Smith, Peter Van Ness, John S. Taylor, Freeman Elston, Aaron Brown, Abijah Harrison, Jur., William Matthews, Ira Pierson, Benjamin Condit, John W. Hardman, John Webb, Ira Quinby, James Reynolds, Amos S. Williams, Chester Robinson, William Peck, Samuel H. Gardner, Daniel Reeves, Jonathan Tichenor, Isaac Coe, Lewis Pierson, Daniel Kilburn, Abraham P. Meeker, Thomas Williams, Jur., Henry Ball, Moses N. Combs, Abram P. Harrison.

RESOLUTIONS PASSED.

1st. Resolved, That all accounts with the town committee must be presented to them on or before the first day of April next or be laid over until the next year. 2d. That the town committee be authorized to purchase a pasture lot for the use of the township if in there Opinion it would be a public benefit. 3d. That the township raise by Assessment One Thousand Dollars the present year for the support of the poor. 4th. That the Resolution introduced for working the roads by tax be postponed until the next annual town meeting. 5th. That the Next Annual Election open at the house of Matthias Ross in Camptown and close at the house of Daniel Kilburn in Orange. 6th. That the next Annual town meeting Open at the house of Daniel Kilburn in Orange at two O'clock P. M.

Daniel Kilburn, Moderator, Moses S. Harrison, Clk.

1828.

April 14th 1828. The twenty second annual meeting of the Inhabitants of the township of Orange was held at the Church this day, when following named persons were Elected to the offices herein designated; and the following Resolutions passed, viz.

Moderator, Noah Matthews; Town Clerk, Amos A. Harrison; Assessor, John Quinby; Collector, Adonijah Osmun; Judge of Elections, Joel Harrison; Town Committee, Jonas Smith, Abram Winans, Ichabod Condit, Ambrose Condit, Moses Lindsley; Surveyors of Highways, Stephen Condit, Abrm. P. Harrison; Overseers of the Poor, William Williams, Daniel D. Condit; Commissioners of Appeals, Jotham Condit, Joel Harrison, Wheeler Lindsley; Chosen Freeholders, Amos Harrison, Jeptha Baldwin; Constables, John Reock, Jonathan Brown, Ichabod Harrison; Overseers of Highways, Daniel Quinby; George Harrison, Stephen

Hedly, John Ball, Abiathar Harrison, Abram Harrison, John Perrey, Jonathan S. Williams, Ira Condit, Benjamin Townley, Ira Harrison, James Reynolds, Silas D. Condit, Simeon Harrison, Lewis Munn, Thos. Day, Elias Tomkins, William Addison, Moses Crowell, Victor K. Reeves, Noah Matthews, Abrm P. Meeker, Abiel Dodd, Lewis Dodd, Jna. T. Squire, Stephen Harrison Junr.

RESOLUTIONS PASSED.

Resolved 1st. That the public Highways be Worked by Tax; and that the money shall be appropriated in district in which it is assessed. 2d. That the amount of money to be raised for the support of the public roads be equal to all other taxes Jointly for the present year. 3d. That the management of the Town farm be exclusively in the hands of the Overseers of the Poor. 4th. That the sum of Six Hundred Dollars be raised for the support of the poor. 5th. That the sum of Two Hundred dollars be raised for the Education of Indigent Children in the Township; to be appropriated by the Town Committee. 6th. That the next annual Election open at the house of Daniel Squire and close at the widow Lydia Condit's. 7th. That the next annual Town Meeting open at the house of Lydia Condit at two o'clock P. M.

Noah Matthews, Modr. Attest Amos A. Harrison, Clk.

1829.

April 13th, 1829. The twenty third annual meeting of the Inhabitants of the Township of Orange was held at the house of Mrs. Condit's this day—The following named persons were duly elected Town officers, and the following resolutions passed—viz—

Moderator, Noah Matthews; Town Clerk, Charles Condit; Assessor, John Quinby; Collector, Adonijah Osmun; Judge of Election, Noah Matthews; Town Committee, Moses Lindsley, Ichabod Condit, Ambrose Condit, John Dean, Jonas Smith; Surveyors of Highways, Stephen Condit, Allen Dodd; Overseers of the Poor, William Williams, Daniel D. Condit; Commissioners of Appeals, Joel Harrison, Lewis Dodd, Samuel Brown; Chosen Freeholders, Timothy Williams, Jeptha Baldwin; Constables, John Reock, Ichabod Harrison, Jonathan Brown; School Committee, Daniel Babbit, William Pierson, Jr., Abm. Harrison, Jonathan T. Squier, Ambrose Condit; Overseers of Highways, James Smith, Eleazer B. Porter, Joseph Osborn, Joseph B. Ball, Abijah Harrison, Jr., John Enslee, John Perry, Jotham Condit, John W. Hardman, Benjm. Townley, Smith Williams, James Reynolds, Daniel Williams, Simeon Harrison, John T. Munn, Ezekiel Ball, Thomas D. Kilburn, Allen Osborn, Isaac A. Baldwin, Lewis Pierson, Danl. Kilburn, Ambrose Tomkins, Joseph Munn, Lewis Dodd, Danl. Reeves, Abm. P. Harrison.

RESOLUTIONS PASSED.

Resolved 1. That the sum of six hundred dollars be raised for the support of the poor the present year. 2. That the sum of five dollars be raised for the support of common schools agreeably to the provisions of an act of the legislature. 3. That the sum of two hundred dollars be raised for the education of Indigent children in the Township, to be appropriated by the Town Committee. 4. That the amount of money to be raised for the support of the public roads for the present year, be equal to one half of all the other taxes. 5. That the next annual election be opened at the house of Matthias Ross and close at Danl. Kilburn. 6. That the next town meeting be opened at Matthias Ross in Camptown at 10 O'Clock A. M. 7. That the Town Committee be authorized to alter the road districts, if they think proper.

Noah Matthews Modr. Attest, Chas. Condit, Clk.

1830.

April 12th, 1830. The twenty fourth annual Town Meeting of the Inhabitants of the Township of Orange was held in Camptown this day, —The following named persons were duly elected Town Officers, and the following resolutions passed, viz—

Moderator, Noah Matthews; Town Clerk, Charles Condit; Assessor, John Quinby; Collector, William Condit; Judge of Election, Joel Harrison; Town Committee, Aaron Peck, Ambrose Condit, Daniel Dodd, Jonas Smith, Moses Lindsley; Surveyors of Highways, Stephen Condit, Samuel Brown; Overseers of the Poor, Elias Tomkins, Daniel D. Condit; Commissioners of Appeals, Samuel Williams, Lewis Dodd, Edwin Gray; Chosen Freeholders, Joel Harrison, Jeptha Baldwin; Constables, Matthias W. Ross, John Reock, Ichabod Harrison, John Hedden; School Committee, Daniel Babbitt, William Pierson, Jr., Abraham Harrison, Jonathan T. Squire, Ambrose Condit; Overseers of Highways, Ezra Gildersleeves, Moses Wilson, Freeman Nelson, David I. Beach, Abm. Williams, Albert Matthews, John Perry, Moses Condit, jr., Zebulon Condit, Moses Crowel, Thomas Burnsides, Daniel D. Reynolds, Jotham Pierson, Zebulon Myers, John T. Munn, James Eaton, Jeptha Baldwin, Thomas P. Gales, Isaac A. Baldwin, Ira Hand, John M. Lindsley, Abraham P. Meeker, Ichabod Harrison, Lewis Baldwin, Daniel Squier, Stephen Harrison.

RESOLUTIONS PASSED.

Resolved 1st. That the sum of one thousand Dollars be raised for the support of the poor, for the present year. 2. That the sum of five dollars be raised for the support of common schools agreeably to the provisions of an act of the legislature. 3d. That the amount of money to be raised for the support of the public roads for the present year, be equal to one half of all the other taxes. 4th. That the Next Annual Election be opened at the house of Daniel Squier and close at Isaac A. Smiths. 5th. That the next annual Town Meeting be opened at the house of Isaac A. Smith, at 2 o'clock P. M., and that all the officers, excepting the Moderator, Clerk, and Overseers of Highways be elected by ballot.

Noah Matthews, Modr., Attest, Chas. Condit, Clk.

At a special Town Meeting of the Inhabitants of Orange Township held at the house of Isaac A. Smith, on the 15th day of May 1830 by order of the Town Committee to appoint one Constable one surveyor of the Highway, & two Commissioners of Appeals, on account of the neglect of John Hedden to qualify according to Law as Constable, of Saml. Brown as Surveyor of the Highway, of Edwin Gray & Saml. Williams as Commissioners of appeals, to which offices they were respectively elected at the last Annual Town Meeting & also to consider the propriety of increasing the road tax—Noah Matthews was chosen Moderator. The following officers were then elected—viz

Daniel Reeves Constable; Saml. Brown Surveyor of Highway; Edwin Gray, Samul. Williams, Commissioners of Appeals.

Resolved *unanimously* that the road tax be *not* increased for the present year.

Noah Matthews, Modr. Charles Condit, Clk.

1831.

April 11th 1831. The Twenty fifth annual Town Meeting of the Inhabitants of the Township of Orange was held at the house of Isaac A. Smith, this day. The following named persons were duly elected Town Officers, and the following resolutions passed viz—

Moderator, Daniel Kilburn; Town Clerk, Charles Condit; Assessor, John Quinby; Collector, William Condit; Judge of Election, Henry B. Campbell; Town Committee, Jonas Smith, Ambrose Condit, Daniel Dodd, Aaron Peck, Joel Harrison; Surveyors of Highways, Allen Dodd, Elias Tomkins; Overseers of the Poor, Daniel D. Condit, Moses Lindsley; Commissioners of Appeals, Jotham Condit, Caleb Smith, Lewis Dodd; Chosen Freeholders, Jeptha Baldwin, Timothy Williams; Constables, Elisha R. Hedden, Matthias W. Ross, Richard Barnwell, Ichabod Harrison, jr.; School Committee, William Pierson, jr., Abm. Harrison, Jonathan T. Squier; Overseers of Highway, Jotham Quinby, Alvin Sherman, Enos Baldwin, Benjn. Meeker, Aaron B. Harrison, Abm. Harrison, Lewis Williams, Alvin P. Condit, Ambrose Condit, Joseph A. Pierson, Samuel Condit, Moses Miller, Amzi Condit, Stephen Condit, Jabez Pierson, Joel Harrison, Elias Tomkins, Ira Taylor, Lyman S. Averill, Lewis Pierson, Edward Condit, Henry B. Campbell, William I. Smith, Elias O. Meeker, Lewis Dodd, John Hedden, Stephen Harrison.

RESOLUTIONS PASSED.

Resolved 1st. That the Township own all the stock, farming utensils, &c. belonging to the poor house. 2d. That the contract made between the Overseers of the Poor & the keeper of the poor house be relinquished if it can be consistently effected. 3d. That the next Annual election be opened at the house of Jabez B. Hedden, and close at the house of Danl. Kilburn. 4th. That the next Annual Town Meeting be held at the house of Danl. Kilburn at 2 O'Clock P. M. and that the officers be chosen by ballot. 5th. That the sum of eight hundred dollars be raised for the support of the poor for the present year. 6th. That the sum of five hundred dollars be raised for the purpose of repairing the poor house. 7th. That the public highways be worked by tax. 8th. That the amount of money to be raised for working the roads be equal to one half of all the other taxes.

Danl. Kilburn, Modr. Attest. Chas. Condit, Clk.

1832.

April 9th, 1832. The Twenty Sixth annual Town meeting of the inhabitants of the Township of Orange was held at the house of Benjm. Jarvis this day. The following persons were duly elected Town Officers, and the following resolutions passed. viz—

Moderator, Noah Matthews; Town Clerk, Abrahm. R. Hillyer; Assessor, John Quinby; Collector, William Condit; Judge of Election,

Henry B. Campbell; Town Committee, Lewis Dodd, Stephen Condit, Ambrose Condit, Jonas Smith, Jonathan T. Squier; Surveyors of Highways, Danl. Kilburn, Ichd. Condit; Overseers of the Poor, Wm. Williams, Moses Lindsley; Commissioners of Appeals, Jotham Condit, Joel Harrison, Caleb Smith; Chosen Freeholders, Stephen D. Day, Timothy Williams; Constables, Matthias W. Ross, Ichd. Harrison, Junr., Elisha R. Hedden; School Committee, Wm. Pierson, Jun., Abm. Harrison, Philip Kingsley; Overseers of Highways, Jonas Smith, Richard Terhune, Stephen Hedley, Job Crowel, Eleazer Williams, Moses Harrison, Lewis Williams, Amos W. Condit, Jun., Isaac Condit, Jacob A. Sharpe, Ira Harrison, Daniel Dodd, Bethuel Williams, Chester Robinson, Stephen M. Peck, Moses Stockman, Jonathan Lindsley, Horatio Baldwin, John P. Courter, Lewis Pierson, Wm. Williams, Ziba Tompkins, Abiel Dodd, Henry D. Rowe, Aaron Brown, Stephen Harrison.

RESOLUTIONS PASSED.

Resolved, 1st. That Six Hundred Dollars be raised the ensuing year for the Support of the Poor. 2d. That the Tax on Dogs be raised to Five Dollars. 3d. That the next annual Election be opened at the Columbian School House in South Orange, and close at the house of Benjamin Jarvis. 4th. That the next annual Town meeting be held at Isaac A. Smith at 2 O'clock P. M. 5th. That the amount of money to be raised for working the roads be equal to one half of all the other taxes. 6th. That the sum of Five Dollars be raised for the use of the school committee.

Noah Matthews, Modr.	Attest, A. R. Hillyer, Clk.

On account of the neglect of Joel Harrison to qualify as one of the commissioners of appeals, to which office he was elected at the last annual Town Meeting, the Town Committee met at the house of Benjamin S. Jarvis, on Saturday Oct. 13th at 4 O'clock P. M. at which time Aaron Brown Esq., was appointed as commissioner of appeals, to fill the vacancy made by the neglect of Joel Harrison.

A. R. Hillyer Clk.

Orange, Oct. 13th, 1832.

1833.

April 8th 1833. The Twenty Seventh annual Town Meeting of the Inhabitants of Orange, was held at the house of Isaac A. Smith this day —the following named persons were elected town officers, and the following resolutions passed—viz.

Moderator, Jonas Smith; Town Clerk, Abraham R. Hillyer; Assessor, John Quinby; Collector, William Condit; Judge of Election, Joel Harrison; Town Committee, Lewis Dodd, Stephen Condit, Jonathan T. Squire, Ambrose Condit, Jonas Smith; Surveyors of Highways, Allen Dodd, Ichabod Condit; Overseers of the Poor, William Williams, Daniel Squier; Commissioners of Appeals, Jotham Condit, Jeptha Baldwin, Caleb Smith; Chosen Freeholders, Stephen D. Day, Timothy Williams; Constables, Allen Osborn, Nathaniel Parsons, John Smith; School Committee, Wm. Pierson, Jun., Abraham Harrison, Philip Kingsley; Overseers of Highways, John Quinby, Moses Wilson, Enoz Baldwin, Amzi Ball, Elijah Williams, Jun., Jacob Harrison, Thomas O. Woodruff, Samuel L. Pierson,

Israel B. Condit, Jacob A. Sharp, Thomas Burnsides, Benjamin Condit, Caleb P. Williams, Chester Robinson, Stephen M. Peck, Moses Stockman, Jonathan Lindsley, Isaac R. Passals, William Ball, Samuel P. Brown, Moses S. Harrison, Cyrus Freeman, Abiel Dodd, Henry D. Rowe, Peter Peck, Richard B. Harrison, C. Lighthipe.

RESOLUTIONS PASSED.

Resolved 1st. That the money received for cloths of Alfred Lyon be Paid to Elisha R. Hedden. 2d. That the road tax be equal to one half of all the other taxes. 3d. That Six hundred Dollars be raised for the support of the poor the ensuing Year. 4th. That the Dox tax be One Dollar. 5th. That the next annual Election open at the house now occupied by Jabez B. Hedden in Camptown and close at the house of Isaac A. Smith in Orange. 6th. That the next annual Town Meeting open at the house of Benjamin S. Jarvis at 2 O'clock P. M. 7th. That the sum of Five Dollars be raised to aid the School Fund.

Jonas Smith, Modr. Attest, A. R. Hillyer, Clk.

At a Special Town Meeting of the Inhabitants of the Township of Orange held at the House of Benjn. S. Jarvis on the 22d Day of June 1833 by Order of the Town Committee to appoint an Overseer of the Poor and Two Commissioners of appeals on account of the death of Wm. Williams, Esqr., Overseer of the Poor, and the neglect of Jotham Condit and Jeptha Baldwin to qualify as Commissioners of appeals, to which offices they were respectively elected at the last annual Town Meeting.— Danl. Kilburn was chosen Moderator. The Following officers were then elected—viz—

Moses Lindsley, Overseer of the Poor; Danl. Kilburn, Aaron Brown, Commissioners of Appeals.

Danl. Kilburn, Modr. A. R. Hillyer, Clk.

1834.

April 14th, 1834. The Twenty-Eight annual Meeting of the Inhabitants of the Township of Orange was held at the house of Benjamin S. Jarvis this day. The following named persons were duly elected Town officers, and the following Resolutions passed, viz—

Moderator, Chester Robinson; Town Clerk, Abram R. Hillyer; Assessor, John Quinby; Judge of Election, Henry B. Campbell; Collector, William Condit; Town Committee, Stephen Condit, Edward Gruet, Daniel Dodd, Ambrose Condit, Jonas Smith; Surveyors of Highways, Ichabod Condit, Allen Dodd; Overseers of the Poor, D. D. Condit, Amos W. Condit; Commissioners of Appeals, Caleb Smith, Jotam Condit, Abiel Dodd; Chosen Freeholders, William Pierson, Junr., Stephen D. Day; Constables, Nathaniel Parsons, Moses B. Harrison, Erastus Pierson, Junr., Chester Robinson; School Committee, Philip Kingsley, Albert Pierson, Abraham Harrison; Overseers of Highways, Chester Robinson, Ezra Gildersleeve, Zenas Williams, John S. Enslee, Lewis Williams, Joseph S. Condit, Henry Walker, Jacob A. Sharp, Smith Williams, Moses Miller, Bethuel Williams, Abraham Tompkins, Ichabod Harrison, Lewis Hedden, Adonijah Osmun; Pound Keeper, Abm. Mandeville.

RESOLUTIONS PASSED.

Resolved, 1st. That the trustees of schools that do not make their resport to the school committee on or before the first Mondays in August and February be barred from any advantages arising from the school fund. 2d. That a public pound be established and that it be located between the first and second Churches. 3. That, whereas, great dissatisfaction has been given by the acts of the collector of this township, in regard to the returns of non-payment of taxes, and it being the duty of said Collector by law to return immediately thereafter all those remaining unpaid on the 20th of December— Therefore, Resolved, that the Collector of this Township be required and directed by this Town Meeting to return (without discrimination) as soon as the 26th of December in each and every year hereafter, the names of all delinquents to a magistrate for collection and that the Town Committee be hereby instructed not in any case to remit to the collector any tax that may hereafter not be collected in consequence of his disregard to this resolution. 4th. That the amount of money raised for the support of the highway the present year be equal to one-half of all the other taxes. 5th. That Five hundred dollars be raised for the support of the poor the present year. 6th. That Seven hundred dollars be raised for the purpose of adjusting a settlement with Clinton Township. 7th. That the tax on Dogs for the present year be fifty cents. 8th. That the next annual election be held at the house now occupied by B. S. Jarvis. 9th. That the next annual Town Meeting open at the house of Isaac A. Smith at 2 o'clock P. M. 10th. That Five Dollars be raised to aid the school fund. Adjourned.

Chester Robinson, Moderator.

Attest: A. R. Hillyer, Clk.

At a meeting of the Town Committee held on the 10 of May, 1834, Silas Condit was appointed Overseer of the Highway in the district to which Bethuel Williams was appointed at the Town Meeting, he declining to serve, and Abiel Dodd was re-appointed Commissioner of Appeals.

A. R. Hillyer, Clk.

In consequence of the removal of A. R. Hillyer from the Township of Orange, who had been duly appointed Clerk of said Township, at the last annual Town Meeting, S. D. Day, Esqr., one of the Justices of the Peace in and for the County of Essex, upon application of the Town Committee did advertise a Special Town Meeting, in the manner prescribed by law, to be held at the house of B. S. Jarvis, July 5th, 1834, at five o'clock P. M., for the purpose of choosing a Town Clerk to serve as such from the time of his appointment, until the next annual Town Meeting. In pursuance of said notice the inhabitants convened at the above time and place and organized by appointing S. D. Day, Esqr., Modr., after which Moses Reynolds was chosen Town Clerk to supply the vacancy occasioned by the aforesaid removal.

Stephen D. Day, Moderator.

Moses Reynolds, Clerk.

1835.

April 13th, 1835. The Twenty ninth annual Meeting of the Inhabitants of the Township of Orange was held at the first Presbyterian church this day. The following named persons were duly elected Town officers for the ensuing year—and the following Resolutions passed.—viz.

Moderator, Chester Robinson; Town Clerk, Ichd. Harrison Jun.; Assessor John Quinby; Collector, William Condit; Judge of Election, Henry B. Campbell; Town Committee, Daniel Dodd, Edward Gruet, Stephen Condit, Jonas Smith, Lewis Dodd; Surveyors of Highways, Ichd. Condit, Allen Dodd; Overseers of Poor, Daniel D. Condit, Noah Matthews; Commissioners of Appeals, Abial Dodd, Jotham Condit, Caleb Smith; Chosen Freeholders, Stephen D. Day, William Pierson Jur.; Constables, Nathl. Parsons, Chester Robinson, George McClaud; School Committee, Abm. Harrison, Chs. R. Day, Jesse Williams; Overseers of Highways, Chester Robinson, Jotham Quimby, Abijah Harrison Jur., George Smith, Daniel Pierson, Erastus Pierson, Jur., Ellis F. Condit, Jacob A. Sharp, Smith Williams, Daniel Dodd, Caleb Pierson, Abm. P. Meeker, Cyrus Baldwin, Lewis Baldwin, Adonijah Osmun; Pound Master, Abm. Mandeville.

RESOLUTIONS PASSED.

Resolved 1st. That six Hundred dollars be raised for the support of the poor the ensuing year. 2d. That Four Hundred dollars be raised for the purpose of settlement with Clinton Township. 3d. That five dollars be raised to aid the school fund. 4th. That a Dog Tax be as follows —for every Slut five dollars and every male dog Two dollars. 5th. The Collector be instructed to pay all money raised for Township purposes over to the Town Committee to be expended by them. 6th. That it be recommended to the Trustees of the defint school districts to appropriate the school fund to the education of the Indigent children exclusively. 7th. That the next annual election be held at the House of Isaac A. Smith. 8th. That the next annual Town Meeting be held at the House now occupied by B. S. Jarvis at 2 o'clock P. M. 9th. That the amount of money raised for the support of Highways for the present to equal to one half of all other tax. Adjourned. Chester Robinson, Moderator, Attest, Ichd. Harrison Junr. Clk.

1836.

April 11th, 1836. The thirtieth annual Town meeting of the Inhabitants of the Township of Orange was held at the House of George W. Blake this day. The following named Persons were duly elected Town officers for the following year. And the following Rosons passed—viz.

Moderator, Henry B. Campbell; Town Clerk, Ichabod Harrison, Junr.; Assessor, Jabez Pierson; Collector, William Condit; Judge of Election, Calvin Dodd; Town Committee, Jonathan S. Williams, Daniel Babbit, Daniel Dodd, Lewis Dodd, Abial Dodd; Surveyors of Highways, Charles Harrison, Allen Dodd; Overseers of the Poor, Noah Matthews, Daniel D. Condit; Commissioners of Appeal, Jotham Condit, Caleb Smith, John Harrison; Chosen Freeholders, Stephen D. Day, William Pierson, Junr.; Constables, Samuel L. Pierson, Linas D. Condit, Nathl Parsons, Chester Robinson; School Committee, Aaron Pierson Jur., Abm. Harrison, Chas. R. Day; Pound Master, Abm. Mandeville; Overseers of the Highways, Chester Robinson, Ezra Gildersleeve, Chs. Harrison, Hiram Quimby, John Perry, Moses Condit, Ambrose Condit, Linas Williams, Smith Williams, David A. Smith, Ziba Tompkins, Ths. W. Munn, Lewis Dodd, Ichabod Harrison, Junr.

RESOLUTIONS PASSED.

Resolved 1st. That all Cattle, Horses, Hogs or Sheep running at large may be driven to the Public Pound and the same fees demanded as are allowed in such cases for Cattle trespassing. 2d. That Six Hundred Dollars be raised for the support of the poor the present year. 3d. That the road Tax be equal to the one half of all the other taxes raised. 4th. That the sum of Five Dollars be raised to aid the school fund. 5th. That the tax on Dogs for the present year be Fifty cents. 6th. That the next Annual Election be held at the house of George W. Blake. 7th. That the next annual Town meeting open at the House of Isaac A. Smith at 2 O'clock P. M.

Henry B. Campbell, Modr. Attest, Ichd. Harrison Jur. Clk.

At a meeting of the Town Committee at the House of Isaac A. Smith The district of road known as Park street, William street & King street was set off as a separate district. Aaron Williams was appointed Overseer. The district of road from the Bridge near the House of Calfvin Dodd north to the Bridge near the house of Albt. Sayers, west to the Swinefied road South to the Bridge at the Factory. Calvin Dodd was appointed Overseer.

Attest. Ichd. Harrison, Junr. Clk.

1837.

The thirty first annual Townmeeting of the Inhabitants of the Township of Orange was held at the House of Isaac A. Smith this day— The following named persons were duly elected Town Officers for the ensuing year, and the following Resolutions passed (viz)

Moderator, Henry B. Campbell; Town Clerk, Ichd. Harrison, Junr.; Assessor, Jabez Pierson; Collector, William Condit; Judge of Election, Calvin Dodd; Town Committee, Lewis Dodd, Daniel D. Reynolds, Daniel Babbit, Jonathan S. Williams, Daniel Dodd; Surveyors of Highways, Allen Dodd, Timothy W. Mulford; Overseers of the Poor, Dan'l D. Condit, Noah Matthews; Commissioners of Appeals, Chs. Harrison, Abial Dodd, Jotham Condit; Chosen Freeholders, Henry B. Campbell, Jonas Smith; Constables, Chs. E. Willis, Edward Pierson, Nathl. Parsons, Saml. L. Pierson; School Committee, Philip Kingly, Abm. Harrison, Jessee Williams; Pound Master, Peter Gruet; Overseers of the Highways, Chester Robinson, Daniel Quimby, Abithar Harrison, Moses B. Harrison, Ths. O. Woodruff, William Bodwell, Henry Walker, Daniel S. Williams, Ira Harrison, Daniel Dodd, Rufus Freeman, Israel Dodd, Lewis Dodd, Eason Park, Calvin Dodd, Richd. Kelsall, Jacob Sharp, William Johnson Senr., Silas D. Condit.

RESOLUTIONS PASSED.

Resolved 1st. That the sum of Six Hundred Dollars be raised for the support of the poor the present year. 2d. That the road Tax be equal to the one half of all the other Taxes raised. 3d. That the sum of Five Dollars be raised for to aid the school fund. 4th. That the Tax on Dogs for the present year be Five Dollars. 5th. That this meeting approve the plan of a county poor House. 6th. That the next Election be held at the House of Isaac A. Smith. 7th. That the next Town meeting open at the House of Barnabas Day at 2 o'clock P. M.

Henry B. Campbell, Modr.

Attest, Ichd. Harrison Jur. Town Clerk.

At a meeting of the Town committee at the House of B. Day April 15 1837 the district of road commencing the north side of Main street, at the First Presbyterian church to the Williamsvill road including the street running from Day street to High street—The new road commencing at the turnpike on the west side of Rahway river leading past J. Condits to the swamp road. Silas D. Condit was appointed over seer William Johnson Senr. in the first named District.

Attest, Ichd. Harrison Jr. Clk.

1838.

April 9th, 1838. The thirty second annual Town Meeting of the Inhabitants of the Township of Orange was held at House of Barnbas Day this day. The following named persons were duly Elected Town officers for the ensuing year and the following Resolutions passed (viz.)

Moderator, Henry B. Campbell; Town Clerk, Ichd. Harrison, Junr.; Assessor, Jabez Pierson; Collector, William Condit; Judge of Election, Calvin Dodd; Town Committee, Abithar Harrison, Lewis Dodd, Jonathan S. Williams, Ira Canfield, Daniel Dodd; Surveyors of the Highway, Allen Dodd, Timothy W. Mulford; Overseers of the Poor, Daniel D. Condit, Noah Matthews; Commissioners of Appeals, Chs. Harrison, Jesse Williams, Abial Dodd; Chosen Freeholders, Henry B. Campbell, Jonas Smith; Constables, Daniel Pierson, Chs. E. Willis, Nathl. Parsons, Moses B. Harrison; School Committee, James A. Williams, Jesse Williams, Albert Pierson; Overseers of the Highways, Chester Robinson, Daniel Quimby, Abraham Williams, William Harrison, Lewis Williams, Moses Condit, David H. Lyon, Caleb Pierson, William B. Williams, Daniel Dodd, Henry Williams, Cyrus Baldwin, Amos Baldwin, Richd. B. Harrison, Calvin Dodd, Richd. Kelsall, Jacob Sharp, George Valentine, David W. Condit, Moses Lindsley, Jeptha Baldwin.

RESOLUTIONS PASSED.

Resolved, 1st. That the sum of Six Hundred Dollars be raised for the support of the poor the present year. 2d. That the road Tax be equal to the one half of all other Taxes raised. 3d. That the sum of Five Dollars be raised to aid the school fund. 4th. That the Tax on Dogs, for the present year, be Fifty Cents. 5th. That the next Election be held at the House of Barnabas Day. 6th. That the next Towne Meeting open at the House of Isaac A. Smith at 2 o'clock P. M.

Henry B. Campbell, Modr.

Attest: Ichd. Harrison, Junr. Clerk.

1839.

April 8th 1839. The thirty third annual Town Meeting of the Inhabitants of the Township of Orange was held at the House of Isaac A. Smith this day—The following named Persons was duly Elected Town officers for the ensuing year, and the following Resolutions passed. (viz).

Moderator, Henry B. Campbell; Town Clerk, Ichabod Harrison, Junr.; Assessor, Jabez Pierson; Collector, William Condit; Judge of Election, Calvin Dodd; Town Committee, Jessee Williams, Ira Canfield, Jonathan S. Williams, Abithar Harrison, Daniel Dodd; Surveyors of

Highways, Allen Dodd, Charles Harrison; Overseers of the Poor, Daniel D. Condit, Noah Matthews; Commissioners of Appeal, Abial Dodd, Moses Lindsley, Lewis Dodd; Chosen Freeholders, Jonas Smith, Henry B. Campbell; Constables, Charles Dickerson, Moses B. Harrison, Charles E. Willis, Nathaniel Parsons; School Committee, Albert Pierson, James A. Williams, Jesse Williams; Overseers of Highways, Barnabas Day, Simeon Harrison, James E. Smith, Abrm. Williams, Caleb Matthews, Ths. O. Woodruff, Moses Condit, John W. Herdman, George McCloud, Jesse Williams, Daniel Dodd, Joseph S. Condit, Abial Dodd, Lewis Dodd, Richd. B. Harrison, Calvin Dodd, Richd. Kelsall, Clark Townley, Horace Hedden, Nathl. Stephens, Edwin Gray, Jeptha Baldwin.

RESOLUTIONS PASSED.

Resolved 1th. That the Sum of Seven Hundred Dollars be raised for the support of the Poor the ensuing year. 2d. That the Road Tax be equal to the one half of all other Taxes raised. 3d. That Sum of Ten Dollars be raised to aid the school fund. 4th. That the Tax on Dogs for the ensuing year be One Dollar per head. 5th. That the thanks of this meeting be presented to Peter Sendee for his gratuitous donation of Fifteen Dollars for the support of the Poor. 6th. That the thanks of this meeting be presented to Moses B. Harrison for a donation of Five Dollars for the benefit of Common Schools. 7th. That the district of Road comprising the main Street, be divided into two districts, the division to be left in the hands of the Town Committee. 8th. That the next Annual Election be held at the House of Isaac A. Smith. 9th. That the next Town meeting open at the House of Barnabas Day, at 2 o'clock P. M.

Henry B. Campbell, Moderator.

Attest, Ichd. Harrison, Jur., Clk.

At a meeting of the Town Committee held at the House of B. Day, April 13th 1839, The district of road composing Day Street &c. was dissolved, and attached to the district of Jesse Williams.

Ichd. Harrison, Jur. Clk.
Orange April 13th 1839.

1840.

At a Special town meeting of the Inhabitants of the Township of Orange held at the house of B. Day, on the 8th day of February, 1840 by order of the Town Committee. To take into consideration the expediency of resisting the contemplated encroachments of the township of Clinton, upon the territory of the Township of Orange, and defending by all proper measures the common interests and rights of the Township of Orange.

Henry B. Campbell was chosen Moderator, Philip Kingsly, Jabez Pierson & Calvin Dodd was appointed a committee to report resols. The committee reported the following preamble and resolutions which were unanimously adopted.

Whereas notice has been given and an application pursuant to such notice, made to the Legislature of this State, by certain citizens of the township of Clinton in the county of Essex for an alteration of the boundary line between that Township and Township of Orange—

And Whereas the line sought to be .changed is one accurately established by the deliberate action of the Legislature, on application of the citizens of Orange for a restoration of Territory unjustly and improperly taken from them and without due notice

And Whereas, those who by the proposed alteration would be placed within the limits of Clinton, are unanimously oppossed to such a transfer or change of position and jurisdiction, and have ever strenuously remonstrated against it

Therefore, Resolved by the Citizens of the Township of Orange, in Town meeting assembled, that the existing Boundary line between the Township Clinton and Orange having been established upon a fair, full and impartial investigation of the subject and hearing of parties, ought not to be changed or altered.—

Resolved that we deprecate the rumored attempt to unsettle the existing boundary as harrassing and expensive to those residing near the present line and within the limits of Orange, and who are unanimously opposed to the change, and as an unjustifiable effort to detract from the limits of Orange, a portion of her Territory and Citizens, for a mere acquisition of Taxable property, and without a colorabe pretext that the present line is either incorrect or injurious to those residing in its immediate vicinity.

Resolved, that we will defend the common rights of the Township of Orange by all Lawful means and measures, and in the prosecution of that object will oppose any alteration of the present Boundary Line by which our Territory will be deminished.

Resolved, That the committee on resolutions be directed to draw up a remonstrance to be signed by the Moderator and Clerk in behalf of this meeting, to be presented to the Legislature, and that Daniel Babbit added to said Committee.

Resolved, that Albert Pierson and Stephen D. Day be a committee to present the foregoing proceeding to the Legislature.

Resolved, that the proceedings of this meeting published in the Newark Daily Advertiser.

Henry B. Campbell, Modr.   Attest Ichd. Harrison, Jn. Clerk.

April 13th 1840. The thirty fourth annual Town Meeting of the Inhabitants of the Township of Orange was held at the House of B. Day this day—The following named persons was duly Elected town officers for the ensuing year and the following Resolutions passed. (viz).

Moderator, Henry B. Campbell; Town Clerk, Ichd. Harrison, Junr.; Assessor, Jabez Pierson; Collector, William Condit; Judge of Election, Calvin Dodd; Town Committee, Lewis Dodd, Daniel D. Reynolds, Ira Canfield, Jonathan S. Williams, Abithar Harrison; Surveyors of the Highway, Charles Harrison, Timothy W. Mulford; Overseers of the Poor, James E. Smith, Noah Matthews; Commissioners of Appeal, Edwin Gray, Thomas W. Munn, Jotham Condit; Chosen Freeholders, Henry B. Campbell, Jonas Smith; School Committee, James A. Williams, Albert Pierson, Henry Pierson; Constables, Charles E. Willis, Aaron Quimby, Nathl. Parsons; Overseers of the Highway, Chester Robinson, James E. Smith, Abraham Williams, John H. Matthews, Joseph M. Crane, Uriah Garrabrant, Linas Williams, Uzal Crane, Daniel Dodd, Henry Williams, Abial Dodd, Richd. Harrison, Calvin Dodd, Richd. Kelsall, Jacob Sharp, Lewis Dodd, Jonathan S. Williams, Ira T. Freeman, Jeptha Baldwin.

RESOLUTIONS PASSED.

Resolved 1st. That the sum of Eight Hundred dollars be raised for the support of the Poor the ensuing year. 2d. That the Road Tax for the ensuing year be equal to the one half of all other Taxes raised. 3d. That the sum of Ten Dollars be raised to aid the school fund. 4th. That the Tax on Dogs, for the ensuing year be Fifty cents. 5th. That the Town Committee be authorized to expend money, in case of an attempt to invade the territory of the township of Orange by the neighbouring Townships. 6th. That the next annual Election be held at the House of B. Day. 7th. That the next annual Town Meeting open at the House of Isaac A. Smith at 2 o'clock P. M.

Henry B. Campbell, Moderator.   Ichd. Harrison Jun. Clk.

At a meeting of the Town Committee held at the House of Isaac A. Smith April 18th 1840 The district of Road comprising Day street and the street running from Day street to Robinson's Sand Hill was set of as a separate district—Edwin White was appointed overseer.

1841.

April 12th, 1841. The thirty fifth annual Town Meeting of the Inhabitants of the Township of Orange was held at the House of Isaac A. Smith this day— The following named persons was duly elected Town officers for the ensuing year, and the following Resolutions passed—(viz).

Moderator, Jonas Smith; Town Clerk, Ichd. Harrison junr; Assessor, Jabez Pierson; Collector, William Condit; Judge of Election, Ira Canfield; Town Committee, Jesse Williams, Lewis Dodd, Daniel D. Reynolds, Jonathan S. Williams, Simeon Harrison; Surveyors of Highways, Timothy W. Mulford, Ira Harrison; Overseers of the Poor, James E. Smith, Noah Matthews; Chosen Freeholders, Henry B. Campbell, Jonas Smith; Commissioners of Appeal, Jotham Condit, Edwin Gray, Thomas W. Munn; Constables, John H. Dayton, Charles E. Willis, Aaron Quimby, Nathaniel Parsons; School Committee, James A. Williams, Philip Kingly, William Pierson Junr.; Overseers of the Highways, Chester Robinson, James E. Smith, Abraham Williams, Moses Harrison, John Perry, Hiram Condit, Jotham Pierson, Ira Harrison, William Vreeland, William Bodwell, E. M. Dodd, Richd. B. Harrison, Calvin Dodd, James Matthews, Jacob Sharp, Lewis Dodd, Jonathan S. Williams, Mahlon Freeman, Jeptha Baldwin, John Lindsley, Horrace Hedden, David W. Condit.

RESOLUTIONS PASSED.

Resd. 1st. That the sum of eight Hundred Dollars to be raised for the support of the poor the ensuing year. 2d. That the Road Tax for the ensuing year be equal to the one half of all other Taxes raised. 3d. That the sum of Three Hundred dollars be raised to aid the school fund. 4th. That the Tax on Dogs for the ensuing year be fifty cents. 5th. That the next annual Election be held at the House of Isaac A. Smith. 6th. That the next Town Meeting open at the House of B. Day at 2 o'clock P. M.

Jonas Smith, Moderator, Attest Ichd. Harrison, Ju. Clk.

At a meeting of the Town Committee·held at the House of B. Day on Saturday April 17th 1841 the district of Road known as the Walker district was disolved and added to district of William Bodwell. Attest, Ichd. Harrison Jun. Clk.

1842.

April 11th 1842. The thirty six annual Town Meeting of the Inhabitants of the Township of Orange was held at the House of Barnabas Day this day. The following named persons was duly elected Town officers for the ensuing year, and the following Resolutions passed.

Moderator, Aaron B. Harrison; Town Clerk, Ichd. Harrison, Jr.; Assessor, Jabez Pierson; Collector, William Condit; Judge of Election, William Stites; Town Committee, Jonathan S. Williams, Lewis Mitchel, Isaac Baldwin, John H. Matthews, Cyrus Baldwin; Surveyors of Highways, Timothy W. Mulford, George W. Smith; Overseers of the Poor, James E. Smith, Henry Pierson; Chosen Freeholders, Daniel D. Reynolds, Isaac A. Smith; Commissioners of Appeal, Jotham Condit, Thomas W. Munn, Ira Condit; Constables, Caleb P. Williams, William H. Leonard, Nathaniel Parsons, Aaron Quimby; School Committee, James A. Williams, Eleazer M. Dodd, Uzal W. Condit; Overseers of the Highways, Chester Robinson, Ira Canfield, Abraham Williams, Thomas O. Woodruff, Hiram Condit, George Perry, Ira Harrison, John Mitchel, Ziba E. Tomkins, E. M. Dodd, Richd. B. Harrison, Calvin Dodd, Richd. Kelsall, Jacob Sharp, Lewis Dodd, Jonathan S. Williams, Moses Lindsly, Jeptha Baldwin, John Lindsly, Edmund S. Alvord, David W. Condit.

RESOLUTIONS PASSED.

Resolved 1th. That the sum of Six Hundred dollars be raised for the support of the poor the ensuing year. 2d. That the Road Tax be equal to the one half of all the other Taxes raised. 3d. That the sum of Five dollars be raised to aid the school fund. 4th. That the dog tax for the ensuing year be fifty cents. 5th. That the Town Committee be authorized to resist any attempt to alter the Boundary line of the Township, and that the same be in force until recinded. 6th. That the next Election be held at the House of B. Day. 7th. That the next Town Meeting open at the House of Isaac A. Smith at 2 o'clock P. M.

Aaron B. Harrison, Modr. Attest Ichd. Harrison Jur. Clk.

1843.

April 19th, 1843. The thirty seventh annual Town meeting of the Inhabitants of the Township of Orange was held at the House of Isaac A. Smith this day—The following persons was duly elected Town officers for the ensuing year and the following Resolutions passed.

Moderator, Aaron B. Harrison; Town Clerk, Ichd. Harrison, Jur.; Assessor, Jabez Pierson; Collector, William Condit; Judge of Election, William Stites; The Town Committee, Thomas O. Woodruff, Lewis Mitchel. Issac Baldwin, Joseph A. Condit, Cyrus Baldwin; Surveyors of the Highway, Timothy W. Mulford, George W. Smith; Overseers of the Poor, James E. Smith, Henry Pierson; Chosen Freeholders, Calvin Dodd, Aaron B. Harrison; Commissioners of Appeal, Jotham Condit, Thomas W. Munn, Ira Condit; Constables, Caleb P. Williams, Aaron Quimby,

Nathaniel Parsons, William H. Leonard; School Committee, Uzal W. Condit, Elizar M. Dodd, Abraham Harrison; Overseers of Highways, William Peck, Ira Canfield, Ira Condit, William S. Perry, Hiram Condit, George Perry, Ira Harrison, John Mitchel, Ziba E. Tomkins, Stephen Dodd, Richd. B. Harrison, Calvin Dodd, Richd. Kelsall, Laurance Coaker, Lewis Dodd, Jonathan S. Williams, Edwin Gray, Jeptha Baldwin, Jacob A. Sharp, Edmund S. Alvord, Bethuel Crane.

RESOLUTIONS PASSED.

Resolved 1th. That the sum of Eight Hundred dollars be raised for the support of the poor the ensuing year. 2d. That the Road Tax be equal to the one half of all other Taxes raised. 3d. That the sum of five Dollars be raised to aid the school fund. 4th. That the Dog Tax for the ensuing year be fifty cents. 5th. That the next Election be held at the House of Isaac A. Smith. 6th. That the next Town Meeting open at the House of Barnabas Day at 2 o'clock P. M.

Aaron B. Harrison, Modr. Attest, Ichd. Harrison, Jur. Clk.

1844.

April 8th, 1844. The Thirty eight annual Town Meeting of the Inhabitants of the Township of Orange was held at the House of Barnabas Day this day. The following persons was duly elected Town officers for the ensuing year, and the following Resolutions passed

Moderator, Aaron B. Harrison; Town Clerk, Ichd. Harrison Junr.; Assessor, Jabez Pierson; Collector, William Condit; Judge of Election, William Stites; Town Committee, Cyrus Baldwin, Orlando Quimby, Timothy W. Mulford, Lewis Mitchel, Jonathan S. Williams; Surveyors of the Highways, Allen Dodd, Ira Harrison; Overseers of the Poor, James E. Smith, Aaron Quimby; Chosen Freeholders, Calvin Dodd, Aaron B. Harrison; Commissioners of Appeal, Jonas Smith, Thomas W. Munn, Lewis Dodd; Constables, Aaron Quimby, Nathaniel Parsons, Charles E. Willis, Jonathan DeCamp; School Committee, Abraham Harrison, Eleazer M. Dodd, Uzal W. Condit; Overseers of the Highways, William Peck, Moses B. Canfield, Abraham Williams, Thomas O. Woodruff, Hiram Condit, Daniel S. Williams, Ira Harrison, Daniel Dodd, Ziba E. Tomkins, Eleazer M. Dodd, Richd. B. Harrison, Calvin Dodd, Aaron Williams, Elias Meeker, Noah Baldwin, Jonathan DeCamp, Ira Freeman, John Tomkins, Edward Condit, Robert McChesnee, David W. Condit.

RESOLUTIONS PASSED.

Resolved 1th. That the sum of Eight Hundred dollars be raised for the support of the poor the ensuing year. 2d. That the sum of five hundred dollars be raised by Taxation—which sum shall be expended in the purchase of broken stone to be delivered on the main road between the foot of the mountain and the Newark line, to be used on such portion of the road as are in a proper condition to receive such superstructure. The Town Committee to advertise publickly for proposals for the aforesaid materials, and the contract to be given to the lowest bidder. 3d. That the Resolution directing all money raised for working the roads be expended in district in which it is assessed be rescinded. 4th. That the road Tax for the ensuing year be equal to the one half of all other Taxes. 5th. That the Dog tax for the ensuing year be fifty cents. 6th. That the sum of fifty dollars be raised to aid the school fund. 7th. That the next annual Election be held at the House of Barnabas Day. 8th. That the next Town Meeting open at the House of Isaac A. Smith at 2 o'clock P. M.

Aaron B. Harrison, Moderator. Attest. Ichd. Harrison, Junr. Town Clerk.

At a special Town Meeting of the Inhabitants of the Township of Orange, held at the House of Isaac A. Smith the 4th day of May A. D. 1844 by order of the Town committee to appoint one Overseer of the Poor, one Surveyor of Highway, one commissioner of appeals, those persons elected at the annual Town Meeting having neglected to qualify according to Law—also to reconsider the resolution raising Five hundred dollars extra road tax—when Jabez Pierson was chosen Moderator; James E. Smith Overseer of the Poor; Ira Harrison Surveyor of the Highway; Jonas Smith Commissioner of Appeals, and the following Resolutions adopted:

Resolved 1th. That the resolution raising five hundred dollars extra road tax be reconsidered. 2d. That the above nmed Resolution be annuled.

Jabez Pierson, Moderator, Attest, Ichd. Harrison, Junr. Clerk.

1845.

April 14th 1845. the thirty ninth annual Town meeting of the Inhabitants of the Township of Orange was held at the House of Isaac A. Smith this day. The following officers were duly elected for Town officers for the ensuing year.

Judge of Election, Ichd. Harrison, Jur.; Town Clerk, Eliazor M. Dodd; Assessor, Jabez Pierson; Collector, William Condit; Chosen Freeholders, Charles Harrison, Calvin Dodd; Commissioners of Appeal, Thomas W. Munn, Jonas Smith, Abijah Harrison, Jr.; Overseers of the Poor, Aaron Quinby, James E. Smith; Surveyors of the Highways, Timothy W. Mulford, Ira Harrison; Town Committee, Lewis Dodd, Jonathan S. Williams, Joseph A. Condit, Orlando Quimby, Cyrus Baldwin; School Committee, Abraham Harrison, Daniel Dodd, Jr., Charles R. Day; Constables, Charles E. Willis, Aaron Quinby, William B. Williams, William M. Sayer; Justices of the Peace, Stephen M. Peck, Cyrus Baldwin, Jesse Williams, Aaron Pierson.

There was raised for the support of the poor Eight Hundred dollars. There was raised for school purposes five dollars. The Tax on dogs was fixed at fifty cents. The Amount of Road Tax was not fixed. The next State and County Election to be held at Isaac A. Smith's. The next annual Town to be held at the house of John C. More.

Ichd. Harrison, Jr. Town Clerk.

EARLY TOWN RECORDS

THE ORANGE TOWNSHIP COMMTY BOOK.

The Commity of the Township of Orange meet at the House of Samuel Munns on Tuesday the 21st day of April 1807 10 o'Clock, A. M. present Daniel Williams Abijah Harrison, Thomass Baldwin, John Dean, & Stephen D. Day when they unanimous elected Stephen D Day their chairman for the present year and proceded to bisness by taking Bonds of the following officers viz Nathan Squier as Collector for the Township in the sum of one Thousand Dollars with Aaron Munn his security, John Quinby as Constable in the Township Appeared and his bond for one thousand Dollars and Stephen Peck his security—Noah Matthews Appeared and gave his bond for the sum of one thousand Dollars and David Condit his surety—when John Quinby & Noah Matthews were accordingly quallified in to office—Stephen D. Day was appointed as a commity to enquire as to a residence of the poor.

Fryday 24th April the Township Commity meet at David Reynolds in New Ark at 2 O'clock P. M. in order to make a division of the poor with the Township of New Ark, Present, Stephen D. Day, Thomas Baldwin, John Dean, Daniel Williams & Abijah Harrison and Proceeded to bisness and made such a division as we thought was just and accordingly instructed our overseer to take charge of such poor Persons as belonged to our Township.

Saturday June 20th. the Township Commity meet at Samuel Munns. present Stephen D. Day, Thomas Baldwin, Daniel Williams, John Dean, & Abijah Harrison and proceeded to bisness appointed Doctr. Isaac Pierson & Major Amos Harrison a comity on the part of our Township to meet a committee of the Township of New Ark in order to ascertain the division line betwixt the two Townships they then examined the accounts of Henry Stryker, Esq. Collector for the Last year and found a ballance in his hands and gave Stephen D. Day an order to draw the same the Ballance appeared to be Forty three Dollars Eighty-nine cents.

March 28 the Committee meet at House of Samuel Munn in order to make a settlement of the Business for this year but had so much business on hand that they Adjourned to Meet at Moses Condit on the morning of the Eleventh of April next.

April 11th 1808 the Township meet at the House of Moses Condit Jur. and proceeded to Business and made a settlement with the Collector & Constables of the Township & the chairman of the Committee was Instructed to make out a report to the Town meeting which was accordingly complyed with.

Orange 18th April 1808. The Orange Township Committee meet at the House of Mouses Condit, Jur. present Major Jabez Pierson Capt Thomas Baldwin, Daniel Williams, Samuel Condit Stephen D. Day when Stephen D. Day was nominated for chairman for the ensuing year and unanimously Elected when the committee proceeded to Business they appointed Jabez Pierson & Stephen D. Day a Committee to run the line betwixt the township of New Ark & Orange.

voted that the chairman draw an order on the County Collector for Thirty six Dollars for pay for a black child of Mrs.—— and pauper.

voted that Chairman of the Committee make such arrangements for a settlement betwixt the Township of New Ark as he may think proper Respecting the poor in Dispute betwixt the two Townships.

voted that they should take bounds the following sums viz

John Quinby gave his bond with Hyram Quinby Security for one Thousand Dollars as Collector of the Township Noah Matthews appeared & gave his bond with Moses Condit his security for one thousand dollars as Constable of the Township. Samuel Munn appeared & gave his bond with John Harrison his Surety for one thousand Dollars as Constable. when Noah Matthews and Samuel Munn were Qualifyd in to office.

May 7th 1808. Survey of the lines Betwixt the Townships of Newark & Orange are as follows viz. Beginning at the Turky Eagle Rock, and running from thence South Thirty nine degrees and forty five mints east one hundred and fifteen chain to the middle of Phenius Crane Bridge thence South Sixty degrees & seventeen minuts east seventy nine chain to Silas Dodd, Bridge thence South Thirty degrees & thirty nine minutes East ninety chain to the Boiling Spring thence South twenty nine degrees & forty minutes west seventy three chains and forty Links to peck's Bridge thence South thirty nine degrees fifteen minutes west two hundred and six chain to Sayres, Roberts Bridge at Camp Town thence South forty seven degrees and forty minutes west one hundred and ten chains to a bridge in the Elizabeth town line where it crosses Elizabeth River.

Caleb Quinby appeared and took the oath of office.

Orange 27th May 1808. The Town Committees of Orange and Newark meet at the House of Moses Condit Jur. in order to make a Division of the poor persons that have been in Dispute when Stephen D. Day was Elected chairman and after considerable altercation on the subject they agreed to make a Division which was as follows. The township of Orange was to take J—— R—— and Mrs. H—— P—— and the children that is at present with her.

voted that David D. Crand and Stephen D. Day be a committee to arrange & settle the account between the two townships.

Agreeable to notice the Township Committee of the Townships of Newark and Orange meet at the house of Moses Condit Jur. inkeeper in Orange on the third Day of June, 1808 for the purpose of dividing the poor of the said townships not heretofore agree upon and said Committees amicably agreed to the following division the Township of Orange by their Committee agreed and It was excepted by the Committee of Newark that they take as their quota the following persons and the remainder be provided for by the Township of Newark viz. (Here follow the names of seventeen persons.) The Committees directed their chairman to make out two certificates, one for each Town and sign the same. In conformity to the said order of the Committees we the subscribers do Certify that the foregoing division of the poor is Just and done as agreed upon by the Committees respectively. as witness our hand this Seventeenth day of August, 1808.

D. D. Crane, Chairman of Newark Committee.

Stephen D. Day, Chairman of Orange Committee.

Orange 4th April 1809 The Town Committee of Orange meet at the house of Moses Condit Jrs. present Thomas Baldwin, Daniel Williams, Jabez Pierson, Samuel Condit, & Stephen D. Day.

Noah Matthews, one of the Constables of Said Township made a Return of bad debts and debts that he had not collected all which he promises to Collect If in his power and the Committee agreed that the said Noah Matthews should not be accountable unless he collected the following persons and the sums anexed to their respective names. (Here follow the names of eighteen delinquents, with a total amount of $23.65.)

April 6th 1809 Jabez Roberts give his Note Caleb Tichenor as overseer poor Six Dollar three cents on Demand. $6-3.

April 17th 1809. the Orange township Committee meet at the house of Samuel Munn present Mr. Daniel Williams, Josiah Baldwin, Samuel Condit, Thomas Baldwin, Abraham Winans. When Abraham Winans was nominated for chairman for the ensuing and was Elected · then the Committee proceeded to business voted that the following Bonds Should be taken with Security viz. John Quinby gave his Bond for one thousand dollars with John Porter security as Collector for the township of Orange for one year.

Noah Matthews appeared and gave his Bond for one thousand dollars and Samuel Munn security for Constable the ensuing year and was Qualified into office. Peter Dean appeared & gave his Bond for one thousand dollars with David Condit security as Constable for the township of Orange for one year & was qualified into office. Nathan Tichenor appeared and gave his Bond for one thousand dollars with Joseph B. Ball security as Constable for the township of Orange for one year & was Qualified into office.

voted that the Chairman Should buy a trunk to keep the township Committee Books and papers in and bee paid for by the town.

Voted that Zadock Brown should have fifty five dollars of the town money by giving Job Brown as security for one year wich Note was drawn payable to Abraham Winans Chairman of the town Committee and the Interest was put in for one year wich made fifty Eight dollars Eighty five Cents payable at Newark Bank.

May the 16th 1809. the Orange township Committee meet at the house of Samuel Munns at 2 O'clock in the afternoon. Present Capt Thomas Baldwin, Josiah Baldwin, Daniel Williams, Samuel Condit, Abraham Winans, and proceeded to Business when Enos Tompkins appeared and took his Certificate that he was Chosen one of the Overseers of the highway. the Chairman was otherized to give Aaron Quinby a Certificate if he Required one. We appointed a Committee to settle with the Township Committee of New Ark if it was thought best. the Committee was Thomas Baldwin, Josiah Baldwin and Abraham Winans.

July 8th 1809. Agreeable to notice the Orange Township Committee meet the township Committee of New Ark at the house of Moses Roff in New Ark at 10 O'clock in the morning. present belonging to the Orange township Committee Abraham Winans, Daniel Williams, Josiah Baldwin, Samuel Condit, Thomas Baldwin and proceeded to settle the account of the two townships all of which we settled Except Our proportion of the five hundred dollars wich the town Land was sold for wich we paid the two Sevenths of five hundred dollars when the two townships was together for Carrying on a Law Suit wich settlement will appear by Receipt, given by both of the townships and were signed by the whole of the two town Committees. Except John Dodd he went away on business the Receipt is as follows.

Newark July 8th 1809

on settlement of accompt made this day between the two Town Committees of Orange and New Ark there was a balance found of three dollars Ninety three Cents in favour of Newark township a demand was made of two Seventh of five hundred dollars was made by Orange Township for mones expended in defending the title to town Lands but Newark Committee Refused to act upon it the above balance was paied by us errors excepted Signed by Stephen Hays, Aaron Johnson, James Ventevool Abraham Spier, Newark Committee; Abraham Winans, Daniel Williams, Samuel Condit, Thomas Baldwin, Josiah Baldwin, Orange Committee.

In the settlement there was a balane found in the hand of Henery Stryker Collector for Newark township of twenty three dollars Seventy two Cents wich money they gave the Orange town Committee an order to Receive wich money belongs to Orange according to settlement.

the Orange township is to pay James Edgins for an old accompt that he held against the New Ark township before we was sot of which amounted too thirteen dollars and twenty one Cents $13.21

Orange Novem. 6th 1809.

the Orange Township Committee met at the house of Samuel Munn at 6 o'clock in the afternoon. present Abraham Winans, Daniel Williams, Josiah Baldwin, Samuel Condit, and took into Consideration the Case of Mr. W—— Respecting his Legacy left him by Mr. Ashfield. when there was a number of the neighbors consulted about it when it was agreed that we should give Mr. Stogden a fee and git his opinion on the Case and Abraham Winans & Josiah Baldwin was appointed to do it it was agreed that we Should Send Mr. Stogden by Mr. Chetwood twenty dollars.

Novem. 10th. Mr Baldwin and Abraham Winan called on Mr. Chetwood and it was thought Best that we Should Call on Judge Morris at Brunswick wich we did the same day and got what information we Could Respecting the Business and Came Back and give Mr. Chetwood twenty dollars for a Retaining fee for Mr. Stogden and to get his opinion in Writing.

Orange Decm. 20th 1810

The Orange Township Committee Met at the house of Samuel Munn on Wensday at 6 o'clock in the Evening Present. Abraham Winans, Josiah Baldwin, Daniel Williams, Samuel Condit and proceeded to Business and Abraham Winans and Josiah Baldwin gave what information they had obtained from Mr. Chetwood & Judge Morris and it was thought best to appoint a Committee of two to wait on Mr. Brenkerhoof and see if the Business Could not be Compromised without going to Law with him and Samuel Condit & Caleb Tichenor where appointed no further business they adjourned.

Orange Jany 6th. 1810. * * * the Committee made they Report and it was not agreed to and Samuel Condit was appointed to wait on Mr. Brenkerhoof and get his final answer.

Orange Feby 10th 1810. * * * Samuel Condit made his report and it was thought best that he should wait on Mr. Brenkerhoof once more.

Orange March 19th 1810 * * * Mr. Samuel Condit Informed us that Mr. Brenkerhoof would give Orange township Committee four hundred dollars for N—— W——'s wife's legacy if we would git N—— W—— to administer on his wife's Legacy and git a power of an attorney from said W—— and a Receipt from said W—— in full and we gave him a Receipt in full, all wich we agreed to and Caleb Tichenor & Josiah Baldwin was appointed to go with said W—— and take out Letters of administration wich was done and Mr. Brenkerhoof gave this township four hundred dollars in a Note payable in one & two years without Interest wich was agreed to by the town Committee.

Orange March 26, 1810. The Township Committee of Orange met at the House of Samuel Munn. present. Abm. Winans, Thomas Baldwin, Daniel Williams, Samuel Condit, Jonas Baldwin. Noah Matthews one of the Constables of Said Township made a return of bad debts that he had not collected all which he promises to collect, if in his power & the committee agree that the Said Noah Matthews should not be accountable unless he collected of the following persons & the sums annexed to their respective names, for the bad debts this year. (Here follow the names of thirteen persons, with a total amount of $14.05) Noah Matthews a Constable paid into the hands of the Town Committee Seven Dollars & 80 cents, recd as bad debts not then collected.

April 16th 1810. The Town Committee meet at the House of Moses Condit, on Monday 16th Day April, 1810, when they proceeded to elect a Chairman when Stephen D. Day was unanimously Elected Chairman for one year. present the following Stephen D. Day, Thomas Baldwin, Josiah Baldwin, Samuel Condit, Daniel Williams. (The only business transacted was the taking of the usual bonds in $1,000 each from the various town officials.)

Monday the 28th May for the purpose of Boarding out N—— W—— when they made a Bargain with Josiah Baldwin to take him and find him vittals & Clothing until the first Monday in May 1811 and to return him to the Town as well Clothed as he was when the took him his Clothing to be appraised.

July 12th 1810. A Committee out of the Town Committee meet with the overseers poor to bind out the poor Children and bound out the following viz: (Four names.)

March 26 1811. The Town Committee meet at Moses Condit in order settle with overseers of the poor which went through and made a settlement they then settled Assessor, Town Collector, and different clament against the Township which can be seen as refered to the accounts current. John Hedden, one of the Constables of Orange Township made a return that he could not Collect the following persons Tax but that he would use his best Indavorers to collect them and pay them over to the Town Committee the following are the names of the delinquents & sum annexed to their respective names. (Here follow nine names with a total of $8.82).

Orange 16 April 1811. The Orange Town Committee meet at the house of Samuel Munn present the following viz. Capt. Thomas Baldwin, Daniel Williams, Josiah Baldwin & Stephen D. Day. Absent, Major Abram Harrison, when they proceeded to Elect their Chairman when Stephen D. Day was unanimously Elected (The usual bonds were then taken from the Township officers in $1,000 each.) The Committee then gave out Certificates to such of the overseers of the publick highways as made application No other business appearing before the committee they adjourned.

Orange April 9th 1812. The Township Committee meet at the house of Samuel Munns at nine o'clock in the forenoon present viz: Stephen D. Day, Josiah Baldwin, Capt Thomas Baldwin, Daniel Williams, Major Abraham Harrison, when they proceeded to business they made a Settlement with the Town Collector Constables of the Town Ship, when John Hedden one Constable of the Township made the following Return that he had not been able to Collect the following taxes viz:. (Eleven names follow amounting to $13.61) the Justices and Overseers of the poor of the Township of Orange came into consultation with the Township Committee Respecting S—— B—— daughter of P—— B—— deceased, a Lunatick and It was agreed unanimously that It was propper that the Town should proceed to secure the property of the above named so that she might not become chargeable to the Township.

Orange 18th April 1812. The Orange Town committee meet at the house of Moses Condit present the following viz: Josiah Baldwin, Abijah Harrison, Capt. Abner Crowel, Enos Pierson, Daniel Dodd, When they proceeded to appoint this Chairman Josiah Baldwin being unanimously elected they proceeded to business John Hedden and Noah Matthews appeared and declined serving as Constables agreeable to their appointment at town meeting the township Committee proceeded to and appointed two others viz: Josiah L. Day and Josiah Leonard. (The usual bonds were then taken from the township officers) the town Committee agree to leave Robert Earl's Note which when collected amounted to $6 with Stephen D. Day Esqr., for collection. the Committee gave out a number of Certificates for overseers of highway and agree if any of sd Committee be called upon for Certificate to make out one signed by order of the Chairman no other business appearing before them they adjourned.

1812 June 24 the town committee met at Samuel Munns present Josiah Baldwin, Abijah Harrison, Enos Pierson, and Daniel Dodd, and proceeded to settle the district of mountain road near Cyrus Freemans and appointed Jared Harrison Overseer of sd district.

Orange 5th April 1813. The Township Committee meet at the house of Moses Condit at nine o'clock in the morning present the following viz: Josiah Baldwin, Abijah Harrison Enos Pierson. Abner Crowell and Daniel Dodd when the proceeded to business they made a settlement with the town Collector and Constables of the township Josiah L. Day one of the Constables of the township made the following Return that he had not been able to collect the following taxes. (Here follow eight names amounting to $5.10)

Orange April 19th 1813. The Orange Township Committee Meet at the house of Ira Munn Jr. at 9 o'clock in the Morning. Present Josiah Baldwin, Enos Pierson, Abner Crowell, & Abraham Winans. absent Abijah Harrison. When they proceed to Business and Josiah Baldwin was Elected President of said Board & Abraham Winans Elected Clk. (The usual bonds were taken.) Enos Pierson was appointed to Call on Mr. Brinkerhoof for the money that he owed the town no other business before the Committee they adjourned to Meet at the house of Moses Condit Jr. on the Second Monday in May.

May 9th 1813. The Township Committee meet at the house of Moses Condit Jr. at nine o'clock in the Morning. Present Josiah Baldwin, Cham., Abijah Harrison, Abner Crowell, Enos Pierson, & Abraham Winans Clk. And Proceeded divide the Districts of Road and give the Overseers the portion of Road to keep in order by John Peck, Ezra Gildersleeve, Amos Freeman, Cyrus Freeman, Uzal Dodd, Caleb Harrison, Timothy Williams, Aron Crowell, & William Perry, and then adjourned to Meet the Next Saturday at Ira Muns.

May 15th 1813. The Town Committee meet according to adjournment at the house of Ira Munn. Present Josiah Baldwin, Chm. Abner Crowell, Enos Pierson, Abijah Harrison and Abraham Winans, and proceed to give out Certificates to the overseers of the highway viz. Elihu Crowell, Timothy Ball, Ruben Ward, Jacob Harrison, Benjamin Lindsley, Daniel Dodd, Moses Orsboun, Erastus Pierson, Henry Townley, Stephen Tichenor & Abijah Harrison, no more business we adjourned.

October 12th. on Monday evening the town Committee Meet at the house of Moses Condit jr. present Josiah Baldwin, chairman, Abijah Harrison, Abner Crowell, Enos Pierson & Abraham Winans, and proceed to appoint one overseer of the highway and one Commissioner of appeal when Josiah Frost was chosen for both of the offices. This vacancy was occasioned by the death of Stephen Tichenor and Enos Pierson was appointed to call on Brinkerhoof for money and no more business we adjourned.

April 7th 1814. The Township Committee of Orange meet at the house of Ira Munn at Nine o'clock in the morning. Present Josiah Baldwin, Abner Crowell, Enos Pierson, Abijah Harrison & Abraham Winans, and proceed to settle with the town Collector and all other Persons that appeared to have business with them the Constable made his Return of bad debts that he could not collect of the following. (Eleven names amounting to $8.13).

April 18 1814. The township Committee meet at the house of Moses Condit Jr. at 9 o'clock in the Morning present Josiah Baldwin, Abijah Harrison, Daniel Dodd, Abner Crowell, & Araham Winans, and proceed to bus. when Josiah Baldwin was chosen chairman and Abraham Winans Clk. Josiah Leonard one of the Constables appeared with his security and gave their bonds for one thousand dollars. & John Reock appeared with his security and gave Bond to the amount of one thousand dollars and there where viz. Josiah Leonard & John Reock sworninto office. John Quimby Collector appeared and and give his Bond for one thousand dollars with Hiram Quimby security Jeptha Baldwin one of the overseers of the poor appeared and where sworn into office and we gave out a number of surtifecates to overseers of the Road Isaac Pierson one of the Overseers of Road Came forward and Declared he would not serve as one of the overseers of the Road and he declined to serve, the town Committee ordered the town Clerk to call a town Meeting as soon as Convenient Abraham Baldwin one of the overseers of the poor for Last year appeared and the town committee Settled with him, his own accompt against the town and for the strays and no other business we adjourned.

Orange, April 2d, 1815. the Orange Township Committee Meet at the house of Ira Munn on Monday April 2d, at 10 o'clock in the Morning Present. Josiah Baldwin char. Abijah Harrison, Daniel Dodd, Abner Crowell, & Abraham Winans Clk. and proceeded to settle with John Quimby, Josiah Leonard, John Reock, William Williams, John Lindsley, Daniel Kilbourn, Nathan Williams for damage done to his sheep & Zebina Dodd for damage done to his sheep Nathaniel B. Gardner for damage done to his sheep and adjourned to meet on Friday at Moses Condit at 2 Clk. in the afternoon Abraham Winans Clk.

John Reock returned as bad debts the following Names. (Fifteen names amounting to $14.37).

Orange April 6th 1815 the Orange Township Committee Meet at the house of Moses Condit Jr. at 2 o'clock in the afternoon and there where present (same as above) and proceeded to business and settled with John B. Bald for damag don his sheep by Dogs wich sum $4 dools 8 Cents and proceeded to settle with Jeptha Baldwin.

The Township Committee of Orange Meet at the house of Moses Condit J on the 17th day of April 1815 at Nine o'clock in the morning Present Josiah Baldwin, Abijah Harrison, abner Crowell, Nathan Williams & Abraham Winans and proceed to business when Josiah Baldwin was Chosen Chairman and Abraham Winans Clk. John Reock one of the Constables appeared with his security Daniel Matthews and gave their bond to the township for 1000 dollars for his true performance Daniel Ball one of the Constables appeared with Joseph W. Camp, his security, and gave their Bond for 1000 dolls for his true performance John Quimby appeared with John Porter his security and gave their Bond for 1000 dollar for his true performance as Collector, and a number of the overseers of the Roads appeared and got their Certificats and no further business we adjourned.

The Orange Township Committee Meet at the house of Ira Munn on Wednesday the third day of April 1816 at Nine O'clock in the Morning (Same present as above.) and proceed to Settle with John Quimby Collector, and balance his account and Settled with William Williams and Jeptha Baldwin overseers of the poor and paid Jude Lindsley his Bill for services done the town and appointed William Williams & Jeptha Baldwin to secure the property of the widow Wilson for the town paid John Reock his Bill for services done the town & David Ball for his services done the town and no further Business we adjourned to Meet on Saturday 6 day of April at 1 o'clock in the afternoon at the house of Moses Condit Jr. Bades Debts returned by the Constable John Reock for year 1815 (Two names, $2.25.)

the town Ship Committee meet at the house of Moses Condit Jr. on Saturday the 6th day of April 1816 (All present as above.) and proceed to settle with Stephen D. Day for his services & paid him for one Lamb killed by Dogs $1.50 Cash on it $2.00 and then proceed to make out a Statement to lay before the town Meeting and no further business we adjourned to Meet at the same Place on Monday at Nine O'clock in the morning.

Monday May 8th the Township Committee met and organized and took the customary bonds from the Township officers.

On May 18th the Committee settled with the last year's overseers as usual * * Isaac Pierson applyed for pay for doctoring ——— ——— in the year 1814 by the direction of the overseers of the poor we voted that he should bee paid for his services the time that she was not at perry the farmers of the poors, Jeptha Baldwin presented his Bill for pay for sheep killed by Dogs also Jabez Pierson presented his Bill for the Like wich Bills was left in the trunk and not payed no further business we adjourned.

The meetings of April 8th and April 12th 1817 were devoted to the usual reports of the non-collecting of taxes, and a large number of claims for sheep killed by dogs, all of which were paid.

The next meeting of importance was on May 13th, 1817, when the record reads * * The object of the meeting being to take into consideration the propriety of joining Bloomfied Township in Purchasing a farm, on which to build a Poor House; when it was unanimously agreed That the Town Committee and the Overseers of the Poor should go and view a farm in Bloomfield Township, and meet on Saturday 16th Inst at 12 O'clock at the House of Daniel Kilburns for that purpose.

May 16th 1817, the record reads, The Overseers not attending, we proceeded to Bloomfield and after viewing the aforesaid farm we agreed to let it rest for the present.

December 20th. 1817, the next meeting of the Committee, the record runs, * * The Town Committee met by Request of the Chairman at the House of Moses Condit Junr. to consult on measures respecting a poor house, And having called upon several of the respectable inhabitants of The Township, when after due deliberation it was agreed that the subject be Postponed untill the next annual Town meeting and that all present do promulgate the same.

Ten meetings of the Committee follow with no business transacted that was recorded except on April 9th, 1819. Three children were bound out for Eighty dollars and this memorandum appears. "Abraham Winans gave his private Note to Moses Lindsley which is endorsed on his note of hand in favor of the Town."

From this point on the records are exceedingly meagre and only note the meeting of the Committee, and the perfunctory taking of bonds from the Township officials. The interesting features will hereafter only be noted.

April 20th, 1819. The object of the meeting was to adopt some method of appointing an overseer of the Poor. William Williams declined serving but by persuasion consented to serve.

May 3d, 1819, a resolution was passed "that the Town Collector be instructed to pay over to the Treasurer of the Township all monies by him collected for the use of the Town, of which resolution he has been duly notified."

April 14th, 1821. "Settled with Daniel Dodd treasurer of last year and found a Ballance in his hands of $306 7-100 dollars seven Cents and a note of one hundred dollars signed by Jonas Smith & John Quimby, wich he paid over to the clerk for the present year."

May 10th, 1823. "The committee agreed to set of a destrict of road beginning at Samuel Lindsley running from thence to Wm. Condits taking the road called cone street, also the destrict of road beginning at S. D. Day Esq. running to a gully in said road and appointed Daniel D. Condit, overseer of said road for the ensuing year."

April 15th 1826 The Committee decided to "meet on April 19th at the house of David Munn to view the different farms in the township which are offered for sale for a poor farm."

April 19, "the committee spent the day in going over a number of farms to select the most suitable one to locate the poor farm and appointed William Williams, Joel Harrison and Aaron Peck to get N. Baldwin and Josiah Baldwin's lowest price for their farms."

April 21st. "Abraham Winans, William Williams & Aaron Peck a committee to Call on Neamiah Baldwin & Josiah Baldwin and get their lowest price for their farms."

April 24th 1826. "The committee agreed unanimously to offer Jeptha Baldwin for Uzal Baldwin's farm 2800 hundred dollars which was done and by the chairman and accepted by J. Baldwin provided the said farm does not fall short of 57½ acres and if it does a reduction to be made on all short of 58 acres at 35 dollars per acre. the Chairman appointed William Williams, D. D. Condit & Ichabod Condit to attend on Friday 28th inst. on said farm at 9 o'clock A. M. to run out said farm."

April 29th 1826. "The committee met and settled with Jeptha Baldwin for Uzal Baldwin's farm the committee and overseers of the poor to

Give their not Uzal Baldwin payable the 1st day of January 1827 with
interest for 645.25
Mortgage to Joseph Demarest $500 interest 30................ 530.00
Mortgage to Abraham Ackerman 1500 interest due 60........ 1560.00
____
2735.25

May 20, 1826 "The Committee agreed to offer Doc. I. Pierson
Fifteen dollars to Doctor the poor for one year."

May 22d, The committee agreed to build a milk house.

May 24, The committee appointed Aaron Peck & D. D. Condit to
attend to the building of the milk house.

October 7, 1826. The town committee appointed Abraham Winans,
& William Williams, a committee to superintendent the poor farm.

January 6, 1827. "The Town committee appointed Abraham
Winans, and Joel Harrison to Purchase a lot Chesnt timber."

March 14, 1827. "The town committee appointed Abraham Winans
to Purchase cows for the poor farm."

May 3d, 1828. The town committee meet at Mr. Condit at 3 o'clock
P. M. & agreed to appropriat the following sums to the definit Schools
in Said township. N. Farms, $14.00, W. Destrict, $14.00, Corner, $10.00,
Jeptha Baldwin, $14.00, Camptown, $10.00, South School, $14.00, Spring
School, $14.00, Peck School, $14.00, White school, $14.00, Freeman
School, $14.00, Academy, $28.00, Dodd School, $14.00.

April 10th 1830. "Resolved, that the committee borrow two hundred dollars to pay up the bills for the year which was obtained of Jonas
Smith, Ambrose Condit, Ichabod Condit & Moses Lindsley at 9 months
from the 10th inst."

April 14th 1832. "That Ten dollars be appropriated to the district
of road of which John E. Courter is overseer, an appropriation of Ten
dollars was made to the district of road of which Jonathan Lindsley is
overseer."

October 20th, 1832. "Resolved That Aaron Brown be appointed
Commissioner of Appeal in place of Joel Harrison who neglected to take
the oath of office according to law."

June 13th, 1833. "Resolved that the Town Clerk be instructed to
advertize a Special Town Meeting on Saturday the 22d inst. at 6 o'clock
P. M. at the house of Benjamin S. Jarvis, to appoint an overseer of the
poor in place of William Williams, decd. and two Commissioners of Appeal."

Orange, February 14th, 1834. "Resolved that One hundred Dollars
be appropriated from the funds of the township to defray the expences
of delegates to attend the Legislature now in session at Trenton to oppose the bill now pending to set off a new township in part from the
Township of Orange."

The Township Committees of the Township of Orange and Clinton
met this Twenty-sixth day of April Eighteen hundred and thirty-four
for the purpose of settling and dividing the property between the said
two townships agreeable to the provisions of an act which passed the
legislature of New Jersey February the Nineteenth in the year aforesaid.
And also for the division of the poor belonging to the aforesaid two
townships.

Whereupon it was agreed as follows, viz:—That the Inhabitants of
the Township of Orange shall pay to the Inhabitants of the Township of

Clinton, the sum of Nine Hundred and twenty-five dollars on or before the first day of April eighteen hundred thirty five with Interest from this date untill païd. And the aforesaid Committee have alloted to the Township of Clinton the following poor persons as of right belonging to them viz. A—— O——, J—— B——, H—— W——, S—— O——, G—— L——, and R—— L——, And the said Committees have agreed to let their respective Council decide to which of the said two townships the following persons do of right belong viz,—M—— C—— and her three children. And the aforesaid committees have agreed that the Township of Clinton shall pay one quarter of the expence in supporting the paupers of necessity now chargeable to Orange Township. And the Township of Clinton shall remove all the poor persons belonging to them within three days from this date. And the aforesaid Township of Clinton agrees to receive the aforesaid sum of Nine Hundred twenty five Dollars as their proportion in full of all demands against the aforesaid Township of Orange.

Alvah Sherman,		Jonas Smith,	
Obadiah Meeker,	Committee of Clinton Township.	Stephen Condit,	Committee of Orange Township.
Lewis Pierson,		Edward Gruett,	
James Van Houten,		Danl. Dodd,	
Ezra Durand Jr.		Ambrose Condit.	

May 10th, 1834. "Resolved that an appropriation be made from the funds of the Township sufficient to erect a pound and That Jonas Smith and Daniel Dodd be a Committee to attend to procuring material for the aforesaid purpose."

April 2d, 1836. "The Township Committee met at the house of Benjamin S. Jarvis, and for causes they deemed sufficient adjourned to the house of Isaac A. Smith."

April 11th, 1840. "The Town Committee on settlement with John Strong Superintendent of the Poor Farm, the Town Com. found due him Eighty-nine Dollars when on motion it was resolved the said sum be allowed him with interest from first of April 1840 until paid."

Orange, April 16th, 1842. * * "It was resolved to Present James Crowel with ten dollars for taking care of Mr. Y——, in his last sickness."

April 20th, 1844. * * "Resold. That Jonathan S. Williams take legal advice respecting the resolution past at the annual meeting for the raising the sum of 500 dollars for repairing the main road through Orange."

EARLY CHURCH RECORDS

A manuscript Church Record of Rev. Caleb Smith, from 1756 to the time of his death, together with a similar record by Rev. Jedidiah Chapman, from the beginning of his pastorate to 1784, were found among the old manuscripts of Dr. William Pierson, deceased, and in 1887 were kindly put by his son, Dr. William Pierson, into the possession of Dr. Stephen Wickes, who printed them in his excellent "History of the Oranges," published in 1892, and from which work they are here reproduced. These records are invaluable to those searching for the habitancy and genealogy of the earlier Mountain settlers.

The following is the list of members in communion of the Mountain Society prior to 1756:

Burnet, Silas.
Baldwin, Amos.
Baldwin, Aaron.
Baldwin, Robert
Baldwin, Benjamin.
Campbell, John.
Crane, Stephen.
Crane, William.
Crane, Noah.
Crane, Caleb.
Campbell, Benjamin.
Crane, Lewis, and wife.
Crowell, Recompence.
Croel, Joseph.
Canfield, Ebenezer.
Cundict, Daniel.
Cundict, David.
Cundict, Joanna, wife of David.
Cundict, Samuel, Jr.
Dod, John Jr. and wife.
Dod, Isaac.
Dod, Thomas.
Davies, Timothy and wife.
Freeman, Thomas and wife.
Freeman, Benjamin.
Freeman, John.
Freeman, Timothy and wife.
Gray, William and wife.
Gould, John, Jr.
Hedden, Eleazer, wife of.

Hedden, John.
Hedden, John, Jr.
Hand, William.
Hedden, Jos., wife of.
Harrison, Capt. Amos.
Harrison, David, wife of.
Harrison, Matthew and wife.
Marten, Jeremiah, wife of.
Mun, Joseph, wife of.
Mun, Benjamin.
Ogden, Nath'l; Eunice, wife of
Perry, Arthur.
Pierson, Bethuel.
Pierson, Samuel, Jr., wife of.
Pierson, Elihu, and wife of.
Peck, John.
Peck, Jesse and wife.
Riggs, Joseph.
Smith, John.
Tompkins, Jonathan.
Taylor, Jacob.
Taylor, Rachael, his wife.
Tompkins, ——, widow of
Ward, Ezekiel.
Ward, Abel.
Williams, Isaac.
Williams, Gershom, wife of.
Williams, Timothy, and wife.
Williams, Lieut. David.
Young, Jonathan.

ENTERED INTO COVENANT AFTER 1756

May	8, 1757.	Mary, wife of Silas Burnet.
June	11, 1758.	Hall, Mary.
July	9, 1758.	Joseph Riggs, wife of
Jan.	22, 1759.	Ward, John.
Aug.	17, 1759.	Williams, Capt. Matthew and wife.
Aug.	17, 1759.	Roe, Azel.
		Harrison, Joanna, wife of Stephn Harrison.
June	13, 1760.	Parsonate, George, and wife.
April	11, 1762.	Harrison, Saml, Senr.
June	20, 1762.	Harrison, David.
Aug.	8, 1762.	Young, Kezia, daugh. of Jonathan.

BAPTISMS FROM 1756 TO 1762. BY CALEB SMITH

1756.	Aug. 22.	Cyrus, son of Bethuel Pierson.
	Sept. 5.	David, son of Joseph Croel.
	Sept. 19.	Moses, son of Ezekiel Ward.
		John, son of Joseph Mun.
	Nov. 7.	Sarah, daugh. of Amos Baldwin.

1757.	Jan.		John, son of Widow John Tompkins.
	Jan.		Zadoc, son of John Hedden, Jr.
	Mar.	6.	Mary, daugh. of Daniel Cundict.
	Mar.	6.	Bethuel, son of Benjn Mun.
	April	24.	John, son of Caleb Crane.
	April	24.	Jemima, daugh. Amos Harrison.
	April	24.	Sarah, daugh. Ebenezer Canfield.
	April	24.	Jairus, son of Gershom Williams.
	May	8.	Edmund, son of Silas and Mary Burnet.
	May	8.	A child of William Hand.
	June	19.	Mary, wife of David Baldwin, and three of her children, Joseph, Rhoda, and Hulda.
	Oct.	9.	Sarah, daugh. of Christopher ——.
	Nov.	6.	A son of Arthur Perry.
	Nov.	27.	Moses, son of Timothy Freeman.
	Dec.	4.	Nathaniel, son of Noah Crane.
	Dec.	11.	Enos, son of Thomas Dod.
1758.	Feb.	5.	Aaron, son of Aaron Baldwin.
	Feb.	5.	Abijah, son of Isaac Dod.
	Feb.	25.	Katharine, daugh. of John Campbell.
	Mar.	4.	Jemima, daugh. of Silas Burnet.
	Mar.	4.	David, son of ——— Coleman.
	April	16.	Ebenezer, son of, and Sarah, daugh. of John Dod, Jr.
	May	7.	Phebe, daugh. of Eleazer Hedden.
			Thomas, son of Jeremiah Martin.
	May	14.	Elizabeth, daugh. of Joseph Hedden.
	May	21.	John, son of Jacob and Rachael Taylor.
	May	21.	Harry, servant boy of Lieut. David Williams. His master engaged for his Christian education.
	June	11.	Martha, daugh. of Stephen Crane.
	July	9.	Abijah, Aaron, Amos, Mary, children of Matthew Harrison.
	Aug.	3.	Benjamin Campbell and his two sons, Moses and Aaron.
	Aug.	27.	Charles, son of Lewis Crane.
	Sept.	17.	Jonathan, son of Abel Ward.
	Oct.	1.	Sarah, daugh. of Joseph Mun.
	Nov.	19.	Abigail, daugh. of Benj. Mun.
	Dec.	3.	John, son of Eleakim Crane.
	Dec.	24.	Adonijah, son of Matthew Harrison.
	Dec.	31.	Sarah, daugh. of Benjamin Baldwin.
1759.	Feb.	25.	Amos, son of Daniel Cundict.
	Feb.	25.	Isaac, son of Ezekiel Ward.
	Mar.	11.	Jane, daugh. of Arthur Perry.
	Mar.	18.	Joseph, son of Bethuel Pierson.
	Mar.	18.	Aaron, son of Isaac Williams.
	Mar.	18.	Sarah, daugh. of Samuel Pierson, Jr.
	May	6.	Comfort, daugh. of John Hedden.
	May	6.	A son of Silas Burnet.
	May	13.	Esther, daugh. of Amos Baldwin.
	May	30.	Phebe, daugh. of Jonathan Tompkins.
	June	24.	Martha, Lydia, daughters of David and Joanna Cundict.

	July	29.	Experience, daugh. of Joseph Riggs.
	Aug.	5.	Benjamin, Elizabeth, John, William, Stockman. Their parents being dead, Benj. Freeman, their God-father, solemnly engaged for their Christian education.
	Aug.	5.	Joseph, son of John Peck.
	Aug.	19.	Jemima, daugh., and Moses, son, of Jesse Peck.
	Aug.	19.	Uzal, son of John Dod, Jr.
	Aug.	19.	Jedidiah, son of John Freeman.
	Aug.	19.	A child (sex forgotten) of Gershom Williams.
	Sept.	2.	Samuel, Zenas, sons of Thomas Freeman.
	Oct.	7.	Jonas, Ruth, Peter, Robert, children of Timothy Williams.
	Oct.	7.	Cornelius, son of Timothy Davies.
	Nov.	11.	Abigail, daugh. of Isaac Dod.
1760.	Jan.	6.	Ruth, daugh. of Capt. Amos Harrison.
	Feb.	3.	Hannah, daugh. of Thomas Freeman.
	Feb.	24.	Lydia, daugh. of Jeremiah Marten.
	Mar.	23.	Susannah, daugh. of Aaron Baldwin.
	May	11.	Linus, son of Robert Baldwin.
	May	11.	Lois, daugh. of Stephen Crane.
	May	11.	Stephen, son of John Peck.
	May	25.	Mary, daugh. of Timothy Williams.
	June	13.	John, Nathaniel, sons of George Parsonate.
	June	15.	Charity, daugh. of John Campbell.
	June	22.	John, son of Robert McEndow.
	July	6.	Zadoc, son of William Crane.
			Moses, son of Samuel Condit, Jr.
1762.	Mar.	14.	Job, son of Jonathan Tompkins.
	April	4.	Hannah, daugh. of Elihu Pierson.
	April	4.	Nehemiah, son of Noah Crane.
	April	11.	Eleazer, son of Robert Baldwin.
	May	9.	Joanna, daugh. of Isaac Dod.
	June	13.	Child (name and sex forgotten) of Stephen Crane.
	June	20.	David, Susanna, children of David Harrison.
	June	20.	Sarah, daugh. of John Gould, Jr.
	June	25.	Caleb, son of Isaac Williams.
	Aug.	15.	Katharine, daugh. of Recompence Crowel.
	Aug.	29.	Enos, son of Samuel Pierson, Jr.
	Sept.	26.	Rebecca, daugh. of John Campbell.

The following is the record of the Mountain Society during the pastorate of Rev. Jedidiah Chapman, from 1766 to 1783, inclusive:

ENTERED INTO COVENANT

1766.	Sept.	8.	Abigail, wife of Job Crane.
			Crane, Rhoda, w. of Stephen Crane.
	Nov.	23.	Tompkins, Sarah, dau. of Obadiah.
	Nov.	16.	Cesar, the negro servant of Elder Pierson.
1767.	June	28.	Baldwin, Aaron, and wife.
	Aug.	31.	Freeman, Joseph, and w.
	Nov.	1.	Baldwin, Aaron, Elizth dau. of.

1768.	April 17.	Crane, Eleakim, w. of.
	April 17.	Smith, Joseph, Jr. Phebe, w. of.
	April 17.	Harrison, Jared, and w. Hannah.
	April 17.	Bostedo, Sarah.
	April 17.	Baldwin, Josiah.
	Dec.	Soverill, widow Jane.
		Pierson, Phebe, w. of Dr. Matthias.
		Camfield, Mary.
		Williams, Hannah.
1774.	July 10.	Quimby, Josiah, w. of.
	July 10.	Jones, James, Hannah, w. of.
	July 10.	Mun, Phebe.
	July 10.	Dod, Moses.
	July 10.	Baldwin, Jonathan.
	July 10.	Baldwin, Eunice.
	Oct. 16.	Williams, Saml w. of.
		Jones, Cornelius, Joanna, w. of.
		Harrison, Simeon, Hannah, w. of.
		Harrison, Isaac, w. of.
		Quimby, Moses, Mary w. of.
		Vincent, Levi, Mary w. of.
		Crane, Timothy, and Sarah his w.
		Canfield, Jos., Phebe w. of.
		Smith, Hiram.
		Baldwin, Simeon.
		Akin, William.
		Crane, Elizth.
		Harrison, Phebe.
		Jones, Phebe.
		Mun, Abigail.
		Mun, Sarah.
		Headden, Mary.
		Gray, Elizth.
		Coalman, Mary.
		Crane, Jonathan.
		Crane, Rachael.
		Crane, Matthias, and w. Elizabeth.
1776.	Feb. 23.	Lindsley, Ebenezer, w. of.
		Crane, Samuel.
		Bostedo, Agnes.
		Ward, Bethuel, Hannah, w. of.
1783.	June 1.	Jacob Callahan, and Rachel wife, joined from Horse-neck.
	Sept.	Tompkins, Job.
	Nov.	Bruen, Timothy, w. of.
		Bruen, Charlotte, their daugh.
		Crane, Hannah, w. of Joseph.
	Dec. 21.	Crane, Joseph.
		David Gardner, 1767, John Gildersleeve, 1767, Ebenezer Hedden, 1767, were ch'h. members, and also John Jones, in 1774.

RECORD OF BAPTISMS BY MR. CHAPMAN.

1765.	Oct.	12.	Jared, son of John Peck.
			Rhoda, dau. Daniel Riggs.
			Jane, dau. Timothy Davis.
	Nov.	16.	Gershom, son widow Martha Williams.
1767.	Jan.	18.	Sibel, dau. David Gardiner.
	Feb.	1.	Jane, dau. Arthur Perry.
	Mar.	29.	Mary, dau. Elder Crane.
	May	31.	Nehemiah, son Timothy Ward.
	June	7.	Mary, dau. Silas Baldwin.
	June	28.	Jeptha, son Isaac Dod.
	Aug.	31.	Rachael, Phebe, Samuel, children of Joseph Freeman.
	Aug.	31.	Lois, dau. Stephen Crane.
	Nov.	15.	Lydia, dau. George Parsonette.
			William, son John Gray.
	Dec.	27.	Desire, dau. John Freeman.
1768.	Jan.	18.	Elizabeth, Rachael, twins of Benj. Mun.
	Mar.	7.	Amos, son William Crane.
	April	17.	Eunice, Sarah, daughters Joseph Smith, Jr.
	July	24.	Mary, dau. David Harrison.
1768.	Oct.	2.	Zenas, son of Richard and Elizabeth Harrison.
	Oct.	13.	Joanna, dau. Joseph and Phebe Smith.
	Dec.	25.	Elizabeth, dau. Samuel Dod.
	Dec.	25.	Nancy, Sarah, daus. of Phebe and Dr. Pierson.
1769.	Jan.	1.	Caleb, son Samuel Condit, Jr.
	Jan.	29.	Phebe, dau. Nathaniel and Eunice Ogden.
	Feb.	26.	Esther, dau. Jared and Hannah Harrison.
	April.	9.	Elizabeth, dau. John Peck.
	April	16.	David, son Elihu Pierson, and Elizabeth d. of Jeremiah Martin.
	April	30.	Josiah, son Eliakim Crane.
	May	14.	Phebe, dau. Arthur Perry.
	June	4.	Rachael, dau. John Headden.
	July	2.	Job, son Silas Baldwin.
	July	9.	Silvanus, son Timothy Davis.
	Sept.	3.	Zebulon, Elizabeth, childn Benjamin Baldwin.
	Dec.	6.	Electa, dau. Aaron Baldwin.
1770.	Feb.	18.	Lidia, dau. Benjn Mun.
	Mar.	4.	Jairus, son Isaac Dod.
	Mar.	25.	Wm. Smith, son Jedidiah Chapman, Pastor.
	May	6.	Naomi, dau. Eunice Cundit, widow.
	May	13.	Jeremiah, son Stephen Crane.
	May	27.	Jane, Lois, children of Caesar, Deac. Pierson's negro.
	July	8.	Abigail, d. Timothy Ward, Junr.
	July	22.	Elijah, son John Freeman.
1771.	Aug.	19.	Nehemiah, son Elder Crane (Noah)
	Sept.	9.	Isaac, son Phebe, wife of Matthias Pierson.
	Dec.	6.	Samuel, son of Samuel and Thankful Crowel,
1774.	Feb.	27.	Sarah, dau. of Caleb and Rebecca Baldwin.
	Mar.	13.	Uzal, son Jonathan and Mary Crane.
	Mar.	26.	Mary, dau. Joseph and Esther Baldwin.
	April	1.	Zenas, son Samuel and Mary Crane.

July	10.	Rachael, dau. John and Hannah Jones.
July	10.	Eunice, dau. Benjamin Baldwin.
Aug.	12.	John, Joseph, sons Josiah Quimby.
Aug.	28.	Janne, dau. John and Elizabeth Wright.
Oct.	16.	Smith, Hiram.
Oct.	16.	Headden, Mary.
Oct.	16.	Children (names not given) of Hannah, w. of Simeon Harrison.
Oct.	16.	Lois, Caleb, Jotham, children of Mary, w. of Moses Quimby.
Oct.	16.	Child of Mary, w. of Levi Vincent.
Oct.	23.	Abigail, dau. of Matthias and Elizabeth Crane.
Oct.	30.	Phebe and others, children of Phebe, w. of Isaac Harrison.
Nov.		Naomi, Samuel, Matthias, Nancy and Mary, the children of Cornelius Jones.
1775. Oct.		Mary, dau. of Richard Harrison.
Nov.		Joanna, dau. of Joseph Baldwin.
Nov.	19.	Joanna, Joseph, children of Isaac Mun.
Nov.	12.	Linus, Joseph, sons of John Dod.
Nov.	26.	Katharine and Matthew, children of Thomas Williams, Jr.
Nov.	30.	Amos, son of Isaac Harrison.
Dec.	18.	Jane, dau. of John Freeman.
1776. April	7.	Isaac, Jane, John, children of Bethuel Ward and Hannah, his wife.
April	14.	Mary, dau. of ——— Ward.
April	21.	Martha, dau. of Cornelius Jones.
May	19.	Prudence, dau. of Daniel Crowel.
July	21.	Phebe, dau. David Dod.
		Esther, dau. of Levi Vincent.
July	28.	Samuel, son of Samuel Tomkins.
Aug.	4.	Sarah, dau. Stephen Crane.
		Sarah, dau. of John and Elizabeth Wright.
Sept.		Nathaniel son of Thomas Grant of New York.
		Lydia, dau. Jonas Crane.
1779. Jan.	17.	Stephen Bradford, son of Stephen Crane.
Jan.	17.	Abner, son of Samuel Dod.
1781. Sept.	2.	Robert, son of Aaron Dod.
Sept.	23.	Hannah, dau. of Hannah and Simeon Harrison.
		Bethuel, son of Abigail and Zadox Baldwin.
Oct.		Jesse, son of Dorcas and Thomas Williams, Jr.
Nov.	17.	Mary, dau. of Phebe and Matthias Pierson.
		Unis, dau. of Richard Harrison.
1782. Jan.	20.	Rhoda, dau. Erastus Pierson.
		Hannah, dau. Bethuel Ward.
		Stephen, son of Ruth and John Mun.
Nov.		Elizabeth, dau. of Samuel and Mary Crane, of Horseneck.
1783. Mar.	23.	Mary Valeria, dau. of Jedidiah and Margt. Chapman.
Mar.	30.	James, Benjamin, sons of Mr. ——— Conolly.
April	6.	Mary, dau. Zadoc Hedden.
April	13.	Henry Earl, son Saml. Crowel.

May	16.	Elias, son of Permenas Riggs.
May	23.	Hannah Allen, dau. Joseph Tomkins, of Horseneck.
June	1.	Nancy, Thomas, Phebe, Cyrus, children of Jacob and Rachael Gallahan.
June	22.	Esther Williams, on ac. of John and Mary Tichenor. Martha Williams, on ac. of Jedidiah Freeman and his wife.
June	22.	Anna, Silas, the children of the widow Williams on her account.
July	6.	Timothy, son of Timothy and Sarah Ward.
Sept.		Jonathan, Daniel, sons of Job Tomkins.
Dec.	14.	Hannah, dau, of Jonathan Baldwin.
Dec.	21.	Eleazer, Nathaniel, sons of Joseph Crane.
Dec.	21.	Nancy, Thomas, Jeptha, Hannah, children of Aaron Crane.
1784. Mar.	14.	Isaac, son of John and Ruth Mun.
Mar.	21.	Caleb, son of Joseph and Mary Baldwin.

REMINSCENCES OF AN OCTOGENARIAN

Octogenarian days have their compensations, and there is fun in sitting as a fan on the bleachers of life when advancing years prevent taking an active part on the gridiron or diamond "at the biggest game of all history," from the viewpoint of Rev. Dr. James M. Ludlow, pastor emeritus of the Munn Avenue Presbyterian Church, East Orange, who observed his eightieth birthday Tuesday, March 15, 1921.

In the evening gloaming of life he would not exchange the memories of the past for all his former juvenile anticipations, and although he has "no special job in the present-day world," the fascination of living in "cataclysmic times" continues to hold his interest. Dr. Ludlow was born at Elizabeth, March 15, 1841.

"Yes, I am now an octogenarian," Dr. Ludlow remarked today, "and henceforth I shall be, as an old friend and colleague said after his fourth score birthday, 'super-annu-eightied'." He continued:

"Do I notice that age brings changes in body and mind? Certainly, but none that I would complain of. On the whole I think that between the two boundaries set by the Psalmist, seventy and eighty years, nature intended that a man who had lived with ordinary regard to physical and mental laws should find the most satisfactory stretch of his earthly jaunt.

"Of course, old age accumulates some disabilities, which to youthful ambitions would seem to be afflictions. But a wise man adjusts himself to his environment, as a dog adjusts his body to the unevenness of what he may be lying on. There is 'no fool like an old fool' and the old fool is never more foolish than when he insists upon acting as if he were young. An observing man notes that with the passing of the years bodily changes are matched by mental and dispositional changes, so that the soul can remain master of whatever situation may occur. He is not unlike a good ship that rearranges its sails to meet the varying winds and may make some progress when near head-on to a gale that might swamp it if sidewise or even astern.

"I do not hesitate to confess some of an old man's disabilities, because I am not responsible for their coming. An old bow loses both toughness of fiber and elasticity through exposure to the atmosphere; so do the muscles of the archer, the steadiness of his nerve and the sharpness of his eye, under the stress of years. Few of us can 'come back' in good form to the conflicts of life unless we have a special dispensation from Providence, such as the Patriarch Job had when he said: 'My bow was renewed in my hand.'

"So, having no pull in respect of miracles, I decline to accept your invitation to a five-mile walk unless you will cut it down at least to four, to preach three times a Sunday, to correct proof after candle light, to remain at the club after 11 o'clock P. M. and to take any job, however lucrative, which would interfere with the regularity of my meals, my after-lunch cat-nap or midnight slumber.

"I note also certain mental changes. Possibly they may be due to a little rust on the brain cogs, or to the wearing of the gears of my real automobile. Whether that be the cause, or I may be growing wiser from sheer experience, I have different notions and different tastes from those of former years. I sometimes—though not often—re-read bits of my printed stuff, and am confident that, in a sentimentalism and rhetorical phrase, I could not now imitate it if I wanted to and would not want to if I could. Pegasus has grown stiff in the joints, and his wing feathers are moulting beyond recuperation. Clio and Urania are still quite neighborly, but Calliope, Euterpe and the rest of the Muses seldom call.

"Among other changes I notice what seems to be an incipient aphasia, or word-forgetfulness. My book of memory has suffered many deletions, or at least blurrings of the type, in respect to proper names, scientific and philosophical terms, in which I used to be comparatively glib. Mr. What-d'ye-call-him is more frequently introduced; and in public speaking I find that it is judicious for me to jot down certain significant words, for I have neither mnemonic trick nor verbal inspiration to help me.

"I am, however, reconciled to this loss by the fact that so far at least it affects only my ability to express myself without hesitation and with ready precision when speaking to others. I know that it does not impede the process of thinking, shallow the depths of emotion, or lessen my appreciation of the beauty and force of choice diction as I hear and read it in others. It only humiliates me that at times I must appear in somewhat scant and hole-worn garments when I try to match minds with those who have up-to-date wardrobes of verbiage in which to clothe their ideas.

"I try to comfort myself for these lapses of verbal memory by a theory that it is a part of old people for that life which is just ahead of them when all uttered language shall have been relegated back to this world of sense and sounds—that telepathic heaven St. Paul believed in, where we will 'know even as we are known,' and which Augustine anticipated as a psychic condition in which thought will mingle nakedly with thought without the necessity of speech.

"In looking back over the years it seems to me that my life has been over-active for my personal good. I have been until recently compelled to think continually of things, at least of other people's thoughts, and have not had time to get acquainted with myself. I have had to swim so hastily that I have had little time to take a dive into my own depths. Only in these later years of partial retirement have I learned somewhat about myself that I ought to have discovered long ago.

"I left college at twenty, at twenty-three was pastor of the historic Presbyterian Church of Albany, having in my congregation men and women of mental caliber beyond my own; from twenty-seven and for eight years I had to keep my necktie well starched in the Collegiate Dutch Church of New York (now St. Nicholas), whose edifice was built during my pastorate. Seven years I served the Westminster Presbyterian Church in Brooklyn and twenty-four years the Munn Avenue Church in East Orange, until by various means I succeeded in convincing the people that they needed a better man. All this time I was a chip in the torrent of all sorts of social, charitable and religious work.

"Besides this too engrossing occupation I was persuaded by publishers to write books, although I did not yield to this temptation until I had passed my forty-fifth year, a time when even Dr. Osler admitted that it would be safe for an ordinary man to yield to some indulgence. At sixty-eight I retired from the clerical deck and took my place as a passenger for the rest of the voyage.

"I say I have now retired; to speak more accurately I will only say that I have tried to. How do I like this later life? It is fine—except for certain drawbacks; for example, when a beautiful young lady, to whom the men in the trolley car had offered almost as many seats as there were male passengers, insisted on offering the seat to me, doubtless remembering the infirmities of her grandfather; or when visiting a church in the city the committee on strangers which I had organized a half century before, conducted me to a seat, asked my name and address, and invited me to come again; or when I walk along a street in almost every house of which I have officiated at baptism, wedding or funeral, and realize that I now know scarcely the name of an occupant; or when I think over the list of my church boys and girls, some of whom have become leaders of their generation in politics, business, literature and social life, and many of whom have already finished their course and only 'their works do follow them,' or when I sit in life's evening gloaming and metaphorically whistle for familiar ghosts, and hear in response only the whisper of the wind that bore them away.

"But octogenarian days have their compensations. If we no longer are fascinated by the delights that sparkle on the brim of the cup of life, we may find that the cup is even more exhilarating near the bottom.

"And the present-day world; is it not mine, too, although I have no special job in it? What a world! I have reveled in history, but the ages have had nothing like it for fascination. We are living in catacylsmic times, when once slow-moving historic processes are moving with celerity toward wonderful denouements, such as the Prophets did not foresee. Racial forces coming to the crash of their long antagonisms, having reached the point where they must have new resultants. Science opening vistas in undreamed directions and vastness! Literature bedecking every field where thought wanders!

"It is not necessary for an old man to be feeling the temperature of his colder blood, and so become sluggish in mind. We can keep up all our interest in life, debate its problems and fight its battles on the fields of intellect. Indeed, we can still be partizans, and ought to be for everything that is right. If we cannot play our part down on the gridiron or diamond we can sit on the bleachers, watch the game and cheer the champions of what we believe in. There is fun in being even a 'fan' at the biggest game of all history that is now on. In this sense I hope to be a sport until the call 'Time's Up!' rings out for me.

"And then? Well, there are doubtless bigger problems and ventures Over There. I feel like an explorer. The 'Valley of the Shadow' does not frighten me; for there are clearly revealed though dimly outlined heights on the other side."

NOTE—This paper is taken from "The Newark Evening News," March 12, 1921.

INDEX

ERRATA

Page 10, 26th line from top, paragraph beginning, "The text of Scriptures," etc., should read, "obedience to an overruling Providence," and not "of an overruling Providence."

Page 91, 6th line from top, beginning, "the Revolutionary Days," "had a public house," should read "had been a public house," etc.

Page 553, third paragraph, "M. F. Fitzsimmons" should read "M. A. Fitzsimmons."

Page 491, second paragraph, fourth line, "Mayor John A. Rodgers" should read "Mayor John R. Rodgers."